A totally new selection of letters to *The Times* — among them ones by Evelyn Waugh on earning an honest dollar, Sir Thomas Beecham on tempo, Reginald Bosanquet on Army nicknames, Patience Strong on 'God Save the Queen', Marie Stopes on pocket money, Agatha Christie on Shakespeare, A. L. Rowse on General de Gaulle, Katharine White-horn on how to end a letter, Joyce Grenfell on 'glamoramas', John le Carré on the Foreign Office Iris Murdoch on the selection principle in education, Robert Graves on the bliss of being ignored, John Betjeman on old churches, Ravel on *Daphnis and Chloë,* Rebecca West on the Prince Consort's death chamber and many, many more.

This time he has been able to include running correspondence on trouser turn-ups, the origin of marmalade, the whereabouts of Ruritania, hygiene and the Communion cup, military nicknames and perfect manners — and individual letters on topics as diverse as hip baths, top hats, how to get a message to an express train, *Brideshead Revisited,* oarswomen's dress, war in the Falklands, Oliver Cromwell's head, the sinking of the Titanic — and cuckoos à la Beethoven.

D1151259

THE SECOND
CUCKOO

THE SECOND CUCKOO

A further selection of witty,
amusing and memorable letters to
THE TIMES

Chosen and introduced
by
KENNETH GREGORY

London
UNWIN PAPERBACKS
Boston   Sydney

First published in Great Britain by George Allen & Unwin 1983
First published by Unwin Paperbacks 1984

UNWIN®PAPERBACKS
40 Museum Street, London WC1 1LU,UK

Unwin Paperbacks
Park Lane, Hemel Hempstead, Herts HP2 4TE, UK

George Allen & Unwin Australia Pty Ltd
8 Napier Street, North Sydney, NSW 2060, Australia

ISBN 0-04-808049-7

Printed in Great Britain by Guernsey Press Co. Ltd, Guernsey,
Channel Islands

ACKNOWLEDGEMENTS

The editor and publishers wish to thank all those who have so readily given permission for inclusion of the letters which appear in this volume. The many writers, literary agents and executors to whom thanks are owed are too numerous to be named individually here but their friendly help and many interesting comments and postscripts have been invaluable.

Every effort has been made to trace the writers of the letters or their heirs and executors. Inevitably, we have not always met with success in tracking down the writers of letters in some cases published as many as eighty years ago. To those whom it has proved impossible to trace we would offer our sincerest apologies and express the earnest hope that they will find pleasure in the reproduction of their letters in these pages.

Kenneth Gregory would also personally like to thank all those who have helped him in his researches, including Sir Roger Bannister; Cyril Beazer; Eric Davis; Charles Lewington; Gordon Phillips, former Archivist of *The Times*; the New Zealand High Commission; and, especially, the staff of the Bath Public Reference Library.

CONTENTS

INTRODUCTION

by Kenneth Gregory

Cuckoo-hatching is fun. As the first bird was being spruced up, delightful letters started rolling in. The nonagenarian Sir Clough Williams-Ellis reminisced copiously on numerous topics, the most important the art of after-dinner speaking. Yes, Bernard Shaw had been very good – so, too, Norman Birkett and Bernard Darwin. Sir Clough gave the palm to A. P. Herbert, who was perfect without apparently trying. Coincidentally, Clifford Curzon fired off a cable from Italy, promising deeper thoughts from home. When these materialized, the great pianist agreed he had not *yet* been faded out by the BBC – or had he without knowing? When, finally, *The First Cuckoo* left the nest, Kenneth Tynan opened tentative negotiations by phone. Intrigued that Shaw should have roused a bishop by writing 'the suggestion, gratification, and education of sexual emotion is one of the main uses and glories of the theatre', Mr Tynan discussed the possibility of working Shaw in to a sequel to *Oh! Calcutta!*

Yet the life of a *Cuckoo* anthologist can be off-putting. He is always open to reproach. As he was concluding the present volume – dawdling, it must be confessed, over Shaw versus the Church Militant in 1913 – a snorter dropped through the letter-box. *The First Cuckoo* had ignored a gentleman's master-piece; he could not recall the date when it had appeared, but awaited an apology. In spite of returning at once to 1913 – when the Bishop of Kensington reported lewdness at the Palace Theatre (an actress appearing in the revue *A la Carte* had actually powdered her *stockinged* legs); when Shaw replied, only to be denounced by a prebendary as 'a mere cynic, with no real desire to uplift his fellows' – the anthologist felt low. Like P. G. Wodehouse after the Master had been called 'a burbling pixie', the anthologist fretted and refused to eat his cereal.

Until, that is, he recalled one abiding joy of his work. He was acquiring a smattering of irrelevance. As late as the thirties, *The Times* published letters on more than one page; consequently the eye was constantly being side-tracked. Seek-

1

ing 'Nourishment in Food' by Julian Huxley, which appeared shortly after the accession of King Edward VIII, the eye caught a quotation from the Oxford University Labour Club Bulletin – 'Magdalen Man Makes Good'. Dr Huxley and proteins were forgotten. So, too, a blistering letter on postal delays in 1928 was pushed aside by a list of the pall-bearers at the funeral of Thomas Hardy: Stanley Baldwin, Ramsay MacDonald, the Master of Magdalene College, Cambridge, the Pro-Provost of Queen's College, Oxford, J. M. Barrie, John Galsworthy, Edmund Gosse, A. E. Housman, Rudyard Kipling and Bernard Shaw. But before 1914 the layout of *The Times* tended to be chaotic: *there was no letters page*. Readers' profoundest thoughts were cast haphazardly into vacant spaces anywhere. Would there be letters on top of the weather map? At the foot of the Court page alongside a review of Covent Garden's *Traviata* which did not mention the conductor? Or jostling an advertisement for a cook-general? As a grace note to the Bishop of Kensington's eruption, *The Times* appended intelligence concerning the Olympic Games Fund. To this the Reverend N. Stick had contributed two shillings and sixpence, Miss Annie Wilson one shilling and sixpence.

WHAT THE SPRING MEANS

A MORAL CHALLENGE

HARDLY A SONG TO BE ECHOED

TO THE EDITOR OF THE TIMES

Sir,—On Sunday morning last, while delivering my sermon on the meaning of Responsibility in Family Life, I was interrupted by a cuckoo.
I am, Sir, your obedient servant,

OSRIC CANTUAR

The Athenaeum.

From the Introduction to *The First Cuckoo*

Tribute must be paid to those *Times* correspondents whose letters appeared in *The First Cuckoo*. It was through them

2

that in 1982 the relationship between the paper and the nation was finally rumbled. The French publishing house of Denoël asked the Academician Jean Dutourd to write a preface to *Le Premier Coucou*. With a discerning eye M. Dutourd went to work:

'L'Anglais est un animal religieux. Il croit à des puissances surnaturelles, à des intercesseurs entre lui et quelque chose de très haut et de très vague qui est l'âme britannique. L'Anglais aime les cérémonies, les rites et les monuments où ils se déroulent. Le *Times* est tout cela en même temps. Il est le Saint-Espirit, le saint patron par l'intermédiaire de qui l'on parle au Seigneur, l'église dans laquelle on fait ses prières et le missel où l'on suit l'office du jour.'

A preface which begins thus, then suggests that the removal of the deaths column from the front page of *The Times* in 1966 was more affecting than the disappearance of the Commonwealth, goes on to liken this loss to a removal of the bas-reliefs from the Arc de Triomphe and their replacement 'par des statues de Giacometti', and concludes that 'L'Angleterre est imprégnée d'humour comme elle est imprégnée de l'odeur

---

CE QUE LE PRINTEMPS SIGNIFIE

UN DÉFI MORAL

UN CHANT QUI N'AURA GUERE D'ÉCHO

A LA RÉDACTION DU "TIMES"

Monsieur, Dimanche matin, alors que je faisais mon sermon sur le sens de la Responsabilité dans la vie de famille, j'ai été interrompu par un coucou. Je suis, Monsieur, votre obéissant serviteur,

OSRIC CANTUAR

The Athenaeum.

From the Introduction to *Le Premier Coucou*

du tabac blond' – such a preface demands that *Times* correspondents shall celebrate. The toast?

'L'Homo britannicus, fils fabuleux de la reine Victoria et d'Oscar Wilde.'

The Editor of *The Times* will not be surprised to learn that it is impossible to find a newspaper 'plus britannique, plus chic et plus vénérable' than his, nor that 'La Grande-Bretagne est un club d'excentriques'. He is, after all, president of the club. Two letters in *Le Premier Coucou* met with a unanimous response from French reviewers: Shaw describing a night at the opera in 1905 when the lady in front of him appeared to have the corpse of a large white bird nailed to her head, and Neville Chamberlain reporting his encounter with a grey wagtail in St James's Park. So that was what the British Chancellor of the Exchequer did in 1933 – he watched birds! If only French Ministers of Finance could be persuaded to indulge in similarly civilized pastimes!

'Quel document sur Albion! Quelle mine pour les historiens et les sociologues! Et aussi quelle source de poésie pure!'

The reader who has recently had a letter acknowledged but not published by *The Times* will doubtless resent that 'pure'. He may be consoled by the thought that they do these things differently in the Soviet Union. *Pravda* receives more than nine times as many letters as does *The Times*. Each Russian letter is read, sorted, classified, and passed on to the relevant ministry or local authority. *Pravda* does not concern itself with 'poésie pure', rather with a Churchillian 'Action this day', or something less immediate. It would be pleasant to think of certain of *The Second Cuckoo*'s letters being shunted to ministries (after publication, of course), and of the ensuing delays. But such is the catholicity of taste of readers of *The Times* that at least a score of additional ministries would be needed. Some potential ministers of wit spring to mind, none of them politicians.

At the start of the century 'the Queen believed in herself, and we believed in her'. A mood of high seriousness governed the correspondence columns of *The Times*. The type was infinitesimally small. Writers fed upon the paper's soberly majestic image. Letters tended to echo the rhythm of the leading article of 23 January 1901: Queen Victoria had died and 'There is much in what we see around us that we may easily and rightly wish to see improved. The *laudator temporis acti* may even

4

contend that we have lost some things that had better been preserved' – which reads like Jeeves in need of fish. But let no one mock that leader writer: 'At the close of the reign we are finding ourselves somewhat less secure of our position than we could desire, and somewhat less abreast of the problems of the age than we ought to be, considering the initial advantages we secured.'

Yet there was always Bernard Shaw. He must for ever remain unique among *Times* correspondents – for the span of his contributions (they lasted from 1898 to shortly before his death in 1950), their high-spirited wisdom and occasionally nonsense, above all for their comprehensive scope. The views of experts have, by some tacit agreement, been at the call of *The Times* since the paper's birth. Shaw alone could, and would, write compellingly in the years prior to the Great War on spelling reform, vivisection, vaccination, polygamy in India, flogging in Egypt, women's suffrage, the battle of the Book Club, motherhood, socialist statistics, supertax, anti-Semitism, emigration, the national theatre, the distribution of wealth, Anglo–German relations, Irving, a monument to Dickens, corporal punishment in the Navy, and electric lighting in Marylebone. Shaw emancipated the correspondence columns of *The Times*. To read a Shavian letter over breakfast cleared one's mind for the day – or at least called forth curses on the man.

At some time or other the newspaper of the Establishment (however that may be defined) changed so that by 1977 it was read by a higher proportion of Labour than of Conservative MPs.* Letters to the Editor also changed, helped considerably by the new bureaucracy. As late as 1939, reaction towards its fatuities was one of injured pride and bewilderment rather than of expectation. *Could* Englishmen behave in this absurd manner? One answer, of course, was that they always had – but not readers of *The Times*. A variation on the 'new morality' was the subject of a letter on 25 January 1947 from Mrs Norah Lofts which was printed in *The First Cuckoo*. One woman had been convicted of inflicting grave hurts on a child, and was fined £10, another of possessing more food ration books than her family of three children entitled her to, and was sent to prison for six months. Mrs Lofts thought a public expression of disgust imperative. Today's initial response might be to

* A MORI Poll found that 89 per cent of Labour MPs read *The Times*, and 81 per cent of Conservative MPs.

associate magistrates with the new bureaucracy and laugh heartily before seeking a remedy.

The mood of *Times* correspondents changed as Britain's fortunes declined. Citizens of the only country which had fought from first to last in the Second World War, *Times* readers awaited the world's thanks. Reality did not appeal and they grew huffy, their sense of humour sadly tested. At home and abroad they searched for logic – *British* logic – and found it rarely. They were saved by modern newspaper costs: they tightened their prose styles. Few correspondents are at their best over 900 words when a third of that number should suffice. Refused space in which to elaborate their theories, they achieved terseness and wit. This anthologist's judgement is that the standard of *Times* letters today surpasses that of any other period.

The Second Cuckoo, like its elder brother now seven years old, does not seek to prove anything. Readability is the key-note. The juxtaposition of letters may sometimes encourage an eyebrow to flicker, shatter a mood of hilarity, or rescue the reader from sombre thoughts. Occasionally, a letter will be discovered out of period simply to emphasize *plus ça change*. The usual bees in bonnets buzz merrily, the sociologist of to-morrow is not forgotten. Bishops are no longer what they were, preferring to concentrate on theology and social problems to the exclusion of wit and the higher idiocy.

In this new selection critics of *The First Cuckoo* have some-times been placated. Not *Cherwell*, which lamented the absence of a fourteen-column letter from Tolstoy, nor Mr Auberon Waugh, who regretted that the addresses of correspondents had been omitted. (Whether Mr Waugh intended to get in touch with certain writers or to trace some esoteric relationship between topics and addresses was not clear.) Those who felt deprived by the absence of any long-running sequence of letters are now indulged. Several sequences are given in their entirety, though not 'Sharing the Cup' – the correspondence about hygiene and Holy Communion which was so prolific that the complete *oeuvre* would have occupied more than one-twentieth of this book. Oddly, though most of the sequences date from the past decade or so, their topics might well have cropped up at almost any time in the present century. *Times* readers are by nature traditionalists.

A cuckoo letter has, of course, been included in this volume. This time readers will not shed a tear over the sad fate of Mr Lydekker, FRS, who, it will be recalled, reported hearing a

Hertfordshire cuckoo in early February 1913, only to confess a week later that he had been betrayed by a bricklayer's labourer highly skilled in his imitation of birds. *The Second Cuckoo* presents the most famous of all the brood, familiar in Peking and Philadelphia, Cape Town and Helsinki, Adelaide and Leningrad. As you might say, the universal and eternal cuckoo linking Uckfield with Bonn and Vienna, and giving conductors some scope to offer different interpretations.

Beethoven's ear, it transpires, was good.

The Happy Reader

[Sir Guy Fleetwood Wilson liked nothing better than to go after tiger on foot. Once charged by a buffalo, he was hurled 10 feet in the air and seriously injured; two days later he rose from his charpoy and said 'I'll get that buffalo!' But that was long ago. On 8 January 1935 Sir Guy lived off Portman Square, within walking distance of his five clubs – Athenaeum, Marlborough, St James's, Travellers, Turf. It was to the last that he adjourned for the purpose of writing a letter. All we need to know of Sir Guy Fleetwood Wilson is that he had been principal private secretary to successive Secretaries for War; that his decorations were (in order of acquisition) CB, KB, KCB, KCMG, GCIE and PC; that in 1912 he had been 'in charge of India during the Viceroy's incapacity owing to a bomb outrage'; and that his publications were *Letters to Nobody*, *Letters to Somebody*, and *Green Peas at Christmas*]

From Sir Guy Fleetwood Wilson   *12 January 1935*

Sir,

A letter in *The Times* of 4 January signed 'A Forty Years' Reader' tempts me to tell you what has led to my having read *The Times* for over 74 years. In October 1857, at Florence, my father called me into his study and said: 'My boy, circumstances beyond my control oblige us to remain in Italy for some years. I want you to be an English boy and to grow into an Englishman. What will do that more than anything else and teach you all about England will be reading *The Times*. Every morning after breakfast you shall read me one or two paragraphs.' I was filled with pride, and the one or two soon became a goodly number.

9

In 1862, when my father died, I had no *Times*; but I managed to obtain a copy when a week old and to keep it for one day. It made a heavy inroad on my slender pocket money. Pride gave way to interest, and I read *The Times* from cover to cover till I started for England in 1868.

In London I at once tried, and succeeded, in obtaining *The Times*, and interest gave way to habit. In 1870 I became a successful 'competition wallah', and since then I have bought or subscribed for *The Times*. I never missed one in Egypt nor in South Africa during the Boer War, nor during my time in India. In 1873 Delane showed me over *The Times* office. I was ill in the spring of last year. *The Times* was carefully kept, and I have devoted the last Christmas Day and the Bank Holiday to reading 13 back numbers. I was happy, for habit had given way to obsession.

Your obedient servant,
GUY FLEETWOOD WILSON

[Having read of the Battle of Britain and other incidents, Sir Guy died on 24 December 1940 aged 90]

Samaritan

From Mrs Hema Archdale   *22 June 1977*

Sir,

As a member of that vast motley crowd who suffers from a chronic and inexplicable ailment, commonly known as 'an urge to write to *The Times*', you can imagine my delight when I came across the following lines on the first page of the *Sunday Times Weekly Review* (The Sex Prophet – Marie Stopes, 19 June).

'She often contemplated suicide: but decided instead to write to *The Times*. Her experience of marriage she informed *The Times* in a letter . . .'

I wonder if *The Times* is aware of the great service it provides in publishing letters from readers – and indeed of the power it has (as in the case of Miss Stopes) of even helping perhaps to save lives?

Yours sincerely,
HEMA ARCHDALE

[The great emancipator certainly wrote to *The Times* (*Marie Stopes*, Ruth Hall, pp. 104–5, 1977), but, as on many other occasions, her letter was not published]

Ideal

From Mr Nicholas Albery   *14 May 1981*

Sir,

You are improving the appearance of *The Times*. But as for the contents, the best and cheapest improvement would be to make fuller use of your resourceful readers by having at least two pages a day of readers' letters (as well as readers' articles) as with *The Sunday Times*'s 'Opinion' page.

My ideal would be a bulky *Times* Readers' Supplement, published separately. The rest of the paper, let's face it, is pretty boring.

Yours faithfully,
NICHOLAS ALBERY

Rousing

[On 17 March 1971 *The Times* printed an advertisement which contained a minimum of letterpress and a maximum of female form]

From Mr C. Pratsides   *19 March 1971*

Sir,

It's disgusting! Disgraceful. Quite plainly, it's too much. How can I, a regular subscriber to this paper, be expected to listen (along with the world) with humble awe when *The Times* speaks, or to enjoy unadulterated food for the Chairman's thoughts when, in all innocence, whilst expecting to come across the Law Report, or the Science Report, or something, I turn to page seven and am suddenly confronted with a full page spread of a naked . . . , that is, of a young . . . , er, of a rather attractive . . .

Well, anyway, Sir, I was shocked. The very foundations of our society have been rocked. Dare I venture to suggest that this is but an omen of things yet to come? The mind boggles at what Chairman Mao is going to do with this.

And it wasn't even in colour. Tut Tut.

Yours faithfully,
C. PRATSIDES

From Mr F. S. Macdonald   *19 March 1971*

Sir,

'Topless People take *The Times*'?

Yours faithfully,
F. S. MACDONALD

'You may marry my daughter if . . .'

From Mrs A. M. Hankin   *13 May 1978*

Sir,

As a daughter, widow, and daughter-in-law of *Times* devotees, may I quote my late husband, when he said 'I don't think I could bear a son-in-law who didn't take *The Times.*' Fortunately they both do. Let us hope that we and the grandchildren may be able to continue doing so.

Yours faithfully,
HELEN HANKIN

Inspirational

From Miss Barbara E. Stirrup   *29 November 1978*

Sir,

Sunt lacrimae rerum . . . I was almost moved to tears by the poignancy of Philip Howard's farewell to *The Times* (17 November). I hope the Editor will see the light and publish this expression of gratitude for all the joy and wisdom *The Times* provides for so many, an inspiration for the health, a refreshment for the sick.

And what higher praise than that of Richard Cobden in Manchester one hundred and twenty-eight years ago: 'I believe it has been said that one copy of *The Times* contains more useful information than the whole of the historical works of Thucydides'?

Yours faithfully,
BARBARA E. STIRRUP

Greater love hath no man

[The following letter so shattered the Letters Editor, the printer or the proof reader that the sender was not accorded 'Mr' in front of his name]

From Stuart J. A. Selkirk   *29 November 1978*

Sir,

Since life will cease to be civilized without *The Times*:

I will start to grow a beard if you do not publish on December 1 and I hope that it won't grow too long. With kind regards to you and your staff for the future,

S. J. A. SELKIRK

[The Selkirk beard achieved three inches of untrimmed growth, being several times appraised by BBC-1. After CBS had dispatched a camera crew, and *Time* magazine a photographer, Mr Selkirk grew weak of spirit and, in July 1979, applied a razor]

Skimmed

From Mr R. W. Middleton   *1 January 1971*

[writing from Switzerland]

Sir,

I finished today's *Times* in four and a half minutes. Is this a record?

Yours faithfully,
R. W. MIDDLETON

Too Serious

From Mr David French   *11 August 1973*

Sir,

May we please have the silly season back?

Yours faithfully,
DAVID FRENCH

Accidents at the Docks

From Mr Ben Tillett   *6 October 1900*

[Secretary of the Dock, Wharf, Riverside and General
Workers' Union from its inception in 1887 to its amal-
gamation with the Transport and General Workers'
Union in 1922; Tillett began his working life at the age
of eight]

Sir,

A Government report has been made giving, it is alleged,
the number of accidents, fatal and non-fatal, at the docks. As
the report is national it is astounding to read that only 100
cases of death by accident occurred at docks, and a few
thousand non-fatal accidents occurred.

I can honestly congratulate the Home Secretary on making
an investigation, and can sympathize with the investigators in
having to face a task of extreme difficulty, when one knows
the way accidents are reported.

But to prove how fallacious the returns are the report of
one hospital will alone prove. At the Poplar Hospital more
men die per year as a result of accident at the docks than are
recorded by the investigators. Non-fatal accidents are also
treated to a greater number than is reported.

The Home Secretary has been as good as any other man in
his position, and every praise is due to him for his work, but
to permit the report to pass without raising a protest as to the
figures would be condoning a neglect which is murderous to
many thousands.

An inquiry, having powers to demand reports from hospitals,
benefit and trade societies, and from private practitioners,
would reveal a state of neglect undreamt of by those who
take an interest in the wellbeing of ship and dock workers.
But even the investigation, so far as it has gone, has proved
the necessity of adopting more stringent measures to protect
the 250,000 men who get more or less a living at the docks.

The factory inspector, when permitted the power to board
ships at all times of working, to examine gear and conditions

of working, will find a docker's life to be more dangerous than a fighter's in the Transvaal. There is not a single factory inspector told off to watch over the interests of more than a quarter of a million men. It is a public scandal, which I trust the Home Office will remedy. The figures given in the investigation in no way indicate the extent or nature of the dangers and unhealthiness of the docker's calling.

Yours sincerely,
BEN TILLETT

English History for French School Children

From Mr Courtney Kenny   *25 May 1900*

[Fellow of Downing College, Cambridge; Downing Professor of Laws of England 1907–18]

Sir,

Much has been said of late as to Continental disapproval of English foreign policy. It is, therefore, interesting, to trace any of the means by which that disapproval is being developed. This week, whilst in the south of France, I purchased at Arles, in the principal bookseller's shop, some of a series of copybooks, the covers of which are devoted to illustrating the Transvaal war by pictures and letterpress. I was told that they enjoy a huge sale. I enclose two specimens of them.

You will see that one gives a vividly coloured drawing of supposed 'Atrocités anglaises à Ladysmith'. One English soldier is depicted whipping a manacled Boer prisoner; whilst another is striking with his rifle a Boer who is lashed to a cannon. The letterpress narrates that 'the English cavalry profited by an armistice to charge a peaceful body of Boers; and maltreated its prisoners'.

The cover of the other copybook has a page descriptive of the English army; and narrates how 'recruiting is the only mode of filling up its ranks. This abominable "white slave trade" is principally carried on in Trafalgar Square. Tramps, beggars, and the dregs of the big towns – these are the sources drawn upon by this shameless recruiting system; which lavishes seductive false promises, and employ gin as one of its most ignoble instruments. Hence drunkenness is one of the most habitual vices of these well-flogged warriors. This is the army of mercenary soldiers which is now taking possession of the Transvaal, whose numerous and important gold mines are the object of England's greed. The sympathies of France have long been given to the brave and upright Transvaalers; and we may hope that our hereditary enemy, who provoked this war, may undergo the defeat she deserves.'

The eight copybooks describe themselves as 'an instructive series, recommended for schools'. If they be the sort of seed sown in French schools, we need not wonder at the fruit which is forthcoming at the voting-urns and in the barracks.

COURTNEY KENNY

['All day long the Angel of Death has been hovering over Osborne House.' Queen Victoria's reign ended on 22 January 1901. As Her Majesty was a very little lady, it was fitting the last letter her reign gave to *The Times* concerned physical standards. Was it right the War Office should shun men of under 5ft 3in, when in Germany those only fractionally over 5ft could serve their Emperor as soldiers? Besides, Field-Marshal Lord Roberts was very small.

Meanwhile Vice-Admiral Sir Cyprian Bridge, who had patrolled the Bay of Bengal during the Indian Mutiny, fired a broadside at mathematicians: 'There have been very few British naval officers whose mental faculties have been strengthened by a course of mathematical study, but personally I have never met one, and they are probably as rare as the great auk.' Sir Cyprian was a former Director of Naval Intelligence.

The new reign called for an intervention from the Athenaeum]

The Style and Title of Edward VII

From Sir Frederick Young   *26 January 1901*

[the author, in 1869, of *Transplantation: the True System of Emigration*; now aged 83, with 13 years to live]

Sir,

In your article in *The Times* of today (25 January), in which you announce that King Edward VII was yesterday proclaimed King of Great Britain and Ireland and Emperor of India, you most truly say that it must have struck many readers of the proclamation that there is room for some amendment in his style and title.

I hope you will permit me cordially to endorse your very excellent suggestion.

As one who has laboured during long years of my life, as far as my humble efforts would allow, to promote the sympathy and closest union between the mother country and the colonies, I earnestly trust that His Majesty may be graciously pleased to add some suitable addition to the style and title under which he was yesterday proclaimed as our Sovereign, in order distinctly to include the colonies by name in the regal designation, which could not fail to be most warmly and deeply appreciated by our countrymen beyond the seas.

I am, Sir, your obedient servant,

FREDERICK YOUNG

[And so 'His Most Excellent Majesty Albert EDWARD the Seventh, by the Grace of God, of the United Kingdom, Great Britain and Ireland, and of all the British Dominions beyond the Seas, Defender of the Faith, Emperor of India']

Motor Cars and Horses

[Sir Edmund Monson, a former Ambassador Extraordinary and Plenipotentiary to the Emperor of Austria, and later to the French Republic, had pointed out that due to motor traffic it was becoming difficult to enjoy one's afternoon carriage drive in the Bois de Boulogne]

From Sir Henry Thompson   *5 September 1901*

[a distinguished surgeon, at this time aged 80]

Sir,

The single source of discomfort which I soon experienced as an alloy to the pleasure derived from the daily use of my motor-car during the last two months, in three adjacent countries, described in your issue of 17 August, was the hostility with which I was regarded by all the drivers of horses I met with. By not a few it was loudly expressed, sometimes in terms inadmissible in these columns. Hence my endeavour to bring about a better feeling between us, and an attempt to show what I felt was error, due solely to want of thought on their part; and I made it my business to show how much gentleness would achieve in the way of improvement.

Naturally, I have been pleased to see how much interest has been taken in the subject, and how many correspondents have expressed their hearty approval of the recommendations made. Others have made suggestions which indicate want of practical knowledge of the motor-car, and one at least has expressed in very strong terms views which demand from me a reply.

As an example of the first-named, one gentleman recommends that as the legal speed is said to be 12 miles per hour, a motor should not be capable of running faster. Had he known anything of the principles of motor construction and driving, he would have been aware that no car thus limited in power would ever ascend a hill. One cannot have less than 16 miles an hour in reserve, or the motor driver would, like a cyclist, have to push his machine up the hill. One requires exchange of speed into power, and in order to ascend a steep hill one often climbs at only four miles an hour, if less steep at eight or 12. But the *minimum* of speed in reserve for all purposes, and there are several, is about 20; and the rate at which I drive on a level, straight, roomy road, where I can see my way well, is a mile in four minutes, producing, with hill climbing, about an average of 12 miles an hour. My car is a $6\frac{1}{2}$ h.p. Tonneau Daimler. With this power in reserve, one descends a hill by the simple weight of the car – no machinery going when all noise ceases, the latter fact being a considerable influence against disturbing horses.

Of the proposal to number motors with conspicuous letters, I need say no more than that if this were adopted it must be applied to carriages of all descriptions without distinction.

Lastly, I must be permitted to refer to the letter of Sir Edmund Monson, which appears in your issue of 31 August. Being old enough to have travelled before any passenger railway existed in this country, I also recollect well the period when railway trains were objects of intense fear to horses and the time it took for them to become accustomed to them; as it subsequently did to the ordinary bicycle. But the sketch of French automobile driving as practised even in the delightful 'Bois' and suburbs of Paris, including as it does such descriptive terms as 'monsters', 'excruciating noise', 'asphyxiating odours', with inmates 'enveloped in gowns, protected by hideous masks', like 'the demons of a travelling circus', giving 'the impression of a diabolical phenomenon', is, I hope, and have no doubt is, intentionally highly coloured. There are other terms of a similar kind, but the above suffice.

I wonder what Sir Edmund's Parisian friends will think of

this picture of French refinement, which we in England have long learned to appreciate and esteem. I can assure him no such scenes are presented in the parks of London, and, I dare say without hesitation, never will be. I have traversed them quietly with my own motor, but no rate approaching to 'at least 40 kilometres an hour' would be attempted. No odour is ever emitted, and it is only exceptionally, as when dust and small fires are prevalent, that I wear any other than my ordinary spectacles. For example, I drove to Bedford from Hemel Hempstead yesterday, 35 miles out, in all 70, in about $5\frac{1}{2}$ hours, about an average of 12 miles an hour, without any other glasses, as recent rains had laid the dust. And when I wear the 'goggles' they are faintly tinted neutral glasses with narrow, pale, coffee-coloured surroundings.

I am glad to see by *The Times* this morning that an English gentleman resident in Paris expresses his belief that Sir Edmund's opinion is hardly fair.

I have expressed myself as briefly as possible and trust I do not occupy too much space.

Your obedient servant,
HENRY THOMPSON

An Historic Handkerchief

From Captain W. Russell Watson   *19 July 1902*

[New South Wales Detachment, Australian Corps]

Sir,
It may not yet have come to your knowledge that one of the gracious acts of his Majesty the King before his departure to Cowes was the signing of his autograph on the handkerchief used as a flag of truce when I demanded the surrender of the Boer capital Pretoria, 4 June 1900. Her Majesty the Queen also signed, so that this handkerchief is now, perhaps, one of the most historical mementoes of the war, bearing as it does the autograph of their Majesties, the Prince of Wales, Earl Roberts, Viscount Kitchener, and the British generals who were present next morning to receive the surrender of the city.

Yours faithfully,
W. RUSSELL WATSON

The Employment of Children on the Stage

[Ellaline Terriss – with Seymour Hicks leading the cast of J. M. Barrie's *Quality Street* at the Vaudeville Theatre – had informed *The Times* that between 20 and 80 children were employed at every performance in that theatre; they were indeed the breadwinners of many families. Deploring the Bill which would prevent children under 14 from performing in public, she added that their gracious Majesties had welcomed juvenile players to Sandringham]

From Mr Bernard Shaw   *25 May 1903*

[this letter was contemporaneous with *Man and Superman*]

Sir,

May I venture to express a hope that when the proposals of the Standing Committee on Trade become law the new authorities will use their licensing powers in such a way as to put an end to the sordid exploitation of children on the stage which has disgraced the theatre for so many years? I do not propose to occupy your space with any criticism of the pretensions of the theatre as a perfect school of character and manners for children. I have no doubt the little girls who are fortunate enough to be in the same theatre as Miss Ellaline Terriss, and who intend to be exactly like her when they grow up, are the better for it, and are a source of innocent comfort and pleasure to her. They are also a source of considerable saving to managers who, if the magistrates did their duty, would have to employ adult dancers and figurants to fill up the stage with moving masses of glittering costumes. As for the parents who are not ashamed to live on the labour of children under 13, their indignation when it is proposed that they shall actually support their children instead of their children supporting them may be imagined. These people feel no shame when little children are described as 'breadwinners'; they would willingly belong to a nation of such breadwinners; and the view that such a nation would deserve nothing better than extermination, and would probably get what it deserved in the international struggle for existence, would seem to them fantastic and indeed unintelligible.

But my present purpose is to protest against this infamy being thrown on the shoulders of the public. No doubt the public is thoughtless enough at best; and the playgoing section of it becomes almost mindless from the total disuse of its brains in the theatre. But the public never asked for children on the stage. When Mr Rosslyn Bruce, in his otherwise excellent letter in your columns, despairingly concludes that 'the British public must have its children's chorus', he is allowing Miss Ellaline Terriss to hypnotize him, just as Miss Ellaline Terriss, with equally innocent intention, is allowing her feelings to be worked on by what is at bottom pure commercial bluff. I assert as a matter of common knowledge that the presence of children on the stage is as unwelcome to the thoughtless playgoer, whom they bore, as to the thoughtful and public-spirited playgoer whose conscience they disturb. I assert that the child 'professional' is not only a social horror and a national scandal, but an artistic nuisance. I assert that if any theatrical employer of child labour were precise enough in his protests to pretend that if he substituted adults for children in his choruses and dances the attendance at his theatre would fall off he would be laughed at; everybody would know that he was simply pleading against an increase in his salary list.

No manager puts children into the parts on which the drawing power of the piece depends. As much nursery sentiment has been worked up for the little princes in the tower as for the babes in the wood; but when Sir Henry Irving revives *Richard III* he takes care to engage Miss Lena Ashwell for his little prince instead of coaching a child in the part. Mr Arthur Collins would not engage children even for the babes in the wood; he knows that the public would prefer Mr Dan Leno and Mr Herbert Campbell. The last time I witnessed that most revolting of social outrages, the exhibition of a baby in arms on the stage late at night as a joke in a farcical comedy, I am glad to say that the solemn, wondering, shrinking, reproachful stare of the baby at all the vulgarity and folly put the audience so completely out of countenance that it killed the comedy;* and if it had killed the magistrate who licensed the transaction as well I cannot pretend that I should have mourned him long or deeply. No doubt he, too, was moved by sympathy for the parents who were depending for a few extra glasses of beer on the sweet little breadwinner, and was convinced that the child's mind would be elevated later by

* *The Club Baby* by Edward G. Knoblauch, Avenue Theatre, April 1898 (*Our Theatres in the Nineties*, vol 111, pp. 374–7). The last evening GBS spent in the theatre as a paid critic of *The Saturday Review*; his comments made the above letter seem benign by comparison.

a precocious initiation into the gossip of the stage, and its taste moulded classically by those masterpieces of English poetry which it would be taught to sing in pantomime choruses.

But it is useless for me to pursue the subject. There are extremities of humbug and depths of baseness with which decent citizens do not stop to argue, and of which statesmen who are worthy of their position make short work. Everything that is now being said for the theatres was formerly said for the Manchester cotton factories when they, too, professed to be teaching and training little children – though even they stopped short of children in arms. And when the country would stand no more of it the parents raised the same cry against being deprived of their breadwinners. Though we did stop that, yet it is but a few years since we were shamed in the face of Europe by the fact that we were behind all the neighbouring nations in fixing the age up to which children are protected from exploitation for commercial profit by employers and parents.

Why that most grossly commercial of all our institutions, the theatre, should be exempted from the regulations to which our factories and workshops are subject does not appear. I hope the Bill will be amended by an iron rule against the employment of children under 14 in theatres. The managers have been warned over and over again that if they persist in abusing their powers by applying for magistrates' licences as they have done, total unconditional prohibition would be the result. They have disregarded the warning; now let them take the consequences.

Yours faithfully,
G. BERNARD SHAW

[Shaw died in 1950 aged 94; Ellaline Terriss, the widow of Sir Seymour Hicks, survived until 1971, dying at 100]

Sensational Newsbills

From Sir Homewood Crawford   *8 February 1905*

Sir,

May I crave the hospitality of your columns to draw public attention to the growing nuisance of the daily issue of sensational newsbills by some of your contemporaries?

Only yesterday, as the holder of an ancient official position and bearer of a statutory title, I was for the second time made the victim of this modern form of increasing circulation by the hasty preparation of the contents bills of two of the evening papers, with the heading, in large type, on one, 'City Solicitor's Tragic Death', and 'City Solicitor's Suicide' on the other; whereas much annoyance and pain might have been saved me and many kind friends and sympathizers by the addition of the indefinite article.

Only a few weeks back my esteemed colleague Sir Forrest Fulton, the Recorder of London, was similarly affected by the appearance of a contents bill of one of your evening contemporaries announcing, 'Recorder's Sudden Death in Court'! The use of the prefix 'A' would have saved him equal annoyance and vexation, to say nothing of the shock to one's relatives.

If you can see your way to giving publicity to this letter, it may possibly lead to greater care being exercised in the preparation of contents bills.

I am, Sir, our obedient servant,
HOMEWOOD CRAWFORD, City Solicitor

The Cheap Tripper

From the Reverend J. P. Bacon-Phillips   *6 August 1908*

Sir,

Give a dog a bad name and hang him is a wise old adage capable of universal and almost infinite application.

The cheap tripper is become almost synonymous with nuisance, and the very name of the one connotes the other. With a view of testing for myself whether this application is justly deserved and merited, I spent the whole of Bank Holiday among the vast crowds of trippers at Brighton yesterday.

It is agreed on all hands that even Brighton, which is so used to enormous crowds, has never been so full as it was then and is now.

Amongst all that vast throng throughout the day and early evening I only saw two cases of drunkenness. It was a huge respectably dressed, well behaved, orderly crowd, and highly appreciative of the various attractions which make Brighton the premier watering-place of the world. It is the glory of Brighton that as a national institution she is able to cater for every class of the community; and he indeed would be a heartless person who would wish to deprive the pent-up city worker from breathing

24

occasionally the matchless air of Brighton. There are a large number of foreigners at Brighton just now, and some of them expressed to me their astonishment at the extreme orderliness of the great crowd. The tripper never intrudes himself on lordly Hove, but even if he did I contend that he should be made welcome.

Faithfully yours,
J. P. BACON-PHILLIPS

Hedge Cutting

From Colonel Willoughby Verner   *13 July 1908*

[Inventor of the luminous magnetic and prismatic compasses; author of the *Military Life of Field Marshal HRH the Duke of Cambridge* (by command of HRH), and of *My Life Among the Wild Birds in Spain*; former Professor of Military Topography at RMC Sandhurst]

Sir,

Before any of your readers may be induced to cut their hedges as suggested by the secretary of the Motor Union they may like to know my experiences of having done so.

Four years ago I cut down the hedges and shrubs to a height of 4ft for 30 yards back from the dangerous crossing in this hamlet. The results were twofold: The following summer my garden was smothered with dust caused by fast-driven cars, and the average pace of the passing cars was considerably increased. This was bad enough, but when culprits secured by the police pleaded that 'it was perfectly safe to go fast' because they 'could see well at the corner', I realised that I had made a mistake. Since then I have let my hedges and shrubs grow, and by planting roses and hops have raised a screen 8ft to 10ft high, by which means the garden is sheltered to some degree from the dust and the speed of many passing cars sensibly diminished. For it is perfectly plain that there are a large number of motorists who can only be induced to go at a reasonable speed at cross-roads by considerations for their own personal safety.

Hence the advantage to the public of automatically fostering this spirit as I am now doing. To cut hedges is a direct encouragement to reckless driving.

Your obedient servant,
WILLOUGHBY VERNER

25

[Colonel Verner lived in Winchfield, Hampshire. On 8 December 1981, *The Times* reported that the Royal Borough of Windsor and Maidenhead had requested a householder to trim his hedge. Its letter began: 'Whereas a hedge situation at Altwood Road, Maidenhead in Berkshire belonging to you overhangs the highway known as Altwood Road, Maidenhead, aforesaid so as to endanger or obstruct the passage of pedestrians . . .']

Mr Haldane and Woman's Suffrage

[Richard Burdon, later Viscount, Haldane: one of our most successful Secretaries of State for War, died unmarried]

From Miss C. Pankhurst   *10 January 1908*

[Organizing Secretary, National Women's Social and Political Union]

Sir,

The fact that Mr Haldane devoted an entire speech at Glasgow to the question of women's enfranchisement is unquestionably a proof of the rapid progress which the woman-suffrage movement has made since the adoption by the Women's Social and Political Union of militant and really political methods of agitation. At the same time, his vague and general remarks to the effect that the time is coming when women's right to the franchise must be recognized will not suffice to reassure and satisfy those women who earnestly desire the vote. What we want from Mr Haldane and other members of the Cabinet is, not vague declarations of sympathy, but an explicit statement as to when the Parliamentary franchise is to be extended to women. Mr Haldane asserts that before the franchise can be extended to women the voice of the nation must be heard, and by this he appears to mean that a general election must be fought upon the question.

If he takes that view, then we beg to remind him that, at a general election, not the voice of the nation but the voice of the men electors only is heard. To expect women to wait for the franchise until men electors have endorsed their claim is not more reasonable than it would have been to expect men to wait for the vote until women had given their consent to the enfranchisement of men. Moreover, Mr Haldane, when he

26

argues that the constitutional change demanded by women cannot be made before the electors have been consulted, is guilty of great inconsistency, because he is one of those who recently announced the probability that the Government will introduce a Bill altering the position of the House of Lords, and will, if the consent of the Peers can be obtained, carry the Bill into law. This is to be done in spite of the fact that the House of Lords question was not before the electors at the last general elections.

Mr Haldane is further reported to have uttered the following remarkable words: 'Women may wage war, but my advice is – do not do it with bodkins; you will only irritate people and provoke them.' Women suffragists may reasonably call upon Mr Haldane to be more explicit, and to indicate clearly the nature of the methods of attack which he seems to advocate. For want of guidance from Mr Haldane on this point we shall continue our militant agitation on the present lines. Mr Haldane's naïve admission that he does not like the protests we make at his meetings naturally affords us keen satisfaction, for we feel certain that, just as dropping water will wear away a stone, so our policy of pin-pricks, as Mr Haldane calls it, steadily and relentlessly pursued, will break down the Liberal Government's opposition to our demand that the vote shall be granted to women this year.

Yours faithfully,
CHRISTABEL PANKHURST

[Women over 30 were enfranchised in 1918, those over 21 in 1928. Of Miss Pankhurst the public speaker, Max Beerbohm wrote: 'She has all the qualities which an actress needs, and of which so few actresses have any.' Her sex enfranchised, this remarkable woman went to the United States, proclaiming a belief in the Second Advent]

A Plea for Bath

From Mr Ernest George   *25 March 1909*

[President the Royal Institute of British Architects, knighted 1911]

Sir,

May I trespass on your valuable space in the interests of a spot which has historic associations and is pleasant of aspect, but which is threatened with destruction?

Bath Street is part of a scheme, laid out with design and dignity in Georgian days, including the Baths and the Pump Room, with their colonnaded spaces and approaches. We have few such examples of studied architectural treatment in our cities.

It is now proposed that one side of Bath Street (one side of the avenue of columns) should be removed for the greater convenience of a new hotel. By this the corporation will obtain an increased rent for the ground; but will not their city suffer proportionately by a loss of its traditions and beauty?

Expediency and monetary considerations seem to be the leading factors in the shaping of our towns.

It is sad if, in this twentieth century, our ideals do not lead us to anything higher than the destruction of that which was thoughtfully and admirably done by our forefathers.

The city council of Bath are now being petitioned by a large and influential part of their community to preserve these threatened buildings, Prebendary Boyd, the rector, having exerted himself earnestly in this cause; and it is hoped that public opinion may influence the council, showing them how important is the trust that they hold.

I am, Sir, yours faithfully,
ERNEST GEORGE

[Sir Osbert Sitwell claimed (*Great Morning*, 1948) that Bath 'has suffered devastation by one of the most Philistine Councils in England']

In the Centre of Bath

From Mr James Lees-Milne   *20 September 1970*

Sir,

Your readers may be interested to learn that we are getting along quite nicely with the demolition of the centre of Bath. This year alone we have swept away several acres between Lansdown Road and the Circus. The whole southern end of Walcot Street (including the early nineteenth-century burial ground with tombstones) has already gone. We are just beginning on Northgate Street and have only knocked down two or three houses in Broad Street this month. But New Bond Street's turn is imminent. All the houses are, or rather were, Georgian, every one.

To set against these civic improvements it has to be admitted that the Bath Preservation Trust, those enemies of progress, have acquired and restored no. 1 Royal Crescent. But what is one old building saved against so many savaged?

'Come to Britain Movement' and foreign travel agencies please take note of the way we treat the finest classical city in Europe.

Yours,
JAMES LEES-MILNE

[In May 1973 *The Architectural Review* estimated that since 1950 well over 2,000 Georgian buildings had been demolished in what was 'a perfect Georgian city'. Until 1969 Robert Adam's Pulteney Bridge had a backcloth of Georgian terraces; whereupon the Beaufort Hotel arose with little sympathy for its setting.

However, when on 1 February 1983 the city council approved a scheme for providing spa water bathing on both a commercial and a charitable basis in the Bath Street area, it announced that the facade of the street's north side would be preserved. At which the shade of Sir Ernest George doubtless smiled]

Links with the Past

From Mrs Forde   *18 July 1910*

Sir,

A year or two ago there was some correspondence in your journal on the subject of 'Links with the Past'. You may possibly think it worth while to insert my case.

My father was born in 1750, and I was born in 1819 (when he was 69). I attained my 91st birthday on the 3rd of last month (June). That is to say, our joint lives have extended 160 years.

My relations think this is unique, and I have been persuaded to let you know, as I am told that it, at any rate, is a record which beats anything that has yet been made public.

I am, yours faithfully,
LETITIA JANE FORDE

From Mr Alfred Heneage Cocks   *20 July 1910*

Sir,

As this subject has again been admitted to your columns, you may perhaps think it worth recording that my father (as a boy) knew an (old) gentleman, who (as a boy) had danced with an (old) lady who (as a little girl) had danced with Charles II.

There were therefore only two lives between my father (born 1815, died 1899) and Charles II.

Yours faithfully,
ALFRED HENEAGE COCKS

From Mr H. J. W. Holt   *21 July 1910*

Sir,

My mother had an uncle (her father's eldest brother) who was born in 1746. My mother is still alive, and enters her 89th year next month. This would appear to be even a longer 'link' for two generations than that mentioned in your issue of the 18th inst.

Yours faithfully,
H. J. W. HOLT

From Mr F. H. Daubeny   *23 July 1910*

Sir,

May I venture to observe, with all deference to Mr Holt, that 'uncle and niece' are not a 'link with the past' in the sense that 'father and child' are?

I have made a point of studying, so far as I could, the many instances which have appeared during the past few years in *The Times* and other journals, and I maintain that I have seen nothing to equal (or even to approximate closely) that of my aunt Mrs Forde. The nearest approach that I have seen is the case of the late Lord Leicester.

I am yours faithfully,
F. H. DAUBENY

[The 2nd Earl of Leicester had died in 1909 aged 86. His father, the 1st Earl, was born in 1754 – a timespan therefore of 154 years]

From Mr Richard Hollick   *23 July 1910*

Sir,

I noticed a reference to above, and thought my father's case would be interesting.

Mr Francis Hollick, of 265, Burbury-street, Birmingham, is still alive, and has birth certificate for his father, who was born in 1750, so that the two lives extend over seven reigns, including the two 'record' ones of George III and Victoria.

Sincerely yours,
RICHARD HOLLICK

From Mr E. C. Davey   *23 July 1910*

Sir,

I am one of a 'few elderly Oxonians' who knew or saw Dr Routh between 60 and 70 years ago. Near Carfax, in 1845, my tutor pointed out a venerable gentleman in the High Street. 'That', he said, 'is Dr Routh. He is 90 years old and walks five miles every day.'

I may add, from the *Quarterly Review* of 1878, that Dr Routh knew a lady whose mother remembered King Charles II walking in the 'Parks' at Oxford during the year of the great plague in London.

Yours faithfully,

E. C. DAVEY

From the Reverend Daniel Radford   *25 July 1910*

Sir,

I do not know whether but dare say there are many family instances like my own, but on this subject it may be of some interest to mention that my great-grandfather was born in the reign of Charles II. If this savour of antiquity it is partly explained by my being more than half-through my 83rd year, the youngest child but one of my father, who had ten children, and who was himself the youngest but one of 25 children by the younger of two wives.

Yours faithfully,

DANIEL RADFORD

From Mrs F. A. Steel   *26 July 1910*

Sir,

My grandmother, who died in 1872, in full possession of her faculties, used to boast that her grandfather was 12 years old when Charles I was beheaded. She said her father was born when his father was in his 82nd year, and that a Gaelic song was made to commemorate the event. She herself was born in her father's 67th year.

Yours truly,

F. A. STEEL

From Mrs D. M. Morris   *20 May 1982*

Sir,

It has been suggested to me that I should seek information, through your columns, on the longevity of tortoises.

Mine was given to my grandfather in 1881 and was supposed to be male until, some decades later, she laid an egg! Like many a good Victorian country dweller her favourite food is porridge and peaches.

I should be interested to know if there are many more of these ancients around.

Yours etc.,
PENELOPE MORRIS

Unmarried Daughters

From Mrs Norman Grosvenor   *7 December 1909*

Sir,

Your article on unmarried daughters will no doubt provoke many replies and various solutions. I should like to bring early to the notice of your readers the solution that seems to me far the most natural and comprehensive. In most middle-class British families of the better sort where there are several sons, one at least, if not more, will be sent out to the Colonies. On ranches in Canada, fruit farms in British Columbia, or stock farms in Australia and Rhodesia these specimens of the very best of our British race are sent to plough their lonely furrow. For the first few years it is probably unavoidable that the furrow should be lonely, but later on, when the colonist is older, and is beginning to see ahead some prospect of reward for his labour, he would, no doubt, gladly share home and prospects with a wife. But it must be the right sort of wife, a hard-working woman, just as he, if he is to succeed, must be a hard-working man. Do we bring up our daughters to be fit wives for such men? The answer is emphatically in the negative.

Parents of daughters should from the first accustom them to the idea that their future happiness will depend on their ability to do without luxuries and their capacity for useful work of all kinds, from the planning out of the money available for housekeeping to the cooking of a plain meal. They must accustom them too to the idea that their hope and their future may be beyond the seas, since a nation cannot send away a large proportion of its sons without having the same proportion of its daughters left lonely and unprovided for. But parents will doubtless answer, 'It is already too late; when our girls were children we did not bring them up to a life of practical usefulness; also, We cannot send our daughters to the Colonies alone and unprotected, on the off-chance of their meeting suitable husbands.'

To the first of these objections I reply, If your daughter is still under 30, if she has in her the ancient inheritance of her race – the spirit of adventure and the longing for a home of her own – it is not too late. There exists in England more than one training home for such girls, where for a very small sum they can, if they choose, learn to be good housekeepers, good workers in a home, and good wives for colonists. To the second I reply that though this is undoubtedly a difficulty it is not insuperable. It should not be beyond the wit of man or woman to devise ways of sending out small groups of girls to work at the minor industries of a new country – dairy work, gardening, poultry and beekeeping – and from such colonies men anxious to find a wife would choose a real companion and helper. Also I would point out that our young men colonists come home occasionally, but that many of them are deterred from seeking out a wife by the knowledge that the girls they meet, charming, pretty, amiable as they may be, are hopelessly unfitted for the life of hard work, but greater expansion, which is all they can offer them. Further, if our daughters were properly trained a young man going abroad would in many cases find the company of a sister an economy and a real assistance. If it became the fashion for settlers to start their new life in such partnerships the Colonies would be provided with a female society of the best kind, and the right type of marriages would inevitably follow. We must face the fact that if this country is becoming too crowded for our young men it is becoming equally crowded for our young women.

I am, Sir, yours faithfully,
CAROLINE GROSVENOR

PS I should like specially to recommend the Colonial Training College, Stoke Prior, Bromsgrove, Worcestershire, where a sum of £15 to £30 will provide a young lady with all the training she requires to become an excellent colonist.

[Another correspondent pointed out that the Canadian North-West was greatly in need of gentlewomen]

Improper Books

From Mr Lindo S. Myers   *6 January 1910*

Sir,
Anent the question as to what libraries may permit to circulate or not, may I call your attention to a decision in one of the police-courts reported in your issue of today as regards

one of Balzac's best-known works? It is quite possible that its translation into English may have been evil in intent, and have produced what your report calls 'an obscene publication', but that the original work by Balzac should, under any circumstances, be suppressed for anybody I think shows how hard it would be to leave this matter of public censure in private hands.

I am, Sir, yours very faithfully,
LINDO S. MYERS

[The magistrate, who regarded the above as a very serious case, commanded that Balzac's *Droll Stories* should be destroyed, and awarded the prosecution five guineas costs]

Help for Shoeless Children

From Lady St Helier   *6 January 1910*

Sir,

I have just read a letter in your yesterday's issue from 'A Former Member of an Argyllshire School Board' regarding the question of providing boots for children.

I am afraid if we carried out his suggestion of letting the children go barefooted as they do in Scotland we should very soon find ourselves in a more serious position as regards the children's health than we do at present.

It would be quite impossible for children to go barefoot in London streets at any time of the year, when we consider the dirt and filth with which they are encumbered, to say nothing of the risk they would run from broken bits of glass, etc., cutting their feet and the obvious danger which must follow the poisoned dirt getting into the wound.

I am sure if your correspondent would inquire at any of the large London hospitals he would be told of the many cases under treatment for poisoned feet and the great difficulty of curing the same, even where children have worn the best boots their parents could afford to give them, and I for one should be very sorry to take the responsibility of urging the experiment of comparing the London streets with the clean hard roads of Scotland, where they can walk with very little danger and where accidents such as I have mentioned could hardly ever occur.

Yours faithfully,
MARY ST HELIER

Sixpenny Telegrams to Canada

From Sir Henniker Heaton   *11 July 1910*

[Conservative Member for Canterbury 1885–1910, baronet
1912; introduced telegraph money orders in England,
parcel post to France]

Sir,
   It will be a great concession, though far from my ideal rate,
to get wireless telegrams to Canada for sixpence a word.
   Recently the magician Marconi announced a reduction of
the rates from London to Canada to 7½d per word.
   A few days ago he wrote me the following note:

Marconi's Wireless Telegraph Company, London,
                                     July 4, 1910.
   Dear Henniker Heaton. In reply to yours, we should be
very pleased to reduce the cost of messages to Eastern
Canada to sixpence per word for all plain English messages,
retaining the 7½d per word only where codes are used,
provided that the British Postmaster-General could see his
way to agree.
                          Yours very truly,
                          G. MARCONI, Chairman

   In reply to my further letter, Marconi telegraphed to me:
'Galway, 6 July. Thanks for your letter. Eastern Canada
includes Montreal, Ottawa, Toronto, Quebec, and all places
where present cable rate is one shilling per word – MARCONI.'
   We are well aware that the chief reason given by the
powerful cable companies against reduction is that the great
merchants now get many of their messages by codes down to
my ideal of one penny a word. But surely a simple declaration
by each sender that he is not using code words should be
accepted.
   It is intolerable that the masses of the people of the Empire
are forbidden the use of telegraph communications through
the prohibitive charges, and only one message in a hundred is
a social message.
                          Your obedient servant,
                          J. HENNIKER HEATON

[In *The Loss of the Titanic* (see note to letter of 20 April
1912), Lawrence Beesley wrote of the rescue of certain

passengers: 'In the midst of our thankfulness for deliverance, one name was mentioned with the deepest feeling of gratitude: that of Marconi. I wish he had been there to hear the chorus of gratitude that went out to him for the wonderful invention that spared us many hours, and perhaps many days, of wandering about the sea in hunger and storm and cold']

Trespassing in Aeroplanes

From Mr H. B. Devey   *27 April 1910*

Sir,

Motor-cars are bad enough, but they do not come into one's house or garden. With aeroplanes total strangers may drop in, through the roof, for a little chat at any time. I fear the law cannot protect one against such intrusion. If aviation becomes popular I shall have spikes, with long strong prongs, fixed on the chimneys of my house, and the word 'Danger' painted in large red letters on a flat part of the roof. If any flying machines come down in my garden I shall send for the police to remove the occupants, whom I shall sue afterwards for any damage to my trees or shrubs.

I am, Sir, your obedient servant,

H. B. DEVEY

From Mr Henry A. De Colyar, KC   *30 April 1910*

Sir,

According to a *dictum* of Lord Ellenborough's in 'Pickering v. Rudd' (1815, 4 Camp., at p. 221), passing over another's land in a balloon is not a trespass. This *dictum*, which is difficult to reconcile with the well-known legal maxim *cujus est solum est quoque usque ad altum*, was, however, approved of, in the Indian case of 'Bagrum v. Khettranath Karformah' (1869, 3 Bengal L.R., O.J.C., p. 43) by Mr Justice Norman, who expressed himself as follows:

'To interfere with the column of air superincumbent upon land is not a trespass. Lord Ellenborough justly ridicules the notion that travellers in a balloon could be deemed trespassers on the property of those over whose land the balloon might pass.'

I am yours faithfully,

HENRY A. DE COLYAR

[Bernard Shaw's *Misalliance* had been presented in London on 23 February 1910, Lina Szczepanowska emerging from an aeroplane which had crashed on a glass house]

The Sensation of Flying

[In July 1910, a year after Blériot had crossed the Channel, an air display was held at Bournemouth. Drexel climbed to 2,490 feet, the Belgian Christiaens flew for 2 hours and 20 minutes at 39 miles per hour; taking part in the alighting prize competition, the Hon. C. S. Rolls crashed. He was the tenth airman, and first Englishman, to die while piloting a powered machine]

From Mr Arnold White   *18 July 1910*

Sir,

In *The Times* of today your Special Correspondent at Bournemouth reports the fact that yesterday at noon Mr Grahame-White 'took up one of his mechanics for a short flight'. As I had the good fortune to be the passenger referred to, and had never seen an aeroplane before yesterday, it is possible that your readers may be interested in knowing the sensations of a sedentary sexagenarian who finds himself in the air for the first time.

The closest approach to an aeroplane in a stiff breeze is to be on the bridge of a torpedo-boat in half a gale. The switchback motion is delightful when ascending, but the downward swoop is terrifying when near the ground because nothing but the personality of the skipper is present to suggest that the machine will not strike the ground with fatal effects on captain and passenger.

When the first shock of a new environment is over the sense of a new force beats in on one's intelligence, a force that is like nothing on earth or in water, but which recalls the dream experience most people know of effortless gliding, especially when the wind is abaft the aeroplane.

As we passed over the spot where the tragedy of the previous day had occurred it seemed obvious that it was as reasonable to stop a battle when the first men fell before the enemy's shot as to stop aviation meetings because aviators are killed. The battle with the air has begun and will take its toll of human life until the air is conquered.

The combination of moral, intellectual, and physical qualities required for the making of a good aviator are substantially those wanted in a naval officer. Personality in the air is of the same importance as personality in sea-war. Of the brave men who are striving to win the battle with the air one can only speak with reverence and admiration, especially as, in my humble experience, the pleasantest moment was that in which the machine was induced to come safely to a standstill on the ground.

I am, Sir, your obedient servant,

ARNOLD WHITE

From Miss Money Coutts   *21 July 1910*

[writing from the Aero Club]

Sir,

I also made my first flight in the air on Saturday at Bournemouth, so I read Mr Arnold White's letter with interest and amusement.

M. Morane took me in his big two-seated Blériot to an altitude of about 400ft, the highest that a passenger was taken at Bournemouth, but 'the pleasantest moment' was certainly not 'that in which the machine was induced to come to a standstill'! Neither did I find that 'the downward swoop is terrifying when near the ground'.

I found Morane's superb *vol plané* the supreme moment of the exhilaration of flying, and the graceful way he alights, springs up, and then alights again is quite unterrifying.

The only moment of fear was the start, I thought, which Mr White does not mention. The rush and leap into the air that takes one's breath and sight away for a minute may be quite unique to Morane, however, for he rockets into the air as no one else does. As Blériot says, he is *un virtuose* in the art of flying.

This 'new force' Mr White speaks of seems to me to be most unlike the usual dream of 'effortless gliding', because I got the impression of immense, almost terrific, power, both in the aeroplane's strength, and speed and in the genius of the young pilot conquering undreamt-of difficulties beside me.

I am, however, in agreement with Mr White as to 'personality', because, unhappily perhaps for aviation at present, it seems the most important factor in flying. Take Morane as an example, who has only flown for three months, and is now perhaps the finest of them all. Blériot calls this favourite pupil his 'Benjamin' with fatherly pride.

'Oh, yes, it beats every game in the world,' I heard an enthusiastic young flying-man say to another, and as a humble passenger I fully endorse the remark.

I remain yours faithfully,
ELEANORA MONEY COUTTS

[Less than a year later – on 12 April 1911 – a French airman, Pierre Prier, flew non-stop from London to Paris (Hendon to Issy-les-Moulineaux) at 60 miles an hour]

Cromwell's Head

['I to Westminster-hall where I . . . saw the heads of Cromwell, Bradshaw, and Ireton set up upon the further end of the hall.' – Samuel Pepys' *Diary*, 5 February 1661]

From Mr C. R. Haines   *11 April 1911*

Sir,

Now that the identity of Cromwell's embalmed head is generally acknowledged, is it not high time that some steps should be taken to put an end to the national scandal of keeping this ghastly relic as a curio? Cromwell was one of the greatest men the English race has ever produced. Only two of our long list of Kings deserve to be named in the same breath with him. He became King because he was the best and ablest man in the country, a thing that has happened but once besides in our history. In war he was one of the very few generals who were never beaten. He was a true patriot, and made England great and feared among the nations of Europe. He was a doer and not a talker, and, to the great benefit of the nation, he shut up for a time the House of Commons.

Surely it is possible for the Government or some public body to recover this head of Cromwell by purchase or otherwise and restore it to its grave in the Abbey. He deserves to rest in an honoured grave far more, to say the least, than Charles II. Where is the Nonconformist conscience that allows this desecration of the remains of the greatest (in the realm of action) of all Nonconformists?

I am sure the Rev. H. R. Wilkinson, the present owner, would be horrified if the skull of an eminent parishioner whom he had buried were exhumed and kept as a curio in a box.

41

When a perfectly innocent and justifiable proposal was made to open the grave of Shakespeare and inspect its contents for historical purposes, a deafening outcry was raised, but what would have been thought if his skull were in private hands?

May I appeal to you, Sir, to use your great influence in this matter?

I am, Sir, etc.,

C. R. HAINES

[The Reverend, later Canon, Wilkinson, vicar of Stoke-by-Nayland, Colchester, had inherited Cromwell's head. He later bequeathed it to Sidney Sussex College, Cambridge, where Cromwell had been a Fellow Commoner, 1616–17]

An Aristocracy of Character

From Sir Bartle C. Frere   *2 January 1911*

[Bartle Compton Frere, 2nd Baronet and son of Sir Bartle Frere, Empire builder; writing from the Athenaeum]

Sir,

In a very interesting leading article in *The Times* of today, you wisely depreciate ignorant rulers of the people, and go on: 'There is always a real aristocracy, the aristocracy of brains, of patient study', etc.

But you do not seem to refer specifically to the greatest aristocracy of all, that of character.

Yet the wealthy aristocracy, under whose control England had hitherto reached an unexampled height of well-being, was largely endowed with men of high character.

To conserve wealth through many generations needs a strong strain of the best character, as the proverb (not 'made in England') of 'Three generations from shirtsleeves to shirtsleeves' goes to prove. The allurements that are trailed around the path of the wealthy are so compelling that nothing but strong family character can withstand them.

I am not wishing to refer here solely to any abnormal or sublime heights of character, and would include such unpretentious qualities as go with what is known as strong common sense, equally with the fervour of patriotic duty and the high pride which says that *noblesse oblige*.

I can quite conceive that the British aristocracy would

welcome to their midst such a man as Abraham Lincoln, rail-splitter as he was; for their instinct would tell them that he would both fortify their order and safeguard their country.

The demagogues give us an overabundant supply of mere cleverness and talent, but something very distinct from these gifts is also required in the leaders of solidly prosperous nations.

The English are, I suppose, the stupidest race that were ever created, but their love of character has been a talisman that has thus far preserved them and been a more than efficient substitute for many sparkling qualities.

I beg to remain, Sir, your obedient servant,

BARTLE C. FRERE

[*The Shorter Oxford Dictionary* defines 'stupid' thus: 'of the lower animals: irrational, senseless, dull']

Mr Watson and Mr Kipling

[When necessary the Letters Editor will use four words, insert them between commas, and reflect the spirit of *The Times*]

From Mr William Watson   *23 March 1912*

[Knighted 1917]

Sir,

I have only just discovered, on returning from a visit to America, that I have been represented as saying to a New York interviewer: — 'I do not as a rule consider that what Kipling writes signifies much'. Will you kindly give me the opportunity of saying most emphatically in your columns that I never uttered either the words above quoted or anything in the least resembling them?

I am, Sir, &c.,

WILLIAM WATSON

*** No such statement, we need hardly add, has appeared in *The Times*.

Oxygen and the Olympics

From Sir E. Ray Lankester   *22 March 1912*

[physiologist who had held chairs at the Universities of London and Oxford]

Sir,

The competitors in the 'Marathon Race' at Stockholm will (presumably) be allowed to consume refreshments as they run. Such was the case when the race took place in London. Will you allow me to ask the authorities at the Olympian Games to be held at Stockholm to state in your columns whether a competitor will be allowed to breathe (as he runs) oxygen from a bag carried by him? It would be extremely interesting to see whether such 'breathing' is of material assistance to the runner, and, as oxygen is not a drug but as natural an article of consumption as water, there seems to be no reason why a runner should be disqualified for refreshing himself with it as he may with water or soup.

Yours faithfully,

E. RAY LANKESTER

[The Stockholm marathon was run in a heat wave on 14 July, national flags being periodically raised in the stadium to denote the leaders. Generally the Finnish flag suggested the seemingly inevitable; then suddenly two Union Jacks took pride of place. So it was at the finish: (1) K. K. McArthur, (2) C. W. Gitsham – both South Africans.

Sir Ray Lankester's letter, hitherto unanswered, has drawn this comment from Sir Roger Bannister: 'There is little doubt that speed of running is limited by the amount of oxygen extracted from atmospheric air. Of course any equipment carried by the athlete and delivering the oxygen would have the disadvantage of increasing the athlete's weight and wind resistance. It might be science but it would hardly have anything to do with sport – at any rate as we once knew it!'

Sir Ray Lankester consoled himself during the remainder of 1912 by informing *The Times* of his views on the National Portrait Gallery, and the sinking of the *Titanic*]

Lessons of the Titanic

From Mr Lawrence Beesley   *20 April 1912*

[a former science master at Dulwich College who was a 2nd-class passenger on ss *Titanic* which, on 10 April 1912, left Southampton for New York on her maiden voyage. The following telegram was sent from the Cornell University Club, New York, on 19 April]

Sir,

As one of the few surviving Englishmen from the steamship *Titanic*, which sank in mid-Atlantic on Monday morning last, I am asking you to lay before your readers a few facts concerning the disaster in the hope that something may be done in the near future to ensure the safety of that portion of the travelling public who use the Atlantic highway for business or pleasure.

I wish to dissociate myself entirely from any report that would seek to fix the responsibility on any person or persons or body of people, and by simply calling attention to matters of fact, the authenticity of which is, I think, beyond question and can be established in any Court of Inquiry, to allow your readers to draw their own conclusions as to the responsibility for the collision.

First, that it was known to those in charge of the *Titanic* that we were in the iceberg region; that the atmospheric and temperature conditions suggested the near presence of icebergs; that a wireless message was received from a ship ahead of us warning us that they had been seen in the locality of which latitude and longitude were given.

Second, that at the time of the collision the *Titanic* was running at a high rate of speed.

Third, that the accommodation for saving passengers and crew was totally inadequate, being sufficient only for a total of about 950. This gave, with the highest possible complement of 3,400, a less than one in three chance of being saved in the case of accident.

Fourth, that the number landed in the *Carpathia*, approximately 700, is a high percentage of the possible 950, and bears excellent testimony to the courage, resource, and devotion to duty of the officers and crew of the vessel; many instances of their nobility and personal self-sacrifice are within our possession, and we know that they did all they could do with the means at their disposal.

Fifth, that the practice of running mail and passenger vessels through fog and iceberg regions at a high speed is a common one; they are timed to run almost as an express train is run, and they cannot, therefore, slow down more than a few knots in time of possible danger.

I have neither knowledge nor experience to say what remedies I consider should be applied; but perhaps the following suggestions may serve as a help:

First, that no vessel should be allowed to leave a British

port without sufficient boat and other accommodation to allow each passenger and member of the crew a seat, and that at the time of booking this fact should be pointed out to a passenger, and the number of the seat in the particular boat allotted to him then.

Second, that as soon as is practicable after sailing, each passenger should go through boat drill in company with the crew assigned to his boat.

Third, that each passenger boat engaged in the Trans-atlantic service should be instructed to slow down to a few knots when in the iceberg region, and should be fitted with an efficient searchlight.

I am, Sir, yours faithfully,
LAWRENCE BEESLEY

[Official inquiries revealed that although there were 2,207 passengers and crew on board, lifeboats could accommodate only 1,178. A mere 703 persons were saved. The *Frankfurter Zeitung* stated that the provision of lifeboats was even more unsatisfactory on the larger ships of the *Nord-Deutscher* and *Hamburg-Amerika* lines.

Mr Beesley's superb account, *The Loss of the Titanic*, appeared in 1912]

Hoops in Rotten Row

From Mr L. Macassey, KC   *11 February 1913*

[Knighted 1917]

Sir,

A serious and growing danger now attends riding in Hyde Park – that is, hoop-trundling alongside and across the Row. An erratic hoop evades its small owner, dives under the railing into the Row, and falls under the feet of some unsuspecting pony, usually that of some child riding for security's sake near the railing. With the best-mannered pony in the world, entanglement in a stout wooden or iron hoop means disaster.

On Saturday forenoon I saw two children, assisted by a governess, playing at rolling their hoops through a gap in the Row rails. They got them through at last, right under the legs of a small girl's pony, almost bringing it down. On Saturday afternoon another pony did not escape. My small daughter, aged 5, when galloping had her pony's feet entangled in a hoop. There was a bad smash. She was carried home seriously injured.

The danger is recognized; there have been many complaints, but nothing is done. It is the old story of divided responsibility. The police and the Office of Works have overlapping jurisdiction. What is clear is that the Office of Works could deal with the matter by 'a rule of the park', under the Parks Regulation Act, 1872, and that if such a rule were made, the police could enforce it.

I am, &c.,

LYNDEN MACASSEY

May Day Celebrations

From Lady Macdonell   *3 May 1913*

Sir,

I have just read in *The Times* of today the very interesting article on the lost celebrations of May Day. The writer tells of many May Day rites now gone. May I tell you of one spot in England where some are still honoured, and have been for generations? Early this morning the children of Penzance were out in the fields gathering the 'May', or boughs of green. They will probably be cheered on their way by slices of bread and cream at the hospitable farmhouses. Yesterday the boys would bring out their May horns and be running about blowing them. If you asked them what they were doing, they would probably tell you they were 'scaring away the devil'. I have one of these May horns by me as I write. They are made of tin, varying from a foot to a yard in length and shaped like a herald's trumpet. They can evoke a tremendous blast. Some persons, only inured to the sound of motor horns, object to them.

It is a curious fact, though I have never heard attention drawn to it, that in the ancient carved chancel screen of the old church of Sancreed, a few miles from Penzance, there is a figure that recalls to one's mind the urchins in Penzance streets with their May horns. It is the figure of a youth with puffed-out cheeks, blowing a long horn, while before him a huge serpent writhes in graceful coils lifting a spiteful head with outstretched tongue. May this not be a medieval representation of a local – or perhaps not entirely local – custom of 'scaring the devil' before the coming of May? Perhaps someone better informed than I can answer the question.

Yours truly,

AGNES MACDONELL

A Philosophy of Eggs

From Mr Edward Brown   *23 December 1913*

Sir,

The descriptions or inscriptions adopted by retailers with eggs are many and varied. Terms used frequently mean something totally different in shops within the same street. Districts in this respect have to be taken into consideration. What would be called a 'new-laid' egg in Bermondsey might not rise above the 'cooker' class in Bayswater. A 'new-laid' in Hammersmith probably would be a 'breakfast egg' in Hampstead. Quality is an abstract element determined, so far as food products are concerned, by the degree of palate education in consumers. It is not like a yard measure, absolute in extent, 36 inches, neither more nor less.

A case has recently been tried before the stipendiary magistrate at Burslem, Staffordshire, of a retailer for selling Russian eggs as 'new-laid', and for which a fine with heavy costs was imposed. In the course of the evidence submitted for the defence, it was claimed that if an egg possesses all the characteristics of an English new-laid egg then it is a new-laid egg, with which I agree, provided, however, the English is really what is stated. Such could never be applied to a Russian egg. It might be to a proportion of French and Dutch eggs, but I know of no others which come up to the standard of quality required.

The term 'new-laid' means what it says, namely, of recent production, and something more. Selected for size, shape, brightness, and smoothness of shell, it must be full – that is, the air space very small – clear when tested by light, and firm in both the white and the yolk. Within a very few days the contents shrink by evaporation, the air space enlarges, and the albumen becomes cloudy. Anything in the shape of interior blacks or spots disqualify an egg for this class. No long-distance imported or native egg more than a few days old can possibly retain the features named.

It is frequently thought that the designations 'new-laid' and 'fresh' are synonymous and interchangeable. I have said what the former means. The latter term indicates that it has not been preserved and nothing more. A 'fresh' egg may be three months old, but it cannot be called 'new-laid' by the greatest effort of imagination. In Germany this word includes all that are not preserved. To me the fact of an egg being so labelled is a warning to avoid it as far as possible.

What we want to arrive at on the part of producers, traders, and consumers alike is a clear appreciation of terms used, which in the best trade are:

'New-laid.' – Three to five days old in accordance with the season of year, and in other aspects as laid down above. These alone are recommended for boiling;

'Breakfast.' – In all respects the same save that as they are a few days older there is a slight shrinkage and the bright appearance has gone. For poaching or frying these are excellent;

'Fresh.' – Not preserved. Good eggs for cooking, but nothing more. Usually foreign and inferior native supplies, in which value has been lost by delays in marketing;

'Cookers.' – A varied class, including 'pickles', often very doubtful indeed. Faith is necessary for their consumption; and

'Eggs.' – Upon these the curtain may be drawn. A scrap-heap for other classes.

Yours faithfully,
EDWARD BROWN

[Bayswater, Hampstead, Hammersmith, Bermondsey: where Westminster (Mr Brown's address) ranked in the London hierarchy is not clear]

A Drain on the Family Removed

[On 16 March 1914 the price of *The Times* was reduced to one penny]

From Mr Alfred de Rothschild   *17 March 1914*

Sir,

I hope I may be allowed to send you my most heartfelt congratulations. *The Times* has hitherto been a luxury, but now it will become a household word.

Yours very sincerely,
ALFRED DE ROTHSCHILD

[The word 'luxury' had been used impersonally; prior to 16 March 1914 *The Times* had cost something like £2 11s 8d a year, subscriptions to Mr de Rothschild's six clubs £61 19s]

The Golden Age of the Central Line

[A correspondent had written on the Poetry of Speed –
the reluctance of buses to decant or pick up passengers in
the Bayswater Road]

From Mr Stuart Sankey   *17 March 1914*

Sir,

To Colonel Bethell's generous advocacy of the fine sporting
tone of London's traffic I would add my humble tribute to that
of the Central London Railway, now also in the humorous grip
of the great combine.

This service used to be content to carry passengers to their
destination in an ordinary humdrum way, mostly seated it is
true, but with no fun for their money. Now, any morning in
these parts* you may see gents, presumably on their way to
play marbles in the City, gleefully betting on the platform as to
whether the next train will stop or run through. Having at last
captured a tired train there is the further sporting chance as
to whether it will stop or pass through the station at which
they had thought to alight. In order not to kill joy the company
carefully refrains from placing any indicator on the car, as is
done on less sporting lines, while the guard, busy in harvesting
and flattening out for further circulation derelict newspapers,
takes good care not to give the show away.

In heavy storms or if for other reasons an especially crowded
time occurs, the management display a lawky humour in re-
ducing the cars to three, or even two; any Sunday morning
much amusement may be cheaply gained by observing bevies
of ladies in all their bravery, armed with prayer-books, relegated to the smoking car, two to each strap, apparently using
devotional language.

Then again, what more mirth-compelling than to watch the
guard at some wayside station, say the Bank, sternly admon-
ishing his flattened sardines to 'hurry up' out of the one
practicable door of an end car before his train speeds on its
way to some really busy place.

'In case of fire' I will – 'turn out the guard'.

This up-to-date railway has recently discovered a clever
artist; there are plenty of subjects awaiting his pencil.

Yours obediently,

STUART SANKEY

[*Probably Lancaster Gate]

Women in the Saddle

[Kaiser Wilhelm II had forbidden the wives of German Army officers to continue riding astride, influenced perhaps by the refusal of King George V to witness any exhibition of women riding astride at Olympia. One correspondent claimed that until the twelfth century all women rode astride; doctors conceded that by using this method young girls acquired a 'buoyant carriage']

From Miss Eva Christy   *19 March 1914*

Sir,

I have been interested in the remarks in your paper concerning women riding cross-saddle.

As I have made a life-long study of side-saddle riding, and for a number of years also the points of difference between it and cross-saddle riding, it is possible that the following remarks on the subject may be of interest to some of your readers.

When riding quietly on the road, or on horses which may be called reasonably quiet, there is a great amount of pleasure to be obtained from riding cross-saddle, with comparatively little strain to the muscles. There is perhaps less fatigue in this manner of riding than in the other when going slowly, as one generally does when 'hacking'. I have consulted four doctors on the matter of whether a woman runs any risk of injury to herself riding thus, and they all agree that they see no reason why harm should arise from it.

It is certainly a fact that given a cross-saddle rider and a side-saddle rider of equal physical capacity, the cross rider has the least firm seat of the two – that is to say, in order to remain in the saddle when hunting, where jumping is included, the cross rider will have the greater strain of muscle of the two, and consequently will be more fatigued in the effort of keeping his or her seat. I cannot be surprised, therefore, that some doctors condemn the practice of women hunting in the cross-saddle on account of the risk which might cause injury to certain organs; but it seems hardly fair to entirely condemn the practice of cross riding for women because it is unwise to hunt in this manner.

I advocate the side-saddle for most women because a more secure seat can be obtained in it than can ever be obtained in the cross-saddle, but I am often asked why I ride in the cross-saddle quite as often as in the side; my answer is that, although I always prefer to enjoy the security of the side seat when

going across country or jumping, I use the cross seat generally
for teaching, the principal reason for which is that it is more
convenient for that purpose.

One of your correspondents speaks of the 'straight seat', by
which, I suppose, he means the cross seat! Is it not a little
hard on those who ride in the side-saddle with the backbone as
absolutely straight as any rider in the cross-saddle to have this
implied slur cast upon them? I must admit that there are far
fewer good riders in the side-saddle than there are in the cross-
saddle, but this need not imply that the side rider cannot ride
straight if she is properly taught.

Side riding is the more difficult to teach of the two, and
unfortunately it is usually done on the same principles as cross
riding, which is a mistake if good results are to be obtained.

Yours faithfully,

Eva Christy

Daphnis et Chloë

From M Maurice Ravel   *9 June 1914*

Sir,

My most important work, *Daphnis et Chloë,* is to be produced at the Drury Lane Theatre on 9 June. I was overjoyed,
and, fully appreciating the great honour done to me, considered the event as one of the weightiest in my artistic career.

Now I learn that what will be produced before the London
public is not my work in its original form, but a makeshift
arrangement which I had agreed to write at M. Diaghilew's
special request in order to facilitate production in certain
minor centres. M. Diaghilew probably considers London as one
of those 'minor centres', since he is about to produce at Drury
Lane, in spite of his positive word, the new version without
chorus.

I am deeply surprised and grieved; and I consider the proceeding is disrespectful towards the London public as well as
towards the composer. I shall, therefore, be extremely thankful
to you if you will kindly print this letter.

Offering you thanks in anticipation, I remain,

dear Sir, faithfully yours,

Maurice Ravel

[Notwithstanding, 9 June 1914 was a memorable evening.
Thomas Beecham conducted Balakirev's *Thamar* for
Karsavina and Boln, Pierre Monteux *Daphnis et Chloë*
for Karsavina and Fokine]

Dogs during the Season

[Insisting that 'most people worth anything love dogs', a correspondent had deplored the banishment of her dog ('better behaved than most children') to the guard's van while she travelled first-class]

From Lady Constance Emmott   *13 July 1914*

Sir,

I am glad to see Lady Alderson's impartial, sensible letter in *The Times* of yesterday on the travelling dog owner's grievances and rights. If the travelling dog owner has rights so have householders – and for the sake of London dog owners I would ask the same question of those representatives of what Lady Alderson rightly calls a 'cross minority of nervous, fussy people', who, as chairmen and members of squares and gardens committees, rule out dogs, even when led, from the use and enjoyment of those air spaces.

Householders having access to such gardens on a South Kensington property (and there are others equally inhumanely treated) pay two guineas or more per annum for the privilege of sitting under the besooted shade of a plane tree on a hot summer's day. Yet, if they avail themselves of this privilege they must leave their panting little companions indoors – for no better reason than some old ladies 'cannot bear dogs' and are 'terrified' of them. Surely London must be unsuitable for such sufferers. In any case, when the gardens are left in sole possession of hundreds of cats and frozen solid during winter, seats unoccupied by nervous ladies or nursery-maids in charge of perambulators, might not the poor dog have 'his day'?

House agents in these districts know well that this is one of the many causes which lie behind the too obvious board notices of 'This house to be let or sold', 'Apply within' – to find, often, only the cat in charge. I plead for dogs obliged to remain in town during the season.

Yours, etc.,
CONSTANCE H. EMMOTT

[A male correspondent counterattacked Lady Alderson: if she dared to travel with her dog as companion, he would bring his monkey]

Travelling from Germany

[On 4 August 1914 Britain entered the war against Germany]

From Mr Alison Phillips   *7 August 1914*

[a former foreign correspondent of *The Times*; Professor of Modern History in the University of Dublin 1914–39]

Sir,

May I add my testimony to that of Lady Phillips published in your issue of today? I started from Germany at 3 o'clock p.m. on Saturday last, with my wife and sister-in-law, and during the whole of our trying and anxious journey we experienced nothing but the utmost kindness and courtesy from both people and officials.

Perhaps I may add one thing more. It is too late to believe in the *bona fides* of the German Government; but in that of the German people I still believe. During my short visit I had conversations with many Germans of various classes. All believed that Russia had provoked the war in order to establish the Slav hegemony over the Germans, and that France was an accomplice in the spirit of *revanche*. All hated the idea of war – the look in their faces haunts me yet – but accepted it with a high courage because they believed it to be necessary for the safety of their country.

The German people, believe me, are better than their Government. We have to fight them, but let us do so in the spirit of gentlemen, giving them full credit for the admirable and amiable qualities to which those who know them best bear loudest witness.

W. ALISON PHILLIPS

To English Girls

From Mr Henry Arthur Jones   *29 August 1914*

[author of *The Liars, Mrs Dane's Defence*, and many other plays, whose entry in *Who's Who* included 'Recreation: hunting sedition']

Sir,

Yesterday morning came the news of a serious set-back to our armies. Yesterday afternoon, while Lord Kitchener was telling of the bravery of our wounded and dead, while he was asking for men to take their places, every lawn tennis court in the space near me was crowded by strapping young Englishmen and girls.

Is there no way of shaming these laggards?

The English girl who will not know the man – lover, brother, friend – that cannot show an overwhelming reason for not taking up arms – that girl will do her duty and will give good help to her country.

Your obedient servant,
HENRY ARTHUR JONES

[The critic GBS had written of his friend, 'His qualities are creative imagination, curious observation, inventive humour, original sympathy, and sincerity']

Fighting and Foxhunting

From Field Marshal Sir Evelyn Wood, VC   14 December 1914

Sir,

I forward herewith a copy of a letter received a few days ago by the honorary secretary of the local hunt. It was written by a general officer who distinguished himself in South Africa as a colonel, in command of a column, 14 years ago, and who has recently added to his reputation. He is not well off, and so, when hunting with this pack, rode 'boarded-out horses', on which he was always in the first flight. It seems to me, however, that he is rich in generous self-sacrifice and thought for others, which is as remarkable as is his military value.

Your faithful servant,
EVELYN WOOD, FM

On Active Service
30 November 1914

Dear Sir,

The soldiers out here doing our share to keep the flag flying feel very grateful to those 'Stalwarts' who are doing their share to keep foxhunting on its legs. We know that you subscribe to our wants, and we feel that we should contribute to the cost of maintaining hunts, in case any of us again have the pleasure of enjoying the 'sport of kings'.

In memory of Auld Lang Syne I enclose a cheque for

the Essex Hunt and £5 toward the Hunt servants, who no doubt will feel the pinch of war as much as anyone.

Yours truly,
'SPORTSMAN'

The Honorary Secretary, Essex Hunt.

Private Letters and the Censorship

From Mr Edmund Gosse   *27 January 1915*

[critic, author of *Father and Son*; knighted 1925]

Sir,

May I appeal to you on a matter which interests a large number of persons, who, like myself, must be at a loss to know how to act?

Before Christmas I wrote a letter to my friend Mr Compton Mackenzie, the novelist, who lives in Capri. It was delivered, after a very long delay (of which we make no complaint), but it was accompanied by a curtly-worded communication from the English censorship, desiring Mr Mackenzie to tell his correspondent that, in future, if the latter wished his letters to be delivered he must write 'shortly and clearly'. As far as 'clearness' is concerned, my handwriting, whatever its demerits, is as clear as print. As far as 'shortness' is concerned, my letter was not longer than one is accustomed to write to a friend abroad. I wrote exclusively about a literary matter interesting to Mr Compton Mackenzie and myself. Political questions, even the war itself, were not mentioned or approached. Mr Mackenzie's reply, which was as long as my letter, and dealt with precisely the same subject, came to me without delay, and without having been opened.

As I desire nothing less than to incommode a busy public department, I wrote privately to the Censor, stating what I have mentioned above, and asking for definite instructions. I have had a civil reply, but not the least explanation or information. Can you, Sir, therefore inform me what number of words the Censor permits a friend in England to address to a friend in a neutral country?

I am, Sir, your obedient servant,
EDMUND GOSSE

No War Profits

[On 11 December 1915 Mr Lloyd George, Minister of Munitions, had delivered a virtuoso speech to the TUC at Bristol. 'We have controlled profits by an Act of Parliament . . . We have nationalised the industries of this country']

From the Headmaster
of Shrewsbury School   *14 September 1915*

[who briefly employed Neville Cardus as his secretary; Dr Alington became headmaster of Eton in 1916, and in 1933 Dean of Durham]

Sir,

It is becoming plain to the average observer of events that there is only one thing which can cause us to lose this war, or can force us to conclude an unsatisfactory peace, and that is the suspicion between different classes in the nation. It is not my purpose to discuss the question whether this suspicion is justified; it is enough that it exists, and that is a statement which you, Sir, are under no temptation to deny.

So far as one can see the suspicion rages mainly round two topics, the rise in the price of necessaries and the amount of war profits; but these two are really one, for the rise in prices would lose half its sting, but for the idea that it is caused by the undue profits of middlemen. The real question before the Government is, therefore, that of the abolition of all war profits; till that is done suspicion will inevitably continue.

And what is the obstacle? It is not undue sympathy on the part of the Government with profit-makers; Mr Lloyd George's speech at Bristol has made that plain. It is not the fear of protests in the Press; you have, if I am not mistaken, repeatedly supported such a measure. It is most assuredly not the fear of public opinion, which would be overwhelmingly on the side of such legislation. The professional classes have borne their own burdens as best they could, but they have no more sympathy than the working classes with the abnormal profits made out of the country's need.

It is time, in fact, to ask the plain question, Who *does* want to make profit out of the crisis? When that question has been answered it will be time for the nation to decide what shall be allowed, but I am much mistaken if the demand will be either loud or clear. When every class has given of its own flesh

57

and blood with such splendid readiness, it is impossible to believe that any will haggle over money. We are told that the Government have already dealt with profits in munition factories, and it is no doubt their intention to deal with other war profits by way of taxation. The purpose of this letter is to implore them to make their actions and their intentions plain beyond the possibility of mistake. Vague assertions do not quiet vague suspicions.

When once a clear principle is laid down, be it abolition or curtailment, the question resolves itself into one of fact, and suspicion will die for lack of food. There can be no objection to the fullest representation of working-class opinion on the committee which is to carry out the principle into action. The present situation of half-hearted promises and forced concessions is both humiliating and demoralizing, and to the average man it seems frankly intolerable that a Government in which we all have good reasons to believe should be unable to give expression to an elementary principle of political morality and should allow us to drift, as we are drifting, into a great and needless danger.

I am, &c.,

C. A. ALINGTON

[If there came to be a link between Dr Alington's fears, the inflated Honours lists of 1917–23, and Mr Lloyd George's £2m secret fund, it showed how wise some had been to spend the war involved in distilling, brewing, shipping, coal, and the manufacture of soap and custard powders]

Commissions to Schoolboys

[A correspondent had pointed out that, although Lord Kitchener, the Secretary for War, frowned on the granting of commissions to boys under 18, his order was not being obeyed]

From Canon Wood   *14 December 1915*

Sir,

May I say one word in reply to the letter of a 'Public School Master', which appears in *The Times* of today (11 December). As an old headmaster, I am not likely to underestimate the value of school discipline. But long experience has convinced me that we keep our boys at school too long. And, as to the commissions to boys, Clive sailed to India at the age of 17; Wolfe, 'a lanky stripling of 15', carried the colours of the 12th Regiment of Foot; Wellington was ensign in the 73rd Regiment at the age of 17; Colin Campbell gained his commission in the 9th Regiment of Foot at the age of 16. We keep our boys in leading strings too long.

I am, Sir, your obedient servant,

JOSEPH WOOD

[The writer was successively headmaster (1870–1910) of Leamington College, Tonbridge School and Harrow School]

The Swords of Fallen Officers

2 January 1915

Sir,

Many swords sent home from the front by the regimental authorities have been so badly labelled that it has been impossible to identify them, and they lie derelict. Some also are said to have disappeared en route. The pain caused to relatives by the non-receipt of a lost one's sword is great. Every care should be taken in the transmission of so precious a relic.

Yours,

THE FATHER OF AN OFFICER KILLED IN ACTION

Shooting at Aeroplanes

[A correspondent had insisted that any good shot (possibly King George V?) should be able to hit an aeroplane. But what should he aim at?]

From Mr Percy Bono   *6 January 1915*

Sir,

The Infantry Training Manual, 1914, page 130, gives instructions for firing at hostile aircraft. It says:

'In the case of rifle fire at aeroplanes men should be instructed to aim six times the length of the machine in front, and in the case of airships at the nose of the envelope.'

Yours obediently,

PERCY BONO

[This correspondent lived in the West End of London]

[Sir George Birdwood, a former Professor of Anatomy and Physiology at Grant Medical College, Bombay, was an authority on incense and carrots, whose letter on the 'mosquito plant' (*Ocimum viride*) appeared in *The First Cuckoo*. During the Great War he was quick to display his wide-ranging interests]

The Hibernation of Flies

From Sir George Birdwood   *4 January 1916*

Sir,

The question of the hibernation of flies having swarmed in the correspondence columns of *The Times* from before St Thomas's Day, as if we were still in 'Bartholomew tide', it may interest some of your readers, if, by your kind favour, I am allowed to place on public record the following instance of the habit, in a particular fly, that came under my own close observation – not scientific, but simply sympathetic; for being half-Hinduized in my philosophy of life, I fully recognize flies as fellow human creatures, and comparatively high up in the scale of 'the 84 millions of millions of transmigrations' through which the soul of Nature gradually ascends from atoms up to man.

In November 1912, a lady taking tea, letting a drop from the cup fall on the back of her left hand, a half-starved fly, that had been warming itself on the shade of an overhanging lamp, at once flew down to sip of it; and was left so to do, until 'well fed up', and with a blessing on its head, it flew back to its hiding-place behind, as was afterwards found, the pier-glass above the mantelpiece. The fly repeated its visits every night of that winter; and after the following spring and summer had passed, repeated them in November of 1913, but for 14 nights only, after which it disapeared for ever.

One of the most humanizing sights of Old Bombay was of the stricter Hindus, of certain castes, feeding with sugar the insects, chiefly ants, among the grass of the 'Esplanade', stretched flush with the sea along the spacious breezy curve of Back Bay; and that notwithstanding their familiar proverb: 'The scorpion bears poison in its tail, the fly in its head.'

I have the honour to be, Sir,
your most obedient servant,
GEORGE BIRDWOOD
St Sylvester's Day, Patron of the Hon East India Co

60

The Kilt in Warfare

From Sir George Birdwood   *7 March 1916*

Sir,

As one always interested in the subject, permit me to comment on two of the questions revived in my mind by the article in *The Times* of Saturday last on 'The Kilt in Warfare'.

The 'feminalia' – i.e. 'femuralia' – of the Romans were swathes or bandages for the thighs, as the 'tibularia' were for the shins: in other words, the Indian *patti* (cf., *pattis*, Daniel 3: 21), *anglice* 'puttee', or 'bandages', just now so familiar among ourselves as the 'leggings' of Lord Kitchener's impromptu levies. The hosen – a German word – of the Scots Highlanders may have been derived from these 'rollers' or 'fillets', for the Romans had apparently no socks or stockings, 'soccus' with them meaning a slipper. But both the Gaelic word 'philabeg' and the Swedish 'kilt' mean a closely plaited, heavily folded – fold upon fold – short skirt, trussed or bunched up, about the thighs, weighing, with the attached sporan or 'purse', over 20lb.

The khaki 'loin-cloth' as at first supplied to 'Kitchener's Army' was not only an egregious, but an absolutely 'odious' travesty of the historical and right manly philabeg; the French term *laideur* used in *The Times* of it really applying it in the stronger sense of the original Old German *laid*.

> I have the honour to be, Sir,
> your most obedient servant,
> GEORGE BIRDWOOD

Soldiers Shot by Firing Squad

From Mr A. J. Smith   *2 May 1972*

Sir,

Regarding 'Facts on 300 soldiers shot by firing squad during the First World War' (April 26), since this implies the incredible average of more than one a week during four and a quarter years of that war the total would seem a matter for verification, though it is generally known that the extreme penalty could be inflicted for a grave dereliction of duty in the field during the Great War.

In this connexion, I recall reading one dank evening in the autumn, 1917, some GHQ orders, that had been fixed on sandbags outside battery billets, at Ypres. These stated that Private so-and-so (giving his full name and regiment) had been tried by court martial and found guilty of absenting himself from support trenches, when under orders to go forward, until apprehended in a forest behind the fighting zone.

He was, the orders grimly went on, sentenced to death by shooting. Then below a line of typographical symbols on the order sheet was the laconic announcement that the sentence had been duly carried out at dawn on such-and-such a day. Thus was an instance of Rudyard Kipling's pregnantly-sombre lines 'I was afraid of death so they took me to meet him blindfold' – even if actually not the whole truth.

Between the two world wars the military law on the subject was changed by Parliament, and offences incurring the irrevocable penalty drastically restricted.

Yours faithfully,
A. J. Smith

On the Eton Word 'Rouge'

From Mr William Warren Vernon   *13 October 1917*

Sir,

I was once, about 30 years ago, discussing the Eton word 'rouge' and the verb 'to rouge' among some English friends at Florence, one of whom was the Hon Alethea Lawley, sister of Lord Wenlock, of Escrick, in East Yorkshire. (NB – She has been for several years married to a Venetian, Signor Wiel, formerly Librarian of the Biblioteca Marciana.) Miss Lawley exclaimed: 'Oh, but "to rouge" is quite a common word in our part of Yorkshire, meaning "to push one's way through anything", and I have often, when two people are quarrelling, heard one of them say, "Now don't ye come a-rouging against me!"' even as at Eton we might have said: 'There was an awful crowd, but I soon rouged my way through it!' Whenever I see a doubtful East Yorkshire word, I always turn to Vigfussen's *Icelandic Dictionary*, wherein I have occasionally found the solution of some difficulties both in Norwegian as well as in East Yorkshire provincialisms. I find in Vigfussen, s.v.: *Rydja* (more anciently *hrjóda*) – *rydja sér til rúms*= 'to make oneself room': again, *rydja sér til rikis*= 'to clear the way to a kingdom, *i.e.*, to conquer it'; and III, 'to clear one's way, to make great havoc – to throng, to crowd'. I never can ignore the possible Scandinavian origin of any word, if it be in use in the east of England.

To give another instance. On one occasion I was reading in Ibsen's *Peer Gynt*, where that rascal is relating a lying tale to his foolish old mother of how he sprang on to the back of a wounded buck and galloped along the Gendin Edge, when suddenly

> 'paa en raadlös braabraet plet
> for ivrejret rype-*steggan*
> flaksed, kaglende, forskraemt
> fra den knart, hvor han sad gemt
> klods for bukkens fod paa eggen.'

'*Steggan*' did not appear in any Norwegian dictionary that I possessed at that time, though it is given in Iver Aasen's *Dictionary of Provincial Dialects*, but I bethought me of Vigfussen, and I found '*Steggr* m. *Steggi*, a.m. (properly a mounter); in Yorkshire a *steg* is a gander, from *stiga* (to mount); a he bird. *Andar Steggi* a male duck,' &c. Therefore the lines translate:

> '(All at once – at a desperate break-neck spot)
> Rose a great cock ptarmigan,
> Flapping, cackling, terrified,
> From the crack where he lay hidden
> (at the buck's feet on the Edge).'

Had I not known from Miss Lawley (30 years ago) that the word 'rouge' is in common use round Escrick, I might not have thought more about it; but as it is, I cannot agree that it is the same in sound and meaning as 'scrooge' (pronounced scroodge) whereas 'rouge' is pronounced exactly like the French equivalent of 'red'.

As it may possibly interest some old Etonians who know Scandinavia, I venture to send you this for what it may be worth.

I remain yours faithfully,
WILLIAM WARREN VERNON

** The word 'rudge' is given in Wright's English Dialect Dictionary, as used in Northumberland, Yorkshire, Lincolnshire, Wilts, and Cornwall, meaning 'to push about', 'handle a person roughly'; reference is also given to 'rooge' or 'rouge', 'to labour hard' (Cornwall).

Stonehenge

From Canon H. D. Rawnsley   *28 September 1918*

Sir,

We can none of us be too grateful to Mr Chubb for his public-spirited gift of Stonehenge to the nation. It may not be feasible, but the thought constantly recurs, why not make this great meeting-place of an ancient British race who worshipped the sun a national memorial of the immortal dead who have laid down their lives that the Sun of Righteousness might arise with healing in His wings for the whole civilized world?

Salisbury Plain as a military training ground has done much towards winning the war. What could be more fitting than that here, in the midst of Salisbury Plain, there should be at this old meeting-place of pre-historic tribesmen and warriors an assemblage on Midsummer Day of each year, or at stated intervals; and that a solemn service should be held in memory not only of Wiltshire men but of all the men of the British Empire who have died for right against might – for justice, freedom, and peace?

The gates of the great stone pylons stand open wide to all the quarters of the heavens, and seem to invite the going forth of light and liberty to all the world. Nothing would be needed but a huge stone Celtic cross in the neighbourhood of the circle, with a simple dedication thereon to the imperishable memory of the gallant dead.

I feel that such a monument in the solemn propinquity of this great British shrine would be preferable to a Priapic monument of cones and Eastern Welis* on a huge bare platform in Hyde Park.

Yours truly,
H. D. RAWNSLEY

[*The tomb or shrine of a Mohammedan saint]

Home in Cattle Trucks

From Mr M. F. Healy   *27 February 1919*

Sir,

Let me add a word to the correspondence in your columns about soldiers travelling in cattle trucks. I left Cologne on 7 February in a train consisting of cattle trucks for the men and uncushioned and unheated third-class carriages for the officers. There was also a 'kitchen car' – a truck with two kitchen ranges and two boilers in it. The best comment on the temperature lies in the fact, to which I pledge my word, that in this kitchen car, with its four fires, any water spilled froze instantly on the floor. Blankets of a very wretched quality were provided: they were translucent, and only served to cover us with hair. As I had been ill, I had provided myself with a hot-water bottle, which I refilled at the engine every couple of hours. Nevertheless, the water in that froze long before it could be renewed. In the trucks for the men was a little straw in some, a small stove in a few. The journey to Dunkirk took 51 hours, and we were met by the query, 'The Adjutant's compliments, and was it true that four men had died of exposure during the journey?' Fortunately the alarm was ill-founded.

My only point in writing is to state in contrast that we left Cologne station full of steam-heated trains – devoted to the German civil population, who are limited to the shortest of journeys! If their journeyings are necessary, why not allow them to use the cattle trucks; or any steam-heated carriages left over when due provision has been made for the comfort of the men who were dragged from their homes by the crimes of these same German people and should not now be returned to these homes in a condition which, with an epidemic raging, invites a fatal disease?

Let me add that from embarkation at Dunkirk there was no reasonable ground for complaint – except, perhaps, that the admirable through trains to the different dispersal stations might also be heated. But these were comfortable trains with cushioned seats, in no way to be compared to the bestial accommodation provided across the Channel.

Yours faithfully,
MAURICE F. HEALY

Turned-up Trousers

From Sir Henry Bashford   *19 April 1952*

Sir,

Forgive this aside in troubled times; but even in such times justice should be done. It was at Oxford, in the early nineties, that I first beheld, as a small boy, the astonishing spectacle of a host of god-like young men, all of whom were wearing – on a fine summer's day – the ends of their trousers turned up. Did this fashion originate at Oxford, and is the originator known? I feel that he must be by somebody. Yet if so, why is it not general knowledge? No philosopher, dictator, hero, or statesman – indeed, nobody else in the history of mankind – can ever have set an example so long and so fervently followed by so many millions of the human species. Is he alive in an ignoring world? If he is dead, why does he lack a monument?

Yours, etc.,

H. H. BASHFORD

From the Assistant Editor, The Outfitter   *21 April 1952*

Sir,

Indeed justice should be done, as your correspondent suggests. Our records show that the first big change in the styling of men's trousers came in 1898 when some Cambridge undergraduates turned up the bottoms of their trousers to show their brightly coloured socks. A great controversy raged around the new style, and shortly afterwards 'turn-ups' became popular. But I believe the originator is still unknown. The fashion of creasing the trousers down the front was started by King Edward VII, creases being at the sides before this. Now the trend is to abandon 'turn-ups' on trousers in a return to Edwardian styling.

Yours faithfully,

CHARLES E. CLARK

From Mr G. McFarlane   *22 April 1952*

Sir,

At Cambridge in the middle nineties some of us turned up
our trouser-ends, but the practice must have been regarded by
the authorities as faintly raffish, for a man presenting himself
for a degree in the Senate House was always required to turn
them down. When I took my degree in 1897 I was in the same
bunch as my friend the late H. H. Thomas, FRS. Being a man
of originality he had turned his ends up. But he was quickly
spotted by the Proctor (or was it the Esquire Bedell?) and
was hustled into the wings (so to speak), whence he emerged
demurely, ends down, to kneel before the Vice-Chancellor.

Your obedient servant,

G. McFARLANE

From Major C. E. Pym   *22 April 1952*

Sir,

Could the fashion of turned-up trousers have originated at
Eton? When I went there in May 1892, we wore all our
trousers turned up, whether they were those which were worn
with tailcoats and Eton jackets, 'fives bags', or change suits;
and of course the bottom buttons of waistcoats were left un-
done. I do not know how long before this date these fashions
had started, but they were well established then.

Yours, etc.,

C. E. PYM

From Sir Roderick Jones   *23 April 1952*

Sir,

Timid by nature, I am shy of questioning the pronounce-
ments of the *Outfitter*, pontifical in its domain. But 60 years
ago the *jeunesse dorée* (chiefly Civil Servants and lawyers) of
Pretoria, then the capital of the Transvaal Republic, were
fastidious about the frontal crease in their trousers. And
Jerome K. Jerome, in his celebrated *Idle Thoughts of an Idle
Fellow* (published in 1889), advised his contemporaries who
could not afford a valet to put their trousers under the bed
when they retired for the night. This obliged him to explain
to a youth who had taken the advice literally and been disappointed with the result that 'under the mattress' obviously
was intended. It was only at a later date that King Edward VII
started the fashion of the crease down the side, but it never

68

became popular and did not endure. In other words, the frontal crease preceded the side crease, and has long survived it.

I have the honour to be, Sir, your most obedient servant,

RODERICK JONES

From Mr E. V. Knox   *23 April 1952*

Sir,

The trousers of Dr Grace
Were not folded at the base,
But surely those of Mr Burnup
Had a turn-up.

Yours faithfully,
E. V. KNOX

[Which may, or may not, explain why Mr C. J. Burnup of Kent headed the first-class batting averages in 1906]

From Mr J. B. Oldham   *23 April 1952*

Sir,

The legend, whether true or not, current at Oxford at the turn of the century, was that the practice of turning up trousers, then a peculiarity at Oxford, was originated by Wilde and the aesthetes to display the highly embroidered socks which they affected in their parades down 'the High'.

Yours faithfully,
J. B. OLDHAM

From Mr J. H. H. Sutcliffe   *24 April 1952*

Sir,

On the subject of fashions in dress in his undergraduate days the late Dr T. G. Bonney, who went up to St John's College, Cambridge, in the Michaelmas term of 1852, wrote in his *Memories of a Long Life*: 'We did not go about, except on wet days, with our trousers turned up, and to have had them stitched into that position would have evoked merciless chaff, and deservedly, for the custom is only surpassed in folly by that of a woman who totters about on narrowing heels two inches high.'

I am, Sir, your obedient servant,
J. H. H. SUTCLIFFE

Sir,

I would be loth to enter a controversy between Cambridge and Eton over turned-up trousers: may I, however, give a French reason for this fashion? In the days of my youth I was told that one fine June day Edward VII, then Prince of Wales, after attending the races at Auteuil prepared to cross the large sandy square opposite the exit, noticed that it had been too well watered, and turned his grey trousers up. The smart young men of the day copied what they thought to be a new royal fashion.

> Yours faithfully,
> MAURICE VIGNON

From Mr M. C. Collier   *25 April 1952*

Sir,

I am pretty sure it was an Eton tailor who introduced 'turn-ups' to trousers, his dictum being that the extra weight of the 'turn-up' gave a better setting to the trousers and prevented bagging at the knees. All upper boys wore turned-up trousers when I left in 1891. Further, I think the Eleven at Lord's had their trousers turned up to show their immaculate white boots. Eton set other sartorial fashions, to wit, the bottom button of waistcoat unbuttoned, and the watchchain across the chest and not across the tummy.

> Yours faithfully,
> M. C. COLLIER

From Sir Guy Nott-Bower   *25 April 1952*

Sir,

> The fact that Mr Burnup's
> Trousers had 'turn-ups'
> Underlined Dr Grace's
> Need for braces.

> Yours, &c.,
> GUY NOTT-BOWER

Sir,

The late Horace de Vere Cole used to claim that it was he who first started the fashion of turned-up trousers when an undergraduate at Cambridge.

Yours faithfully,
AUGUSTUS JOHN

From Mr Eric Parker   29 *April 1952*

Sir,

May I try to suggest a date? I was at Eton from 1883 to 1889. In the eighties, if I remember rightly, the only people who wore turned-up trousers were boys who were members of 'Pop' – the Eton Society. In any case, could not the date be settled by photographs?

Yours faithfully,
ERIC PARKER

From Mr C. F. Simond   29 *April 1952*

Sir,

In the early nineties men were prohibited by the casino authorities in Monte Carlo from entering the gaming rooms with turned-up trousers. This was not on account of any sartorial objection, but it appeared that it was easy to flick a coin off the tables into the 'turn-up'. At least that was the reason given to me by an attendant.

Yours faithfully,
C. F. SIMOND

From Sir Claud Russell   30 *April 1952*

Sir,

If further data are required in the matter of trouser-ends, I recall that, in 1905, at the British Embassy in Paris, a junior attaché, who had been invited to luncheon, made his appearance with trouser-ends turned up. His chief, Sir Francis Bertie, after a look at the young man, directed a glance at the ceiling, as though to see if it was raining, and then, after a closer inspection of the floor, asked his guest whether he considered the drawing-room carpet so muddy as to require him to turn up his trouser-ends.

Yours faithfully,
CLAUD RUSSELL

Sir,

In the Eton mess photograph, taken in 1889, in which Mr Eric Parker is one of the fag masters and I hold a kettle, no one has his trousers turned up. The same holds true for the college photograph of 1889; not even the wearers of white flannels were thus distinguished. In the college photograph of 1893, on the other hand, both the wearers of white flannels had them turned up, as also had a few of the other 68.

Your obedient servant,

R. E. MARTIN

From Sir Henry Bashford   *3 May 1952*

Sir,

Will you allow me to thank the correspondents who have tried to identify the originator of turned-up trousers as a world-wide custom? King Edward VII, Oscar Wilde, Mr Horace de Vere Cole, and some past presidents of 'Pop' have all been suggested, and Oxford, Cambridge, Eton, and Auteuil as possible places of origin – but none, I fear, with the conviction of certainty. The display of socks, the prevention of bagginess, and an intra-school distinction have been put forward as motives. But even if these were the first motives, they could not, I think, account for a response so almost immediate, so international, and, for more than two generations of mankind, so pertinaciously clung to. Some far deeper and more universal aesthetic need must have been diagnosed by somebody – though perhaps unwittingly – and, by this simple device, satisfied. What this was, and why it became manifest when it did, could hardly be dealt with in the scope of a letter. But a clue to the latter can, I think, be found in the minor change that took place, almost concurrently, in the threading of boot and shoes laces. The former involves the mystery underlying all that is embraced in the word 'art'.

Yours, etc.,

H. H. BASHFORD

From the Editor, The Tailor and Cutter   *5 May 1952*

Sir,

Your correspondence concerning the original date and derivation of trouser turn-ups has become so prolonged, and so many factions are now involved, that I feel it my public duty to settle the dispute. In the year 1858 a Mr Aloysius Bredloser (a highly successful kitchen-range manufacturer of the period) attended for a final fitting at his tailor's in Albemarle Street only to find that the trousers were too long. To mark the alteration his tailor turned the bottoms up to the required length. Casually inquiring the price of the suit, Mr Bredloser was startled to find it somewhat beyond his sartorial budget, and taking advantage of his tailor's temporary absence (he had gone for a piece of chalk) Bredloser hot-footed it for home leaving his old suit in part exchange. As the trouser alteration had never been effected, Bredloser was compelled to retain the turned up portions – swearing that he preferred them that way. The apparent idiosyncrasy caught on among his friends and finally became a fashion.

The day of Mr Bredloser's fitting (research discloses) was 1 April 1858; and the time at which he silently pulled the door to behind him and launched himself upon Albemarle Street and society with his trousers turned up was 3.46 p.m. I trust that you will now close this correspondence and oblige

Yours faithfully,

JOHN TAYLOR

Wages near Slough

From His Honour F. R. Y. Radcliffe, KC   *14 March 1919*

Sir,

There has been some controversy as to the wages paid by the Government to labourers on the Cippenham site, near Slough. Here is a concrete case proved before me on oath in a workman's compensation case last month. The applicant was a labourer, about 40 years old, who could neither read nor write. He was employed in loading up cinders near Windsor into motor-lorries and carting them to Slough. He was employed from 13 August 1918 to 4 September 1918, when he met with an accident. His wages, proved from the employers' books, averaged £4 11s 8d a week.

Your obedient servant,

FRANCIS R. Y. RADCLIFFE

Undergraduates' Coal at Oxford

From the Bursar, University College, Oxford   15 January 1919

Sir,

While war lasted I hesitated to complain. The armistice justifies me in making public a wrong which is being deliberately done to the university. The coal allowance for an undergraduate is 7lb per diem. He is denied a daily fire. Even on alternate days he cannot keep a fire all day, for college rooms are large, and not within a house door. So no private study is possible, and, unless a college has very many and large common rooms, study in public rooms is carried on at great disadvantage. The Board of Trade authorized its official to inform the Bursars in September that no appeal from this allowance would succeed. 'They might appeal, if they liked.'

Since then, except once to repudiate its divisional officer, the Board has neither considered nor acknowledged any letter of mine! Mr Prothero [Conservative MP for Oxford University] kindly opened the subject with the Fuel Controller about 2 December. An inquiry 'before next term' was promised. The papers were then, no doubt, pigeon-holed, and nothing has happened! Government officials, not content with commandeering and unduly retaining our buildings and injuring us by delays over dilapidations, must needs cheat the men who fought for them and the younger generation out of their university life. We are treated far worse than an elementary school. This heartless incompetence requires the pen of a Dickens, and I could indicate more than one Sir Tite Barnacle.

Yours faithfully,

A. B. POYNTON

[Robert Graves (*Goodbye To All That*, 1929) rented a cottage from John Masefield on Boar's Hill, though he makes no mention of chopping wood]

Undergraduates' Bedmakers at Cambridge

From the Bursar, Pembroke College, Cambridge 10 April 1919

Sir,

In your issue of today, in a paragraph reporting meetings held in Cambridge on the subject of wages paid to bedmakers, it is stated that 'at Pembroke a bedmaker with nine sets to attend and no "help" receives 12s 9d'. The statement is not correct. All bedmakers in Pembroke College are paid £1 a week, and this wage is paid for 52 weeks in the year. Furthermore, all bedmakers with nine sets of rooms have 'helps', who are paid 15s 6d a week.

I am, yours etc.,
LEONARD WHIBLEY

Locking up Juries

From Mr A. G. Armstrong   *22 September 1919*

Sir,

I was the foreman of the jury which heard the Finsbury Park murder case, and therefore, with my fellow jurors, was locked up for the night of 17 September at the Old Bailey. The jury had to spend the night in one room, on camp beds, with, of course, the two bailiffs in charge – 14 people in one room, who spent a very uncomfortable night. There were no proper conveniences for washing, shaving, &c. Only four jurors were able, at short notice, to obtain their night attire. It should be mentioned, however, that, by the kindness of the Sheriffs, the jury was provided with a very excellent dinner. I am informed that it would have been quite possible to have provided for the accommodation of a jury in such circumstances when the new Central Criminal Court was built, but that to do so would have rendered the premises liable to 'inhabited house duty'.

Yours faithfully,
A. G. ARMSTRONG

Land Values and Inflation

From Lord Hugh Cecil   *24 April 1919*

[Conservative MP for Oxford University 1910–37, later Lord Quickswood]

Sir,

I read of such expressions as 'artificial value' and 'inflated value' of land at the present time. Would it not make the discussion about the compulsory acquisition of land more lucid if these expressions were carefully and exactly expounded? I see nothing specially 'artificial' about the value of land just now. It depends, like all other values, on demand; and if demand may have been stimulated by the Corn Production Act, it must also have been depressed by vague threatenings of a confiscatory kind, and by the requirement made by public opinion that owners of land – or at least large owners of land – should manage their property not only with honesty and integrity, but with a certain graceful generosity, the proper limits of which naturally tend to be wider in the judgement of the public than in that of the owner of whom it is exacted. Indeed, it is obvious that these influences are bringing a great deal of land into the market.

And is the value of land 'inflated' in proportion to other commodities? 'Inflation' means, I suppose, a temporary value which will soon disappear. I have not yet seen anything which seems to show that the general value of agricultural land has risen in price to a greater degree than most commodities. In short, the 'inflation' of the value of land seems to be only the depreciation of the value of money. If that is so, the suggestion that landowners should be compelled to sell at the market value of the year 1913 would merely mean that they should be bought out with a depreciated currency – as it were with dummy half-crowns. This, I am sure, cannot be the intention of any honest person.

But the point which seems to me most to need explanation is why it should be thought that the price which purchasers are now voluntarily ready to give for agricultural land should be a bad bargain for the State or for the smallholders on whose behalf the State is purchasing. Purchasers are not philanthropists; and if they are paying a price, must be assumed to think that they will not lose by it. The only explanation that occurs to me is that purchasers are believed to be paying for the supposed amenities of landownership, and not for that agricultural utility on which the success of a smallholding will depend. But even so, it can hardly be suggested that the landowner ought to be deprived of the value of the amenities of his land. If the State wishes to save the smallholder the burden of the cost of those amenities, it must bear the difference itself.

I am, yours faithfully,

HUGH CECIL

[The internal purchasing power of the £ in terms of 1913 was as follows: 1913 £1; 1920 8s (40p); 1929 12s 2½d (61p); 1938 12s 9½d (64p); 1946 7s 7d (38p). Thereafter . . .]

Children and Cinemas

From the Reverend Dr E. Lyttelton   *21 May 1920*

[Captain of the Cambridge side which beat the Australians by an innings in 1878; Headmaster of Haileybury 1890–1905, of Eton College 1905–16]

Sir,

The statement that Devonshire House is to be turned into a cinema moves me to ask your favour for a suggestion. We dispute as to whether a cinema is good educationally or bad. This is a waste of time. It may be very good; it may be very bad; and that depends, not only on the films – the quality – but on the rapidity and frequency with which they are shown to children – the quantity. Everything that is good for children, even food and kindness, may become terribly mischievous if overdone. Now after having tried, mostly unavailingly, for 40 years to induce young English people to use their brains rightly, that is to think, let me say with emphasis that all pictures are a baneful strain on young children if they are shown quickly. They demand the same expenditure of effort, if they are to be instructive, as making out a half-obliterated inscription does for any adult, or the interpretation of one of your financial articles for an ignoramus. That is true, no matter how good the films may be.

What is going on, then, is this: Being allowed to sit for three hours on end, the more alert-brained children struggle to keep up with the passing shows, and after a time sink into a torpor – the natural defence of our boys against being over-taught. The duller lot sink into that condition at once. In either case they feel as if they were learning when they are not, and become incapable of any true intellectual effort whatever. As now exhibited, this is the films' peculiar spell. I say nothing about their selection: that may be good, though many people doubt it: but there is something in this invention which makes it necessary to represent all life at best as a hustle and a chaos. Elephants are shown scuttling about like antelopes, and the onlooker's mind is violently wrenched from the siege of ancient Babylon to a modern love story, without a word of warning or a second's pause. I am well aware that we none of us really know what good education is; but it certainly is not the soaking of little minds with misleading impressions at the cost of three hours of carbonic acid in the lungs instead of daylight and play.

What, then, ought to be done? Restrict the cinemas for all children under 16 (or 18) to one hour a week: give them a few pictures connected with the history or natural science they have been doing in school, and let each picture be explained by some one who can talk plain English in a clean accent; and let the windows be open, and the light shine through them as often as may be. I am aware of the practical difficulties, but assume they are not insurmountable.

Yours faithfully,
E. LYTTELTON

The St James's Park Kiosk

From Brigadier-General C. J. Markham   *7 December 1922*

Sir,

Some six months ago I wrote to enlist your sympathy on behalf of Mrs Orford, the owner of the refreshment kiosk in St James's Park.

As is now known to all, her kiosk has been pulled down – the site, as I understand, being required for the war memorial of the Brigade of Guards – and a new one on another site has been erected. I have this morning received a letter from Mrs Orford, in which she tells me that she is 64 years of age, and is now without any means of livelihood; for, in spite of the fact that she made a tender of £50 for the new kiosk, her tender was not accepted, and a caterer has, she hears, secured the business at three times that figure. Furthermore, her application for some compensation for this loss has been refused by the government department concerned.

There is, I venture to think, something pitifully mean about this transaction; for the sake of the paltry sum of £100 a year this poor woman has been deprived of her livelihood and a connexion of three centuries has been ruthlessly severed. Protest, I know, is useless, and indignation a waste of energy; but if you, Sir, with your great power and authority, could find means of obtaining some redress for Mrs Orford, I, for one, should be deeply grateful.

I am, Sir, your obedient servant,
C. J. MARKHAM

[The First Commissioner of Works insisted that, even if Mrs Orford could prove lineal descent from any of the stallholders of Stuart times, modern conditions demanded a commercial basis for negotiations]

Women Medical Students

From Dr Charles H. Pring   *9 March 1922*

Sir,

The majority of your correspondents – the ladies in particular – wholly miss the essential objection to mixed medical classes, whether at the London Hospital or elsewhere. Whether a particular lady lecturer feels 'no embarrassment' when dealing with nauseating subjects in her class of boys and girls is beside the mark, save that such absence helps the argument. There is no desire to 'ban' women doctors, nor to bid them keep to their obvious duties in the home, still less to hinder their 'occasional flirtations', the golden opportunities for which are to be found in the mixed schools.

No, the objection is that when young women consort with young men under conditions where ordinary delicacy and modesty are necessarily absent, the normal high standard of conduct is lowered. No matter how choice the demeanour and character of the feminine neophyte, after a few months of the students' common room she becomes coarse, immodest and vulgar. It is because mixed classes have *not* 'put a stop to the reiteration of salacious stories' that such stories are passed on to and readily absorbed by 'the boys in gowns'; that all sweetness and refinement is repudiated; that death itself is made the subject of jest. It is because of these things that those of us who have daughters view the prospect of their possible association with the advancing sisterhood with misgiving and dismay.

Yours, etc.,

CHARLES H. PRING, MA (Fellow of the Royal Society of Medicine)

Purification of Sport

From the Dean of Durham   *11 November 1922*

[Bishop of Calcutta 1898–1902, sometime Headmaster of Harrow School]

Sir,

If it is not inopportune, in the days immediately preceding a general Parliamentary election, to dwell upon a subject of high social, though not political, interest, will you allow me to support the appeal so strongly made in your leading article for the purification of British sport?

Sport is, or once was, a synonym for honourable conduct. The spirit of sport was the spirit of integrity, nay, of chivalry. But it has, of late, been corrupted, partly by the increasing popularity of cruel and brutal pastimes, such as the bull-fights which have been imported from Spain into Southern France; pigeon shooting in its most callous form at Monte Carlo; and, in England itself, the rabbit-coursing which tends to become simple butchery, and, I must frankly add, the boxing-matches which constitute a practical resuscitation of the prize-ring, but partly, too, and perhaps still more, by the abuses which have, in a peculiar degree, invaded the football field, such as the 'barracking', to use the term current in Australia, the refusal not only of the spectators but of the players themselves to accept the decision of the umpires, and the bribery which, according to unimpeachable testimony, has now and again deterred players from doing their best to win their matches at Association football.

Mr Stanley Harris, in a letter which you published on 24 October, says explicitly:

There can be little doubt in the mind of any person who has watched any professional football of late years that sportsmanship is practically non-existent . . . The crowd, as a whole, has no sense of sport whatever. They are there to see their own side win, and they have not much interest as to how that result is accomplished, but do their best, by fair means or foul, to bring it about.

It is probable that the root of the evil in Association football, as elsewhere, is gambling. For, where the love of money comes in, the love of sport for its own sake dies out. The evil, I am afraid, must be acknowledged as being widely spread; but the remedy for it is not easily discoverable. Something may be done by legislation, something, too, by the authorities of the Football Association, if they adopt drastic measures in reference both to the offending players and to the grounds upon which the offences are perpetrated or tolerated. But an enlightened public opinion is the only effective safeguard of the sporting spirit; and I have thought at times that the teachers in secondary and elementary schools might well avail themselves of such opportunities as occur to impress, directly or indirectly, upon their pupils what is the true nature of sport, and how vital is the duty of keeping it clean and pure.

I remain, Sir, your obedient servant,

J. E. C. WELLDON

[In September 1903 Bishop Welldon had been a passenger on the *Orantes* along with P. F. Warner's MCC party en route to Australia. Asked if it was wrong to pray to beat Australians, the Bishop replied 'My dear Warner, anything which tends to the prestige of England is worth praying for.']

Women Barristers and Wigs

From Sir Herbert Stephen   1 April 1922

[Clerk of Assize for the Northern Circuit 1899–1927]

Sir,

I am glad to say that I do not know the name of any member of the Committee of Judges and Benchers of the Inns of Court whose recommendations concerning the forensic costume of women barristers you publish this morning 31 March. I can therefore criticize their 'wishes' without fear or favour.

I have no fault to find with what they recommend about gowns, bands, or dresses. As to wigs, I think they are hopelessly wrong. A wig is, historically and essentially, not a covering, but a substitute for natural hair. I believe the history of the forensic wig to be in substance as follows. About the period of the Restoration, some of the leaders of fashion in France, for reasons of cleanliness and health, took to shaving their heads. They accordingly wore wigs, which soon became very large and elaborate. The fashion found such favour that for something like a century all gentlemen, when fully dressed, wore wigs. During this time they either shaved their heads, or cropped their hair very close, and probably also wore nightcaps when in bed.

Then the wig gradually disappeared, and the modern method of cutting the hair short, but just long enough to make an efficient covering for the head, was gradually adopted. Judges and barristers followed this practice like other people, but found that, as long as the hair was short, the wig formed a distinctive, dignified, and convenient headdress for use in court. If women barristers are going to cut their hair short as we cut ours, our wigs will suit them well enough, but I do not believe they will do anything of the kind.

The Committee wish that their wigs 'should completely cover and conceal the hair'. Why they entertain this wish I cannot imagine. Our wigs by no means completely cover and conceal our hair. Suppose a woman barrister wears her hair 'bobbed'. Her wig, if it completely conceals her hair, will certainly not be an 'ordinary barrister's wig'. Suppose she has plenty of hair, and wears it coiled in one of the usual ways. She will then want one pattern of wig when fashion places the coils on top of her head, another when they are resting on the back of her neck, and a third when they approach the situation of the old fashioned chignon, high up on the back of the head. Each of the three will impart to the wearer a hydrocephalous, ungainly, and ludicrous appearance.

It must be apparent to every one, except the Committee, that women barristers ought to wear a distinctive, and probably dark-coloured, headdress, in approximately the form of a biretta, a turban, or a toque. I use each of these terms with very great diffidence.

I am, Sir, your obedient servant,
HERBERT STEPHEN

[In 1974 Miss Rose Heilbron, QC, became a Judge of the High Court; Sir Herbert Stephen was by then dead]

The Pig in Legend

From Mr Edwin Brough   *7 June 1923*

Sir,

'Tantony' is a new name to me for the small one of a litter of pigs or dogs. Some years ago I made the following collection of names all in use in various parts of the country:

Nisgil (Midlands), Nisledrige and Nestletripe (Devon), Darling, Daniel, Dolly and Harry (Hants), Underling, Rickling, Reckling, Little David (Kent), Dillin, Dilling (Stratford-on-Avon), Cad, Gramper, Nestletribe, Nestledrag, Nestlebird, Dab-Chick, Wastrill, Weed, Dandlin, Anthony, Runt, Parson's Pig (the least valuable to be devoted to tithe purposes), Nest Squab, Putman, Ratling, Dorneedy (Scottish), The Tit-man (Vermont), Nestledraft, Pigot, Rutland, Luchan, Piggy-Widden.

Yours faithfully,
EDWIN BROUGH

Who is Respectable?

From Mr A. P. Herbert   *8 February 1923*

[later Independent MP for Oxford University 1935–50; knighted 1945; Companion of Honour 1970]

Sir,

Is it not time that the official categories of respectability were revised?

In order to secure the renewal of a passport, it is necessary to obtain a signed declaration of identity and fitness from a mayor, magistrate, justice of the peace, minister of religion, barrister-at-law, physician, surgeon, solicitor, or bank manager, with whom the applicant is personally acquainted; and similar lists are found on many other official forms. On what principle they were compiled I know not, but they cause considerable inconvenience, and defeat their own end.

I never knew a mayor. But I have known many Civil servants of reasonable integrity, and in my neighbourhood are two or three not more unscrupulous than the rest of their profession; I am friendly with two editors; I know a peer; several stockbrokers, baronets, novelists, and Members of Parliament would readily swear that I am a fit and proper person to go to France. But these gentlemen are not worthy, and I am forced to search any casual acquaintance for magistrates and dental surgeons, who, in fact, know nothing about me.

For persons even poorer than myself the difficulty is more serious. As a rule, the only 'respectable' people they know are the physician and the clergyman, and why should these alone be bothered with the things? Why not the policeman, the postman, the landlord, the tax collector? Things have come to a pretty pass in this democratic age if the word of an attorney is more than the word of a publisher: and if we cannot trust a policeman, whom can we trust?

The result, in most cases, is that the applicant obtains a solemn declaration from that one of his acquaintance who knows least about him. This is the kind of trivial official rubbish which is allowed to endure for ever because no one thinks it worth while to protest. I therefore protest that these antiquated and offensive lists should be revised, as above, or, if that be too daring, abolished altogether.

Why not simply 'a householder'?

I am, Sir, yours faithfully,

A. P. HERBERT

Pace of a Bricklayer

[The Director-General of Housing, Ministry of Health, had claimed that the British bricklayer was the best in the world, his target 500 bricks a day. A letter signed 'Builder' decried this effort: not only would a patriotic British bricklayer deal with 2,000 bricks in eight hours, one particular hero had just laid 809 bricks in a single hour. A still greater hero was then discovered]

From Professor H. H. Turner   *5 January 1925*

[Savilian Professor of Astronomy in the University of Oxford, 1893–1930]

Sir,

I was puzzled, probably in company of other readers, to learn that a bricklayer had recently laid 879 bricks in an hour, under supervision. Naturally, I did not expect this record performance to be approached in an average day's work, but believing that the number for a whole day is often a mere fraction of his hourly rate, I ventured to ask my friend, Mr J. E. Drower, whose articles on the housing problem in your columns recently attracted attention, to comment on the very considerable discrepancy. His answer seems to me so interesting that I venture to think you may care to give it publicity in your columns, for which I have obtained Mr Drower's consent.

Yours faithfully,
H. H. TURNER

Dear Turner,

I am quite prepared to accept the statement that a bricklayer has laid 879 bricks in an hour. He must be an exceptional man working under exceptional circumstances; everything must be made easy for him and everything placed ready to his hand. The cost of labourers' attendance that he would want would nullify to a great extent the advantage coming from the extra number of bricks laid per hour. It is a mere *tour de force* and of no value to found any rule upon; a man could not keep it up any more than a sprinter could run at the rate of $9\frac{1}{2}$ secs per 100 yards for six miles.

Eight hundred and seventy-nine bricks with the mortar

weigh three tons. In building them they would have to be moved by the bricklayer: the horizontal component of the movement would be about 4ft and the vertical would average 3ft 6ins. This in itself would be a great effort. Before the war it was considered a very good day's work for a navvy to shovel up two cubic yards of earth from a loose heap so placed that, in dealing with it, the navvy had not to move from his place. Instead of the navvy's simple movement, a bricklayer has to pick up his bricks one by one from one heap, to fill his trowel with mortar from another, to bed and joint the bricks, to plumb and aline them, and occasionally to cut and fit them. Eight hundred and seventy-nine bricks an hour give him 4.10 sec. for each brick. A man would have to be supernaturally clever to turn out good work at such a speed. As I said, it can only be called a *tour de force*, for which parallels can be found in every trade and from which no rule can be deduced.

There is some misunderstanding as to the number of bricks which a bricklayer is allowed under trade union rules to lay in a day. Every job of any size is under the supervision of shop stewards, who settle what they consider a proper day's work should be. The number of bricks varies with the sort of work; it may be as low as 300; it may be a good deal higher, but it is always too low. Just at present men are working very badly when under shop stewards. When the jobs are small and only one or two bricklayers are employed, there is seldom any interference on the part of the trade unions and the men work very much better. In such cases it is not uncommon to get 1,000 bricks a day laid without any pushing or undue exertion. In the good old piece-work days of 10 hours, 1,300 bricks a day were considered to be the maximum. I am speaking throughout of plain straightforward work. The trade union rules regarding restriction of output are not written and are not rigid; they vary with every job and the shop steward is the authority; sometimes he gets a bad half-hour in the trade lodge when the men are dissatisfied with him.

Yours sincerely,
J. E. DROWER

[Mr Drower had been the first Director of the Building Materials Supply for the war-time Ministry of Munitions. Like Professor Turner he was a Fellow of the Royal Astronomical Society.

An internationally known builder was asked in 1982 the

daily achievement of his bricklayers: his reply was '800'. Which would suggest that the 500 bricks a day achieved by Ministry of Health bricklayers in 1925 reflected a civil service tempo]

Longevity Records in 'The Times'

From Mr C. B. Gabb   *1 January 1925*

Sir,

On the front page of *The Times* last year there were reported the deaths of 402 persons of 90 years of age and over. Of these 123 were men (including 18 clerks in holy orders) and 279 women; of the latter 178 were married. The number of those who reached their century is eight; of these two were men and six women, two of whom were 105 and had been married. Four others (two men, one a clerk) were 99. Besides the above named, 95 attained their 90th year, 28 men (six clerks) and 67 women, of whom 30 were married. The number of nonagenarians who have died in the last ten years is 3,153, a yearly average of 315, ranging from 263 in 1918 to last year's big total of 402. The number of centenarians for the same period is 55, the most in one year being 11 in 1923.

In other parts of *The Times* deaths have been reported of 40 others who had been born before or during 1824. Of these four were 103; six, 104; one, 105; four, 106; and one, 107. Under 'News in Brief' on 16 August, John Campbell, of County Antrim, aged 112, is reported dead; and on 18 August, under 'Telegrams in Brief', the same is told of Alexa Vivier, of Manitoba, who had reached the, nowadays, patriarchal age of 113.

I am, etc.,

C. B. GABB

[Mr Gabb's finest hour came on 1 January 1935, the occasion of *The Times*'s 150th birthday, when a column-length letter on longevity took pride of place. Not only had the last surviving Crimean veteran, William Freeman, died in Adelaide aged 104, but Zaro Agha had passed on at 157. Mr Gabb emphasized that this Turk could (and naturally would) have read 46,950 issues of *The Times* – had he not been illiterate]

A Managed Currency

From Mr J. M. Keynes [Baron 1942] *26 March 1925*

Sir,

I hesitate to trespass upon your space yet again. This most
fundamental problem of modern economic society requires a
wider flight of thought and speech than I can expect you to
accommodate. Confined within the birdcage of a column, one
can but hop helplessly from one small perch to another.

But when Mr Wynnard Hooper gives, with your aid, much
prominence to the statement that it is my policy to hand over
to the Treasury the future management of our currency, I am
compelled to send you a disclaimer. The passage in my 'Tract
on Monetary Reform', which Mr Hooper detaches from its
context, concludes an argument in which I maintain that he
who manages the volume of credit is master, that the note-
issue merely follows suit, and that, therefore, when credit is
managed note-issue needs no management at all and may just
as well be left in the hands of the Treasury, who are anyhow
entitled to the profit. Mr Hooper is so steeped in the old idea,
that the management of the note-issue is the essential thing,
that he does not notice how I have deposed it by substituting
the management of credit.

So far from wishing to diminish the authority of the Bank
of England, I regard this great institution as a heaven-sent gift,
ideally suited to be the instrument of the reforms I advocate.
We have here a semi-independent corporation within the State,
with immense prestige and historical traditions, not (in fact)
working for private profit, with no interests whatever except
the public good, yet detached from the wayward influences of
politics. In the last resort the Cabinet and the Chancellor of
the Exchequer must have their way – in the future, as now
and always. But it must be the Bank of England which manages
our credit system day by day and takes its orders from no one
except in the most public way and under public protest.

The Bank of England is a type of that socialism of the future
which is in accord with British instincts of government, and
which – perhaps one may hope – our Commonwealth is evolv-
ing within its womb. The universities are another example of
the semi-independent institutions divested of private interest
which I have in mind. The State is generally sterile and creates
little. New forms and modes spring from the fruitful minds of
individuals. But when a corporation, devised by private resource,

87

has reached a certain age and a certain size it socializes itself, or it becomes an abuse, or it falls away in decay. As time goes on not a few of the institutions which a hundred years ago were individualistic experiments are socializing themselves. But none, perhaps, except the Bank of England – and (should I add?) *The Times* newspaper – has yet completed the process. I differ from the immediate policy of the Bank of England; but it is on the greatness and the prestige of this institution, which no one has done more to increase than the Governor who now holds office, that I rest my hopes for the future.

We still pretend to manage our currency as though we did all our business with lumps of sacred metal. But the pretence wears thinner and thinner. Those who advocate the deliberate management of our credit system from the point of view that our credit-money represents not gold but the actual working capital of our industries must not be in a hurry; for they are proposing a big change in a sphere where those who must settle the matter are necessarily unfamiliar with the intricate reasons for the change. The reformers are impugning an orthodoxy and must expect, therefore, at this stage to be met with 'moral' objections, with 'psychological' prejudices, and with appeals to the immutability of human nature as exhibited in the fashions of today. At present, to debate monetary reform with a City editor (or an ex-City editor) is like debating Darwinism with a bishop 60 years ago. But even bishops – so why not City editors? – move in the end.

J. M. Keynes

The Yale's Horns

From the Master of Christ's College, Cambridge   15 June 1926

Sir,

A few years ago, when the King's Beasts were placed on the bridge over the moat leading to the gateway at Hampton Court Palace, I was distressed beyond measure at the effigy of the Yale. Both its horns were directed backwards! I drew the attention of the late Lord Harcourt to this on more than one occasion, and he was genuinely vexed and said that something must be done. But judging by a picture postcard I have recently received, nothing has been done.

My distress and grief have been increased by the action of those who are responsible for restoring the King's Beasts on the outside of the Royal Chapel at Windsor, for here again the Yale has both horns pointing backwards. The Dean of Windsor kindly lent me for a day or two a little book which clearly shows this appalling lack of appreciation of what a Yale really is. For it is in the very essence of a Yale to have one horn pointing forward over the nose and the other horn pointing backwards. I have traced the history of the Yale back to the fourth or fifth Egyptian dynasty, back to the old kingdom, nearly 3,000 years BC. One finds them repeatedly throughout Egyptian art. Herodotus describes them as δπυνθονδμοι, because their horns curve forward in front of their heads so that it is not possible for them when grazing to move forward, as in that case their horns would become fixed in the ground. Aristotle gives a similar account. Pliny describes their horns as mobile, so that should the front horn be injured in a contest the horns are swivelled round and the hinder horn now comes into action. But in spite of Pliny's uncritical mind and unbridled fancy, he could hardly have invented the Yale. At the present time certain of the domesticated cattle in the great territory of the Bahr-el-Ghazal, to the south of the White Nile, have their horns trained by the natives, one to project forward and one to project backwards.

One of the Canons of Windsor states that the new King's Beast on the outside of the Royal Chapel was copied from one in the interior of the chapel. Should this be the case, those who have been or are responsible for the King's Beasts at Windsor are doubly guilty, for they are misleading the public not only without but within the walls of the sacred edifice. It is impossible to test the accuracy of this statement owing to the present reparations to the building. A distinguished archaeologist in the neighbourhood of Windsor who has been kind enough to inspect for me the false Yales on the outside of the chapel, writes that 'we can do little but mourn'. But surely that is a counsel of despair. At Hampton Court Palace, and still more on or in the Royal Chapel at Windsor, under the very shadow of Royalty, we might at least expect a certain degree of historical and heraldic accuracy in such matters as the King's Beasts, and the horns of the Yales should be set right.

I am, Sir, yours faithfully,
A. E. SHIPLEY

[Sir Arthur Everett Shipley appeared in *The First Cuckoo* as an authority on leeches; one of his main interests was parasitic worms]

A Customs Account

From Mr E. M. Hendley   6 *January 1928*

Sir,

I have received a parcel containing one cushion cover of artificial silk and cotton, value 3s 6d, from India, with declaration all in order. A charge of 1s 4d was made, stating Customs duty 10d and Post Office fee for Customs clearance 6d. The parcel had also been opened by the Post Office, and was delivered last Thursday, the 29th.

E. M. HENDLEY

For Better Elocution

From the Reverend W. Williamson   6 *June 1928*

Sir,

The subject of elocution in the theatre being closely akin to speaking in our churches, may I suggest some few useful rules?

(1) Read or speak so that a person sitting at two-thirds of the total distance of the space to be reached may hear.

(2) Stop at the mental pictures the words are to convey – the punctuation marks are mainly the concern of the grammarian and the printer, e.g., 'There was a man of the Pharisees (slight pause) named Nicodemus.'

(3) The speaker should acquaint himself with the acoustic properties and peculiarities of the building.

(4) If we are young or not too old to learn, a visit to the Law Courts, there to hear our leading barristers, or to the theatre to hear Sir Johnston Forbes-Robertson, who tells us, I believe, that 'our syllables should be like pistol shots', would be helpful.

(5) Our pauses must be at the right pace, lest we say, for instance, 'a man going to see (sea) his wife, desires the prayers of the congregation'.

I am, &c.,
W. WILLIAMSON

The Cook's Vote

From Mr A. A. Milne   *24 October 1928*

Sir,

'In pursuance of the Representation of the People Acts', I have been 'entering below' the 'other names' of 'domestics ordinarily resident on above premises'. To ask one's cook suddenly for her Christian name, and, on being told a little shyly, apparently to reject it and demand an alternative (if any), is a proceeding so unusual in our house that some explanation of it was necessary; and in the course of this the domestic attitude in regard to voting assumed an unexpected clarity, such as might be expressed in the words, 'All stuff and nonsense.' In more parliamentary language, the staff did not appear anxious to exercise the franchise so hardly won for it.

Now what am I to do? Assert my authority as Occupier of a Dwelling-House, Tenement, or Lodgings Let Unfurnished, and insist that the staff shall function civically? Very well. But some further guidance will be necessary. In the first proud moment of full citizenship one tends to shower crosses on all candidates impartially. 'No, no,' I shall say. 'Rather must one concentrate with one cross only on one candidate. I myself, just to give you an example of how the thing works, I myself am concentrating on——.' Well, in short, Sir, I came out of the kitchen full of the discovery that I had three more votes in my pocket; full of envy of the millionaire with 15; and full of admiration of the artist who contrived such a masterpiece of plural voting, and, in the modern manner, framed it upside down and called it 'The Triumph of Democracy.'

Yours, &c.,

A. A. MILNE

The Male Servant Tax

From Mr Geoffrey E. Howard   *6 January 1930*

Sir,

At the beginning of every year one particularly deplores the fact that the late W. S. Gilbert is no longer with us. Successive governments continue to impress upon us the supreme necessity for stemming the tide of unemployment. But those of us who try to contribute our small quota to the solution of this problem by employing men, sometimes unnecessarily, as extra gardeners, footmen, or chauffeurs are rapped over the knuckles by the authorities to the tune of a penalty of 15s for each man we save from the dole.

Yours faithfully,
GEOFFREY E. HOWARD

The Georgians

From Lady Cust   *3 November 1930*

[writing from The Cloisters, Eton College; her husband, Sir Lionel Henry Cust, was Surveyor of the King's Pictures and Works of Art 1901–27]

Sir,

Is it not time that certain of the Victorians stood aside for a little while and stopped finding fault with the present generation? We can hardly pick up a paper nowadays without reading the lamentation of pessimists over England's wretched state. A few days ago, someone writing to *The Times* quoted 'a middle-aged masseur' who considered there was no one left in the country to be trusted. Now another has been bewailing our vanished dignity and the golden days that will never return. Well, were they so very golden? For the comfortable classes in their great houses yes; but what of the Crimean heroes who walked the streets and lanes destitute and hopeless, and the great gulf fixed between rich and poor; derelicts for whom there was nothing save haphazard charity between starvation and the workhouse; and the jerry-built homes that directly caused the slum problems of today?

It is true that the young are not easily discouraged. But it is scarcely helpful to be constantly reminding them that the country is completely decayed, and that they can never hope to do as well as those who have gone before them. When a great life is closed the usual wail is raised about 'the last of his kind' and 'a torch gone out in the dark', and so forth. It is not true. Let our pessimists stop their croaking and watch the glorious achievements of this generation; things unheard of, undreamt of, in their day.

Yours obediently,
SYBIL CUST

The Blackthorn Winter

From Sir Napier Shaw   *25 April 1931*

[Director of the Meteorological Office 1905–20]

Sir,

In your issue of Wednesday 22 April, Mr H. St Barbe, asking for an explanation of a 'blackthorn winter', raises a meteorological question of a more general character than those which form the subjects of official reports. It may be connected with a line of thought concerning the movement of air over the surface of the globe which came into a talk of the BBC in the holiday season last summer; the association is perhaps of sufficient general interest to justify my asking for space to indicate it.

Let us bear in mind that in ordinary circumstances a square foot of surface at sea-level carries about a ton of air, and the movement of air is wind. Next, in the middle of January, the total stock of air on the surface of the northern hemisphere is five billion tons above par, and in the middle of July about the same amount below par. So between January and July 10 billion tons of air are transferred from the northern hemisphere to the southern and brought back again within the year. The process of transfer of those tons of air may have something to do with the question. It is of course merely by-play on the atmospheric stage in which the sun takes the 'star part', and common experience tells us it never repeats itself exactly year after year.

The winter stock of air is kept in cold storage on the great land-areas and the ice-covered polar regions. Not merely the opposite hemisphere, but also the very oceans of their own are preyed upon by the areas which are greedy for cold air. There is a mechanism well known to meteorologists which prevents the store leaking away across its boundary, but with the turn of the sun the mechanism begins to fail, and with January the delivery to the southern hemisphere begins. The blackthorn winter and St Luke's summer, each a month after the equinoxes, when the distribution of pressure over the hemisphere is comparatively speaking featureless, are in the middle of the busiest traffic. Between March and May 3·3 billion tons of air have to be got across the equator, and between September and November 4·2 billion tons have to find their way back.

It may be allowed that the escaping air starts cold and will hug the surface. It would be interesting and it may perhaps be possible to make out its track – certain it is that it cannot get over the backbone of the Eurasian continent; it has to find an easier way than that. The supply may come from different parts of the depôt at different times; northern Asia may come first, north polar regions next, and the commencement of the midnight sun in the north may be the preliminary signal for evacuating the area to the north of us. For us air from the north (if it misses the North Sea) is dry, and air from the south carries moisture; so the scheme fits, for March is our driest month and October our rainiest.

Moreover, we know that the north-east trade winds carrying northern air to the equator are strongest, and the doldrum line, where north and south meet, is farthest south in April – and the south-east trades carrying the air northwards are strongest in September, when the doldrum line is farthest north and the season of West Indian hurricanes at its height.

Let us say, then, that the 'blackthorn winter' arises from the transfer southward of the surplus air of the polar regions, cold when it passes us; and St Luke's summer is part of the process of stocking the northern hemiphere with air for the winter supplied from the southern hemisphere, warm when it passes our islands but chilled on its arrival at the depôt.

This, of course, is outline; some day the filling in will make an interesting scene in the drama of the atmosphere.

I am, etc.,

NAPIER SHAW

Skywriting

From Mr Lionel Curtis   *6 January 1932*

[once a member of Milner's kindergarten in South Africa]

Sir,

After reading your leading article on New Year's Day and drawing new courage for the future, one learns on another page what, in this 'year of opportunity', we English may look to find written in our skies. The magnificent progress of invention is to cover 'this most excellent canopy, the air, look you, this brave overhanging firmament, this majestical roof fretted with golden fire' with advertisements projected by searchlights of 3,000,000,000 candle-power.

Let me quote verbally from the notes of your Correspondent on page 7 of your New Year's issue:

There is perhaps little danger that the night sky will be made ugly by this sort of advertisement, for it occupies comparatively little space, and the rights in the use of the process are being rigidly controlled by the inventors. The authorities have also been consulted since the conclusion of the experimental stage, and *the Admiralty, War Office, and Air Ministry have stated that they have no objection to the use of the device.*

The most precious amenities of our life are entrusted, it seems, to the three Departments of War.

Are we really to understand that Sir Bolton Eyres-Monsell, Lord Hailsham, and Lord Londonderry have knowingly approved a proposal to hand over our common heritage in the glory of the skies to a monopolist syndicate, to be leased in patches to purveyors of soap, cigarettes, patent medicine, and suchlike? Surely these Ministers, when they realize what their offices are said to have done, will allow Parliament to consider the question before, and not after, we are faced by a vested and heavily capitalized interest in the prostitution of the heavens themselves.

'Few starlit nights', we are told, 'are so free from mist as to be unsuitable for projection.' A most valuable fact for the holders of the patent; but I challenge your Correspondent to explain what possible public interest will be served by obscuring the stars with the kind of advertisements that already disfigure the face of the earth. The monetary value of the invention too obviously lies in the fact that advertisements thrown on the clouds involve the most comprehensive vulgarization of Nature that the wit of man can devise.

We are told that 'during the tests arrangements were made to collect evidence from members of the public'. I suggest that *The Times* by inviting comment on this proposal is better qualified than the inventors to discover whether the public really wishes them to exploit the clouds. I therefore appeal to you to do so.

We are told in the article that English and German inventors are joint pioneers in this final outrage of commercialism on the universe. Unless something is done quickly to reserve sky-writing to the government for national purposes only, the night skies in every part of the world will be plastered with advertisements. An example set by us will be followed in all countries in which public interests are not at the mercy of commercial rapacity. Once again England may save not only herself, but the world, by timely exertion. In this 'year of opportunity' 1932 may deserve the motto:

Thou dost preserve the stars from wrong,
And the most ancient heavens, through thee,
are fresh and strong.

I remain, sir, your obedient servant,
L. CURTIS

Cheaper Weddings

From the Reverend Philip Browning   *26 January 1932*

[Vicar of Emmanuel Church, Camberwell]

Sir,

Thank you for your leading article on 'Cheaper Weddings' in *The Times* of 21 January. I have not in one sense halved the wedding fees, but the old regime before I came to Emmanuel was 13s 7d on week days, and double fees on Sundays and holidays.

These double fees were iniquitous, for though on the face of matters it may seem harmless enough, yet in reality it penalized the average couple in this parish because Sunday or a holiday is the only day they can afford to get married upon, and the Church promptly pounced on them and said: 'Very well, if you choose Sunday it shall be at a double price.' For two or three months I carried on this tradition, and then I took counsel with the rural dean, who advised a flat rate.

I should dearly like to abolish all banns and wedding fees, though it would mean a loss to the benefice, because our people are very poor, and when they came and agreed to those high fees I often wondered from where the fees would come.

When working in the diocese of Singapore 'the chaplain had power to remit fees in cases of poverty'. And always when I married the poorer Tamils or Telugus I asked for a packet of candles for the altar and a few cents for the church peon. That was all.

And I think the same principle should apply to any parish where mission work similar to that as in my old diocese obtains. And surely our parish easily comes under that heading.

Yours sincerely,
PHILIP BROWNING

A Wife for Sale

From Dr Cloudesley Brereton   *3 May 1932*

Sir,

The extract on the sale of a wife from *The Times* of 100 years ago, in your issue of today, reminds me of what the late George Danby Kerrison once told me. As a small boy he was riding one day with his uncle down one of our Norfolk roads, when they came across a farmer standing by the wayside with a woman 'with only her shift on' and a rope round her neck, as if she was an animal for sale. She was his wife, and he was offering her to the passers-by for 10s. Another farmer bought her, and the curious thing is that the woman, who lived for several years with her second 'husband', was treated by the neighbours with exactly the same consideration as if she had been his lawful wife. Judging by my friend's age, this must have happened much later than 1832 – round about 1840, in fact.

> Yours faithfully,
> CLOUDESLEY BRERETON

The Abhorred Shears

From Mr F. Warren   *17 October 1932*

Sir,

In the Rhineland two or three years ago, driven to risk even the Prussian haircut, I sat in the barber's chair. After the universal formalities, the operator pushed home a wall plug connected by a length of flex to some gadget in his right hand and prepared to attack from the rear. Before I had time to co-ordinate impressions a hornet, or so it seemed, with power amplifier burst into full song behind my left ear, but any reaction that might have been induced was suppressed when the buzzing atrocity began to crawl and browse about my scalp.

Pride of race gave me self-control. Thought, so far as thought was possible, toyed with short circuits, Sing Sing, voltages, and reaping machines. The ordeal ended with an intimate exploration of the inner ear by the buzzing horror and a query from the barber as to whether we had the instrument in England. With an involuntary 'No! thank Heavens!' I left.

Returning home soon afterwards and visiting my barber I found the Terror to be among us; now one cannot evade it, and I am haunted by the guilty fear that my thoughtless exposure of our immunity may have led to the subsequent invasion. Man is traditionally impotent when in the barber's chair, but now that the type and War Loan conversion schemes are disposed of perhaps *The Times* could voice a protest against the adoption of sheep-shearing apparatus as an aid to hair dressing and restore to the operator his outlet for vocal and muscular expression.

Yours faithfully,
FRANK WARREN

['The Terror' had been introduced into England from the United States soon after 1910; it is even possible the editor of *The Times* had endured it]

British Army in India

From Sir Michael O'Dwyer   *2 May 1932*

Sir,

All who have seen for themselves the splendid discipline and self-control of the British soldier in India under the most trying conditions will welcome Sir Samuel Hoare's [Secretary for India] public refutation (in your issue of 30 April) of the infamous slanders invented by propagandists in India and circulated by their allies here.

May I reinforce his statement by my own experience as Lieutenant-Governor of the Punjab in 1919? The Punjab troubles of that year were caused by similar anti-British calumnies eagerly swallowed by a credulous and excitable population. The most effective were that the British soldier was a demon in human shape; that British troops at Amritsar had fired at and bombed the Sikh Holy of Holies (the Golden Temple) and had outraged Sikh girls there under the pretext of searching for hidden weapons. There was not a word of truth in any of these allegations. But mark the effect on ignorant mobs. To start with they were exhorted to take reprisals on English women. On 10 April in Amritsar City two Europeans were murdered with appalling brutality, and

98

attempts were made to murder two English missionary ladies. On 12 April the train to Lahore was held up at Kasur, two British warrant officers in uniform were clubbed to death, two officers and two NCOs were badly injured but fought their way through; a European lady and her three children were saved by the gallant action of a Muslim inspector.

These facts were known to our British troops and I feared reprisals. On that same date we recovered possession of Lahore City from a rebel mob by a strong military force. To maintain order pockets of British troops from the 4th Sussex were posted in the town hall, waterworks, and at the city gates, and kept up a regular patrol of the main bazaars. Many of these had been deserted by the shopkeepers during the disturbances. In some cases the shops had been left open and unprotected, but the British soldiers effectively prevented any looting by hooligans. After a day or two Hindu shopkeepers began to creep back. They could hardly believe their eyes when they saw their goods and chattels safe; a few days more and they re-opened their shops; in a short time the British soldiers dropped in to purchase fruit, sweetmeats, cigarettes, etc. The now grateful shopkeepers offered them without payment, but to their amazement the soldiers insisted on paying.

So things went on for some weeks till the battalion was ordered to the Frontier to meet the Afghan invasion. At this stage the people of the city sent a deputation to me at Government House to express their contrition for the anti-British outbreak, and their gratitude for the security and protection afforded by the British troops. I well remember their concluding words: 'We were told the *gora log* (soldiers) were *shaitans* (devils); we have found them to be angels.' The British soldier would probably blush at this description; but the British people may well be proud of it and of him.

I am, etc.,
M. F. O'DWYER

[History also recalls that on 13 April 1919 Brigadier-General Reginald Edward Harry Dyer ordered British troops to fire on an unarmed mob in an enclosed area of Amritsar: 1,650 rounds killed 379 Indians and wounded 1,200. In due course the Commander-in-Chief sent General Dyer home, where he was praised in the House of Lords and received £26,000 from a *Morning Post* testimonial]

'True Facts'

From Mr Arthur Horner   *18 May 1933*

Sir,

When you write the leading article on 'True Facts' and similar *clichés* I hope you will deal faithfully with the horrible 'I personally', 'my personal opinion', and other variants of super-egotism. And the monotonous 'special'; why is an interview to 'our special correspondent' invariably 'specially granted'? And why nowadays are the facts 'revealed'? (They used to be elicited, which was worse.)

And 'rushed', too; the mangled pedestrian is always 'rushed' to hospital – how much more humane merely to take him there. But perhaps this last is self-explanatory, as the impression of speed must be given to everything since the Sunday morning church parade was superseded by the Sunday afternoon hire-purchase procession.

Yours faithfully,
ARTHUR HORNER

American Prepositions

From Dr T. R. Glover   *8 February 1933*

[Public Orator in the University of Cambridge 1920–39]

Sir,

'In order to try out the possibilities of these new methods' – did Mr Baldwin really say that at Cambridge on Friday? I cannot believe that you would put an Americanism into his mouth. It is not for a mere MA to criticize his Chancellor; but am I to take it that the Chancellor admitted this phrase, as it were, to an honorary degree? 'To try out' – are we to accept it as English, and Cambridge? Out upon him!

Do you notice how 'out' creeps in? St Paul long ago told us to work out our own salvation; endless people tell us to look out; 'little orphint Annie' (she was American, though, from Indiana) warned us that 'the goblins will get you if you don't watch out'. When Professor Kapitza and his staff have 'tried out' their methods, does Mr Baldwin expect them to 'win out' or to 'lose out'? I respectfully hope neither.

That raises yet another point. Lewis Carroll, when he described Hiawatha's photographing, ended his tale by narrating how –

> He left them in a hurry,
> Left them in a mighty hurry,
> Stating that he would not stand it,
> Stating in emphatic language
> What he'd be before he'd stand it.

Now, though the metre is American (really Finnish, I believe), that is honest English, isn't it? But today in America Hiawatha would say 'he wouldn't stand for it'. I hope Mr Baldwin would *not* say it: and if, as Chancellor, he says he will not 'stand' all this from me, I hope you, Sir, will stand up for me.

Yours, etc.,
T. R. GLOVER

From Professor Ernest Barker   *9 February 1933*

[Professor of Political Science in the University of Cambridge 1928–39; knighted 1944]

Sir,

Dr Glover gambols humorously in regard to American prepositions. But is he not, in this matter of 'try out', mounted upon the wrong elephant?

To 'try out' is to refine and to purify the good stuff of a metal from the clinging dross. The term is a term of Biblical and Tudor English, as other 'Americanisms' sometimes are. *The New English Dictionary* cites the Great Bible of 1539: 'Examen me, O Lord, & prove me; trie out my reynes and my hert.' When Mr Baldwin spoke of 'trying out the possibilities of new methods', he used an apposite metaphor and a piece of fine old English.

I am, Sir, your obedient servant,
ERNEST BARKER

Marmalade at Breakfast

From the Reverend E. S. Haviland   *11 July 1973*

Sir,

    What a dangerous omission. A loyal English knight defends and extols the excellence of the English breakfast without a mention of English *marmalade* (Sir Dingle Foot, special article, 30 June).

Yours faithfully,
EDMUND S. HAVILAND

From Mr Peter Macdonald   *13 July 1973*

Sir,

    Despite the strictures of the Rev. E. S. Haviland, Sir Dingle Foot is undoubtedly correct in omitting marmalade from an English breakfast. Marmalade, like many other inventions, which other nations have sought to appropriate, is of Scottish origin, since it took a canny Scot to see value in the peel that others threw away.

Yours faithfully,
PETER B. MACDONALD

From Mr C. S. Dence   *16 July 1973*

Sir,

    Surely the Rev. E. S. Haviland is correct, and by what right does Peter Macdonald claim English marmalade to be Scottish? These are vital matters of national prestige and I put forward as my authority a certain Gervase Markham (1568–1637) who published a recipe for Marmalade of Oranges in, please note, his *English Huswife.*

    Scottish indeed! Let Peter Macdonald substantiate his prior claim!

Yours faithfully,
COLIN S. DENCE

Sir,

In reference to certain letters on the subject of marmalade, I have heard that it was derived from a confection prepared by the chef for Mary Queen of Scots when she was married to the Dauphin of France and was indisposed. The word 'marmalade' is a corruption of the phrase *Marie est malade.*

This may be a little far-fetched but it has the ring of truth.

Yours faithfully,

JOHN ORR

From Lady Antonia Fraser   *17 July 1973*

Sir,

Alas, I do not think Mr John Orr can be correct in suggesting that marmalade was first prepared for Mary Queen of Scots. I too had been brought up to believe in the story of the chef in the French royal kitchens, hearing of the illness of the child Queen, and muttering frenziedly 'Marie est malade, Marie est malade' over and over again as he stirred a confection of oranges, until they turned by mistake into a delicious golden mixture.

On inspection, this proved to be yet another example of those legends which surely *ought* to be true because they are so appealing – but unfortunately are not. The *Oxford English Dictionary* gives a 1480 date for the word marmalade, deriving from the Portuguese *marmelo* – a quince. A Portuguese origin for marmalade?

Yours faithfully,

ANTONIA FRASER

From Mr G. Pazzi-Axworthy   *19 July 1973*

Sir,

I should like to know the nationality of the people who were enjoying bitter oranges for their afters when Mr Peter Macdonald's canny Scot saw them throw the peel away.

Yours faithfully,

GEORGE PAZZI-AXWORTHY

From Mrs Joan Richards   *20 July 1973*

Sir,

I have read that the Duke of Wellington in the Peninsular Wars much enjoyed the conserves of our ally Portugal and asked his aide-de-camp to send home to England a crate of quince preserve (*marmelada*) and another of orange jam. But the aide-de-camp made a mistake with labelling the crates and Portuguese orange jam was henceforth known in England as marmalade. Before this time marmalade had a broader meaning, referring to conserves made of quinces, oranges and other similar fruits.

This I think is Lady Antonia Fraser's Portuguese origin for marmalade.

Yours faithfully,
JOAN RICHARDS

From Mr Morley Kennerley   *20 July 1973*

Sir,

It would be interesting to know why and when orange marmalade became standard for breakfast here, for abroad one never knows until one sees it on the tray of what fruit the breakfast conserve will be made.

Yours faithfully,
MORLEY KENNERLEY

From Mrs Helen Grant   *23 July 1973*

Sir,

Lady Antonia Fraser is on the right track when she suggests that our marmalade had its origin in the Portuguese *marmelo* – quince. But surely we got the word from the Spanish *mermelada*? In the Spanish Academy Dictionary the derivation of *mermelada* is given as from the Latin *melimelum*, quince. In Spanish *mermelada* means quince jam or jam made from other fruits; so orange marmalade in Spanish is *mermelada de naranja*.

It seems likely that since our marmalade is traditionally made from Seville oranges then it was from Spain that we got the name marmalade for orange jam.

Yours faithfully,
HELEN F. GRANT

Sir,

I too heard that the name of marmalade derived from a confection prepared for Mary Queen of Scots. But my story told that she was prone to seasickness and found this preparation effective for 'Mer Malade'.

Yours very sincerely,
ELIZABETH INMAN

From Mr John Carswell   *23 July 1973*

Sir,

This whole matter, including the answer to the question put by Mr Pazzi-Axworthy, is dealt with in a poem by Hilaire Belloc who wrote:

> The haughty nobles of Seville
> Could find no use for orange peel

Yours etc.,
JOHN CARSWELL

From Emeritus Professor G. E. Trease   *24 July 1973*

Sir,

The Duke of Wellington was by no means the first Englishman to use marmalade. It is mentioned as 'marmaled' in the English translation of Renodaeus' *Dispensatory* published in 1657 by the London apothecary Richard Tomlinson. An earlier reference is in the inventory of Thomas Baskerville, apothecary of Exeter, who died in 1596. This lists 'marmalade 11 lbs, 10 shillings'. Another item, apparently an early form of our biscuits, reads 'biskye bred, 8 lbs 5s 4d'.

Yours faithfully,
G. E. TREASE

From Mr Thomas McLachlan   *30 July 1973*

Sir,

I have read the correspondence about marmalade with considerable interest, but can only conclude that some of your correspondents have not adequately considered the implications of their information.

Lady Antonia Fraser is correct in quoting the date 1480 for the use of the word, as given in the *Oxford Dictionary*, but the *Oxford Dictionary* gives no information about the context in which the word is used.

Professor Trease quotes Renodaeus's *Dispensatory*, but although a reference is given to *Marmaled* in the index as p. 171, I have been unable to find any reference to the word in the book itself. This is not uncommon with books of this period and it would appear that Renodaeus expects his readers to know that marmaled is the same thing as marzipan. He makes no reference to marmalade under either lemon or orange.

My Spanish dictionary makes no mention of oranges being used for marmalade, but describes it as a 'preserve of fruits'. Larousse's large French dictionary devotes some space to *marmalade* as a confection of fruits, which have been reduced to the form of a gruel. The only recipe given is for apple *marmalade*, and at the end the apples are passed through a sieve to smash them up.

I have not had the advantage of seeing Gervase Markham's recipe (16 July), but in 1767 A Lady in *The Art of Cookery Made Plain and Easy* gives recipes for both orange and quince marmalade which would produce a sweet, smooth confection not at all like the marmalade we know.

In spite of Mr Dence's scorn (16 July) it was in 1797 that an extra large shipload of Seville oranges became available at Dundee and the enterprising Mrs Keiller bought them and converted them into marmalade. She was so successful that the firm prospered and her younger son invented a cutting machine to slice the oranges instead of grating them. For many years Keillers marketed their marmalade in white porcelain jars with black print on the front 'James Keiller and Sons Ltd. The Original Dundee Marmalade', and this claim has never been challenged. Orange marmalade, as we know it, is essentially British and comparatively modern.

Yours faithfully,
THOMAS MCLACHLAN

Einstein and Hitlerites

[Adolf Hitler had become Chancellor of Germany on 30 January 1933]

From Professor A. S. Yahuda   *30 March 1933*

[philologist extraordinary]

Sir,

In connexion with the ferocious campaign of Nazis and Nationalists against the Jew Einstein, who is being accused of undermining German prestige abroad for having protested against Hitlerite brutality and barbarism, the following fact may serve as an illustration of such intentions.

When Einstein was invited by Lord Haldane early in 1921 to give a lecture on Relativity at King's College, it was from the very first moment a matter of course for Einstein to address the audience in German. As in certain circles some apprehension was felt, the question arose whether Einstein should not be asked to make use of the French language, as he had some difficulty to express himself in English. Einstein insisted, and said he had complete confidence in the broad-mindedness of the English public, and expressed his conviction that his lecture in German would contribute towards softening English feelings towards Germany and a reopening of the way for establishing the broken scientific relations between Germany and this country.

I was present at that lecture, sitting near the platform next to a few Germans, apparently of some distinction. The large hall of King's College was packed, and scores of students were standing all round the walls. Before Einstein began I heard one of the German gentlemen say to his neighbour in English: 'I wonder whether this meeting will pass without disturbance because Einstein is speaking in German?' I immediately assured him in German that the lecture was announced to be given in German, and that everybody knew it. 'But look at all these crowds of young men,' said he, timidly turning his face towards the walls. 'Do you think they all came here to listen to a lecture on such an abstruse subject as relativity?' 'These are students', I said, 'who came to pay homage to a great scientist. Besides, the number of English students who understand German is much larger than is generally thought.'

The lecture was given amidst most respectful silence, though many of those who understood German did not understand relativity, and some of those who understood relativity did not understand German. A tremendous ovation followed the lecture, lasting a few minutes, and surely not least for his courage. I was later told that the then German Ambassador, Herr Sthamer, who was present, was so overwhelmed by that demonstration of sympathy and admiration that he thanked Einstein in very moving words for the great service he had rendered to Germany. Indeed, there are very few German scholars who have done so much as Einstein to raise German prestige, not only in England, but also in other Allied countries, at a time when the animosity against Germany was still so strong that all the tact and prudence of experienced and far-sighted Germans, like Sthamer, were necessary to restore friendly relations with Germany. And now Einstein is the man of whom millions of Germans are told by those who have done everything to discredit the name and honour of Germany that he is undermining the prestige of their country.

Yours faithfully,
A. S. YAHUDA

[From 1905 to 1931 ten German Jews had been awarded Nobel Prizes for their contributions to science]

The Perfect Lady

From Mr W. Hodgson Burnet   *16 January 1933*

Sir,

Your recent article under the title 'The Perfect Lady' gave some amusing examples of the difficulties with which a Perfect Lady of 1851 had to contend. I have, however, in my possession a book published in 1885 which shows that even at that date the gentle art of correct behaviour was no easy one for either sex.

Great importance was attached to the proper use of that 'accessory of dress and comfort,' the handkerchief. 'Never', says the writer, 'be without a handkerchief. Hold it freely in the hand, and do not roll it into a ball. Hold it by the centre and let the corners form a fan-like expansion. Avoid using it too much. With some persons the habit becomes troublesome and unpleasant.'

To the Perfect Gentleman who is Paying a Visit after a Ball or Party this advice is given: 'Never appear in a drawing-room with mud on your boots. Hold your hat in your hand unless requested to put it down. Then lay it beside you. The gloves should not be removed during a visit.' 'At Evening Parties avoid an excess of jewellery. Do not wear rings on the outside of your gloves.'

It was, however, when the Perfect Lady of 1885 had a gentleman visitor that she must have been sore put to it to know just what she might do. She was on no account to accompany him *all* the way to the door. The writer is most emphatic on this point. 'When your visitor retires,' he says, 'ring for the servant. You may then accompany your guest *as far towards the door as the circumstances of your friendship seem to demand.*' The italics are mine. The onus of deciding how far towards the door she could go was the Perfect Lady's – poor thing! Life in the eighties must have been rather difficult.

Yours, &c.,
W. HODGSON BURNET

Intelligence from The Athenaeum

From Mr H. Pirie-Gordon   *20 September 1934*

Sir,
'A rough-coated dough-faced ploughman strode coughing and hiccoughing through the streets of Scarborough' used to be set as a spelling-test at my prep school at Crowborough in the middle nineties.

I am, Sir, your obedient servant,
H. PIRIE-GORDON

Intelligence from the Reform Club

From Mr Thomas Darling   *29 September 1934*

Sir,
Last week I lifted a potato on my farm, Greys, Royston, Herts, weighing 2 lb 8 oz. The potato is a Sharp's Express.

I am, Sir, your obedient servant,
THOMAS DARLING

An Opera Broadcast

[*Fidelio* (Lotte Lehmann the Leonora, Erna Berger Marzelline, Alexander Kipnis Rocco and Herbert Janssen Don Fernando) had opened the Covent Garden season on 30 April. Part of a fashionable audience arrived late, then talked with animation until loudly cursed by Sir Thomas Beecham]

From Sir Charles Strachey   *26 May 1934*

Sir,

The other day Sir Thomas Beecham, by the interjection of a few timely and well-chosen words, defended his audience from stupid and vulgar interruptions. Listeners to the opera on the wireless have, unfortunately, no such powerful protector.

Last night, just as Sir Thomas had launched his chorus into the serene glory of 'Wach' Auf' – Wagner's most magnificent choral composition – the music was switched off, and 'an announcer' blandly informed us (without apology) that the transmission of *Die Meistersinger* would be suspended in favour of a weather forecast from Daventry. When the opera was resumed that noble hymn was coming to an end, and we had been robbed of one of the most lovely things in the whole range of operatic music. Surely the weather forecast could have been postponed for half an hour or so – when the opera ended. Nobody could possibly prefer a weather forecast, however optimistic, to 'Wach' Auf'. One wonders what words Sir Thomas would have used had he known of this outrage – perpetrated, of course, without his knowledge.

Your obedient servant,
CHARLES STRACHEY

[Sir Thomas always insisted that the BBC once faded him out during the closing pages of the 'Jupiter' symphony in order to broadcast a talk on 'The Sex Life of the Ant']

Fashions in Christian Names

From the Reverend H. M. Larner   *25 May 1934*

Sir,

An analysis of 2,265 names that I made of the 1,363 baptisms, 1895–1925, in the parish of Busbridge, Godalming, showed an extensive and interesting range, in regularity and fluctuation. In the total, 311 were different, a few of them variations, and 151 appeared but once. Individually, sources could be traced to the Bible of 95, to our Calendar of Saints of 34, to our kings and queens of 44, and others to prominent men and women in past and modern times. The most frequent were:

George	102	Mary	85
William	95	Elizabeth	58
Henry	71	Alice	57
John	71	Ann(e)	47
Charles	68	Edith	43
James	66	Lilian	39
Frederick	63	Eileen	38
Thomas	45	Kate	37
Alfred	44	Emily	32
Edward	42	Florence	30
Arthur	39	Margaret	26
Albert	37	Maud	24
Ernest	31	Dorothy	23
Francis	31	May	23

In the Busbridge registers of baptisms there are found the names of all except Adam, Ralph, Roger of those mentioned from the six lists in the *Complete Peerage*, and all in the public school list.

Yours faithfully,
H. M. LARNER

The Cuckoo on the Keys

From the Reverend K. H. MacDermott   25 May 1934

[writing from Uckfield]

Sir,
For many years each spring I have tested the cuckoo's notes with a piano, and have found that they are always within a tone of D and B, or D and B flat (treble stave). It is of interest to observe that Beethoven, a great lover of birds, when he introduced the imitation of the cuckoo at the end of the second movement of his Pastoral Symphony, gave the two notes D and B flat, to be played by the clarionet. As Beethoven was at the time he composed that work (1808) completely deaf

112

one wonders whether it was by chance he selected the correct notes, or merely because they fit in with the key of the movement, or whether his memory of the bird's song had survived after he had been unable to hear it for some years. If the latter, it is fascinating to realize that the cuckoo has not altered the pitch of his notes for over a century.

Yours truly,
K. H. MacDermott

[After taking holy orders Mr MacDermott became an Associate of the Royal College of Music]

What is a Pork Sausage?

From Mr George Wood   *17 January 1934*

Sir,

As one of a family of pork sausage manufacturers, established for nearly 60 years, I claim to be able to answer the questions put by the puzzled 'Grass Widower'. If one may use the term, a 'thoroughbred' pork sausage should contain only the best pork and good seasoning, while a 'half-bred' sausage contains a large percentage of bread or biscuit powder. The colour is accounted for in the making. If a pork sausage appears deadly pale, it contains too much fat meat; and that with a pinky tint contains too much lean meat. There is no such thing as a freckled sausage skin, and the 'Plymouth Rock' appearance of a sausage is due to the herbs used for flavouring showing through its filmy jacket.

In cooking a sausage needs patient coercion, not fierce cremation, and there would be no shrinking or bursting if it were cooked by the old-fashioned Dutch oven; it would then arrive at table brown-jacketed and retaining its rotund dignity. Sausages should never be cooked in fat. A good pork sausage makes its own bed of fat in which to lie, as it is slowly cooked. Never behave harshly to a sausage by pricking it with a fork, for it is found to retaliate by spitting fat at you and bursting before your eyes. As to the opinion of the legal profession, I once knew a circuit judge who gave pork sausages a splendid character, and taking into consideration the millions of sausages consumed – all different in make and flavour – it is remarkable how the palate of the public is so easily satisfied.

Yours truly,
George Wood

'Jubilee Ballyhoo'

[Sir Stafford Cripps, a Wykehamist and a vegetarian, was a highly paid KC between the wars, and a leading member of the post-1945 Labour administration; *The Times* obituary felt he had 'all the virtues and all the weaknesses of a "man with a mission"']

From Mr St John Ervine   *19 June 1935*

[critic, biographer of Bernard Shaw, and author of such plays as *Jane Clegg, John Ferguson*, and *The First Mrs Fraser*]

Sir,

Mr John Inskip quotes a curious passage from a speech lately delivered at Bristol by Sir Stafford Cripps. Sir Stafford, whose references to the Sovereign in the past have been unfortunate, not for his Majesty but for Sir Stafford, asserted, one wonders on what evidence, that 'there are many who feel depressed and discouraged by the Jubilee ballyhoo and the cries of false patriotism'. We may well believe that there are some, Sir Stafford and Communists among them, who feel exceedingly 'depressed and discouraged' by the overwhelming and spontaneous outburst of affection which was shown for the King by his people during his Jubilee celebrations, and it may well be that there were sore hearts in Moscow on Jubilee night; but that, perhaps, is not quite what Sir Stafford means.

Will you permit a puzzled democrat to ask just what Sir Stafford does mean by his singular statement? On what ground does this peculiar proletarian assert that the greetings universally offered to the King were 'cries of false patriotism'? Does he mean that those who gave these greetings were misguided or that they were pretending an affection they were far from feeling? Are the depression and discouragement which 'many' feel at the 'Jubilee ballyhoo' felt by those who have a truer perception of what is meet and proper in government than the rest of us, or are they felt only by the group of 'gunked' people – forgive that Ulster colloquialism! – led by Sir Stafford who are mortified by the discovery that their advice has been ignored even by some of their own sympathizers?

Other questions suggest themselves to this puzzled democrat. At Whitsun the Socialist League, an organization mainly populated by disgruntled dons and ill-tempered members of the middle class, asserted, at what seems to have been a secret session, its general abhorrence of the principle of monarchy and its particular disgust at the pleasure with which his people greeted the King. (Why was the session secret?) Sir Stafford, I gather, was present at this secret session and, presumably, acquiesced in the sentiments proclaimed at it. He certainly has not disclaimed them. Mr Inskip's quotation from his speech at Bristol offers proof that he shared them.

Are we to suppose, then, that if Sir Stafford had been at the head of the Government in May he and they would have ignored the King's Jubilee and would have offered every opposition to its celebration? If so, what becomes of the principle of democracy? The Town Council of Nelson 'ignored' the Jubilee. So did the Mayor of Bermondsey. But the people of Nelson did not ignore it, nor did the people of Bermondsey. On the contrary, they celebrated the Jubilee with a fervour which was, I suspect, increased by the discourtesy their representatives offered to the Head of the State. Does Sir Stafford suggest that the Town Council of Nelson, temporarily in possession of a majority on a municipal authority, were right to flout the manifest will of the people, and that the Mayor of Bermondsey, whose effigy was burnt by his constituents, was equally right in asserting, not their will, but his?

Yours sincerely,
ST JOHN ERVINE

[The Silver Jubilee of King George V and Queen Mary on 6 May 1935 was marked by a thanksgiving service at St Paul's Cathedral. A few days later the King and Queen rode through the poorer quarters of London where the reception was ecstatic. 'I'd no idea they felt like that about me!' said the King. 'I'm beginning to think they must really like me for myself.']

Children's Pocket Money

From Dr Marie C. Stopes   *22 April 1935*

Sir,

The points about children's pocket money raised in the interesting letter by Mr St John Ervine have many bearings of a profoundly fundamental nature, the most vital being character building. The prevalence of regular pocket money is, in my opinion, one of the keys to that lack of adult responsibility

115

about money which is widely deplored. Few parents, however, realize it and think they are being kind to their children when they give them a little money to spend as regular pocket money. They are not being kind; they are wasting one of the most valuable assets they could enlist on the side of independence of character.

I have never given, and never will give, pocket money in my nursery. My son, who is just 11, has earned everything he has spent, with the exception of a few money gifts on recognized occasions, such as birthdays. At the age of four, interested in the household wages book, he asked for a wages book of his own and began to earn money, entering it up in the wages book and signing for it. Looking back in that little record one finds items such as this: to cleaning white paint in drawing-room, 2d; to laying turf straight in garden, 4d; to chopping wood, 2d; to felling a tree, 6d; etc.

An intelligent and thoughtful parent can find innumerable jobs, especially in the country, where a child can give honest work for pence sufficient to supply him with enough or more pocket money than his less fortunate comrades have given to them. That free gift of money bred in their bones the false idea that money is obtainable without work and that they are entitled to a share of the family income without contributing anything in exchange. Were a wages book established in every home, the national character would undoubtedly gain by it and children have a much greater and more real interest in their occupations.

Yours faithfully,
MARIE C. STOPES

The Earwig's Better Nature

From Mr Malcolm Burr   *17 August 1936*

Sir,

Your correspondent can be reassured that the earwigs which annoy her are not more than a minor nuisance. They are really inoffensive creatures; they smell not, neither do they sting. They are, in fact, deserving of our admiration, for they are unique among insects in their personal sense of maternal duty. After the honeymoon in early winter in a gallery dug under a big stone the mother earwigs, when their time draws nigh, expel the fathers from the home, lest they devour their own offspring.

Then they lay their eggs, from January to March, which they cherish and keep clean till the babes come out, and even then do not relax their care. Often one may disturb a nest of young earwigs in the spring, and if the mites are scattered the dam will gather them together again under her capacious abdomen like an old fowl. Meanwhile the fathers lead a bachelor existence until the early summer, when all the parents die off, leaving the youngsters to carry on the species. These come of age about the beginning of August, and rejoicing in their newly found strength and the hardened integument of puberty fare forth into the world to carve out their careers.

I am, Sir, your obedient servant,

MALCOLM BURR

The Art of Hatting

From Mr Frederick Willis   *11 March 1936*

Sir,

As an old hatter I was moved by your leading article on hats. There was a time when a man chose his hat with as much care as he chose his wine. Many famous men have passed through my hands. I had the distinction of fitting Machnow, the Russian giant, with a topper, and I recall his awful majesty when it was placed on his head. The public was spellbound, as well it might be, until that fateful night when a pernickety member of the audience asked, urbanely, if he would have the goodness to remove his hat. Machnow, who understood no English, was unmoved, but his manager's face blanched. He had no choice but to comply with the request; the hat was removed – and the spell broken!

I remember a man, distinguished in the Diplomatic Service, who spent three hours in selecting a hat. I am sure it was longer, but, fearing the incredulity of modern readers, I dare not say so. At the end of this time he declared that he could not settle the matter off-hand but would consult his wife. The next day he came with his wife, who, being a woman of quick decision, made a choice in an hour. That was a man to stir the artistic soul of a true born hatter.

Just before the war, however, we detected signs of decay; men began to show a strange indifference to the important consequences of an eighth-of-an-inch on or off the brim, and they came less frequently for an 'iron-up'. After the war came catastrophe; bronzed young men came in casually for a soft felt, threw it carelessly on their heads and walked out without so much as a look in the glass. I realized then that the art of hatting was dead; anyone could clap a hat on a man's head and throw thirty shillings into the till. I looked back to the spacious days of Sir Squire Bancroft, whose hat was famous in Piccadilly, and Arthur Roberts, who set a fashion with his 'Gentleman Joe', and sorrowfully sought fresh woods and pastures new. But, I raise my hat to Sir Walter Gilbey (whose hat I know well), and wish him every success in his campaign to restore hat-consciousness to an effete generation.

I am, &c.,

FREDERICK WILLIS

['Have there ever been comedians whom *everyone* thought funny? In my experience these number six – Arthur Roberts, G. P. Huntley, Little Tich, George Robey, Charlie Chaplin, and Grock.' – James Agate, *Ego 5*, 1942]

Peers' Coaches

From Major-General Sir Hereward Wake   30 April 1937

Sir,

Is it too late to express the hope that the few peers' state coaches which are appearing at their Majesties' coronation shall proceed to and from the Abbey along the Processional Route?

I understand that only 12 peers have been able to bring out their coaches for the occasion, and that they are to proceed by the back streets. This may be the last opportunity of seeing these historical equipages, so well known before the days of motors.

Yours truly,

HEREWARD WAKE

[According to *The Times*, only four peers brought out their own coaches for the occasion: the Marquess of Bute, the Marquess of Exeter, the Marquess of Londonderry, and Earl Spencer. The last named's granddaughter was to marry King George VI's grandson]

The Singing Mouse . . .

From Miss Alison Holmes   *26 April 1937*

Sir,

In *The Times* of 22 April it was stated that a singing mouse had been found in Wales and that it is to broadcast on 8 May.

It may interest your readers to know that, according to Red Indian mythology, 'Mish-a-boh-quas', the singing mouse, always comes to tell of war.

It may sing at other times, but not to the same extent.

I read of this in Ernest Thompson Seton's wonderful book *Rolf in the Woods*.

I am your obedient servant,
ALISON HOLMES

. . . and a Coal-heaving Mouse

From Mr Dudley Illingworth   *28 April 1937*

Sir,

While two men were working in an outhouse here last week they saw a large mouse carrying pieces of coal, held by the mouth and a front paw, over a wood partition and dropping them into a near-by empty corn bin. The coal is of the size sold as 'nuts', measuring about 4in. by 1in. by 1in. The nuts were so transported with almost incredible rapidity. Unfortunately, before the completion of the mysterious task the owner of the coal disturbed the pilferer, but not before some 30 pieces had been dropped on the corn. He is, however, convinced that the mouse was building for itself a ladder of coal from the corn bin, as two mice had been trapped in it the previous day. I wonder if anyone has ever observed a similar operation to its explanatory conclusion?

Yours faithfully,
D. H. ILLINGWORTH

Painted Finger-nails

From Mr George L. Massy   *3 August 1937*

Sir,

I am credibly informed that the reason why some ladies stain their finger-nails is in order to conceal the traces of black blood that otherwise would be discernible there. Perhaps the knowledge of this may induce ladies who have no black blood to refrain from an unsightly and unpleasing habit. It is understood that this practice arose in America, where the colour line is strictly drawn and traces of black blood have to be concealed if possible. All the more reason for English ladies not to disfigure their nails.

Your obedient servant,
GEORGE L. MASSY

Pronunciation of Latin – Biologist's Plea for the Old Style

From Dr Julian Huxley   *26 January 1938*

[Secretary, the Zoological Society of London, 1935–42, Sir Julian Huxley was Director-General of Unesco, 1946–8]

Sir,

May I add a biologist's plea for the old pronunciation of Latin? There are about 1,250,000 described species of animals and plants, all with so called 'Latin names' (though often derived from Greek, or sometimes Latinized versions of vernacular words or names); there are 'Latin names' for thousands of families, orders and classes; there are Latin and Greek words lavishly employed as technical terms by zoology, botany, anatomy, and medicine.

Much of this biological Latin vocabulary is purely technical, and concerns only the specialist. Even so, difficulties arise. Names of zoological families end in —*ae*, of sub-families in —*i*: the new and old pronunciations reverse the sounds. But there are many names and terms which are also in or on the fringe of general usage: what is to be done about them? First, are 'Latin names' derived from Greek to be pronounced in the new way? It seems impossible to ask biologists to adopt different pronunciations for Latin and Greek words. But if the new pronunciation is to be followed throughout, what of special points like *y* for upsilon? *Hyaena* (as a generic and therefore a 'Latin' name), *Cygnus*, or *coccyx* will be odd enough anyhow; but if the *y* is to be pronounced *ii*, they will be odder still. Secondly, what is to be done with Latinized vernacular names? *Chimpanzee, Bison, Chinchilla, Giraffa* are all names of genera. Is the *g* to be hard, the *ch* transposed to χ?

Then are we to speak of the *Weewerridi* for the civet family, or *Wolpees* for the foxes? It is here that the real objection lies, for the new pronunciation disguises the Latin derivation of current English words – *Woolpees* and vulpine, *Faylis* and feline. The same is true with many anatomical terms. *Acetabulum* with a hard *c* loses its association with acetic acid and vinegar; *humerus, radius, femur* will have two pronunciations; and is the gynaecologist to say *wahgheena*?

Such examples illustrate from a special angle what would seem to be the chief defect of the new pronunciation – that in striving for perfection it has exemplified the proverb that *le mieux, c'est l'ennemi du bien*, since it makes it harder for most people to appreciate the role of Latin in the development of English. Further, as Sir Charles Fortescue-Brickdale said in your issue of Saturday, it gives the average small boy the idea that Latin is an outlandish sort of language. In the same issue, Dr Gilbert Murray admits that he is often driven to adopt both pronunciations according to circumstances. This may serve for a scholar, but puts an undue strain on the ordinary learner.

There remains the added appreciation of Latin said to be conferred by the new pronunciation. On this perhaps I may be allowed to cite my own experience. I had, and I am glad of it, a fairly rigorous classical education during most of my school days, and reached a stage at which I could and did read Homer and Horace and Catullus for pleasure, and sometimes even enjoyed the writing of verse in Latin and Greek (a practice, by the way, which was really extensively enjoyed by my contemporary Alan Parsons, who had an inhibition against expressing his feelings in English verse). The enjoyment was there, in spite of the old pronunciation: that it might have been enhanced a trifle by the new is unimportant if there are countervailing disadvantages.

There is a final point. Why pick on Augustan Latin as standard? Latin pronunciation must have radically changed in the thousand years between the early Republic and the Dark Ages; yet it was in the latter period that Latin was actually contributing to living European languages.

If the new pronunciation leads to confusion and hinders instead of helping appreciation of the part that Latin has played in the evolution of English, we should go back to the old. The issue seems to be one where the expert, as so often, may advise but should not decide. Many points besides accuracy, scholarship, and aesthetic appreciation are at issue. Let

121

specialists use the nearest approach they can devise to correct Augustan pronunciation; but let the bulk of those who learn Latin employ the pronunciation which is least confusing and pragmatically the most useful.

I am, &c.,
JULIAN S. HUXLEY

[Dr Huxley was educated at Eton and Balliol]

Dance Music on the Wireless

From Lieutenant-Colonel Sir Thomas Moore, MP
22 January 1938

[Unionist Member for Ayr Burgh]

Sir,

For many nights, even weeks and months now, I have reluctantly deprived myself of my anticipated digestive: I have cut off my radio. Not because there was an encouraging dissertation on the prevailing fat stock prices, not because there was a seductive description of the immediate effects of a popular cure, not even because there was an appeal on behalf of the charity I have been supporting for so many years. No, Sir, I cut it off because one of my favourite dance orchestras had begun to play.

I admit, of course, that in order to enjoy pleasure we must know pain – the theory of contrast rules it so – but why must the pain be so heavily weighted against the pleasure? For some minutes one's ears are soothed by a tuneful and rhythmic melody, recalling youth perchance, beguiling memory, suggesting romance; when suddenly, while one's thoughts are steeped in gentle solace, a harsh, untuneful mistiming voice breaks into our somnolent enjoyment.

Heaven knows where these voices are found, heaven alone knows how the musical leader himself can endure the noise he has conjured into unhappy life. And surely heaven will not lightly forgive the havoc which that same musician brings into the peaceful home circle. Why, Sir, I ask, must we endure it? Have the BBC no rights, or have they no ear?

Can nothing be done to eliminate this infliction? Surely there are singers with soft, tuneful, and, may I say, cultured voices who will fit in with the harmony of the orchestra?

Why is it that British orchestras alone subordinate themselves
to this hideous cacophony?

Yours faithfully,

THOMAS MOORE

[The above letter is too vague. All we can say is that Sir
Thomas was not listening to the Ambrose orchestra, which
featured Miss Vera Lynn]

Munich

[On 28 September 1938 Neville Chamberlain informed
the House of Commons that he, Daladier (the French
Prime Minister), Hitler and Mussolini were to meet in
Munich]

From Professor E. P. Stebbing   *1 October 1938*

[Head of the Forestry Department, University of Edin-
burgh]

Sir,

Yesterday morning, that momentous 28 September, I was
sitting on a horse, a whipper-in some 20 yards ahead, his
mount and himself a stiff note of interrogation. From the
covert hard by hounds were stirring up the fox cubs, shrill
squeaks of sheer excitement denoting the young entry on the
trail of a rabbit. An old farmer, evidently past hard physical
work, came up and we talked of foxes and their wiles.

Then he abruptly asked, 'And what do you think of the
position, Sir?' Before I could reply he half turned and pointed
down to the Romney Marsh just below, where the mists were
slowly dissipating into fine gauze filaments under the slanting
rays of the new-risen sun. 'On a Sunday evening, Sir, I have
not time of week days, I comes through this field and sits at
yonder point and looks down on the Marsh. Have done so for
40 years and more. Sometimes, when the sheep are newly
shorn, the light slants across and the bright green with the
numbers of glistening white dots scattered over it is wonnerful
beautiful. Is it all going to be spoilt, Sir?'

I looked down on the Marsh showing brilliant green patches
where the mist had cleared and turned to look into those
steady calm grey eyes. 'No!' I said. 'I have often looked at
what you describe so well. No! I can't see it. I can't see that

sky raining down death on this lovely countryside. I have tried to see it for the last few days. But I simply can't.' He nodded gravely. 'There's a God up there,' pointing to the still misty heaven above the Marsh. 'He will surely stop one man from committing so great a crime.'

In that grey eye was faith and confidence. And the same amazing stoical confidence has been exemplified during the past week on this countryside; and, not the least, amongst the women. These people are not likely to be stampeded.

And in the evening came the great news! And I thought of my talk at the dawning with my farmer friend. Was he surprised? I doubt it.

I am, Sir, your obedient servant,

E. P. STEBBING

[The Munich Conference saw the partial dismemberment of Czechoslovakia. However, Chamberlain and Hitler signed a joint declaration in which they regarded the Munich agreement as 'symbolic of our two peoples never to go to war with one another again']

Clocks that Strike Twice

From Mr W. Greenwell Lax   *9 September 1938*

Sir,

It may interest your correspondent Mr Lovell to know that the College Clock in the Great Court of Trinity College, Cambridge, strikes twice. There is a legend that it does so once for Trinity and once for St John's, next door.

As a personal recollection, I may perhaps be permitted to add that those of us who periodically forgathered at the Annual Gathering dinners in June will well remember how that fine athlete, the late Hon. Alfred Lyttelton, often used to run round the Great Court while the clock was striking (twice over) the midnight hour on those occasions – no mean feat!

Yours, &c.,

W. GREENWELL LAX

*** Readers of Wordsworth will remember:

'Near me hung Trinity's loquacious clock,
Who never let the quarters, night or day,
Slip by him unproclaimed, and told the hours
Twice over with a male and female voice.'
—Prelude III, 53.

124

[The Hon. Alfred Lyttelton gained five Blues at Cambridge, became a KC and PC, played both football and cricket for England – and insisted that W. G. Grace did not wash behind his ears]

Germany and the Jews

[On 28 October 1938 Herr Sigismund FitzRandolph, attaché at the German Embassy in London, contributed a column-length letter to *The Times* interpreting the policies of his Government.

On the night of 9–10 November, and following the assassination of the third secretary at the German Embassy in Paris by a German Jewish refugee, the worst pogrom yet to take place in the Third Reich occurred]

From Mr G. M. Young   *17 November 1938*

[author of *Victorian England, Portrait of an Age*]

Sir,

Dr FitzRandolph has undertaken the task, not less honourable than useful, of serving as the interpreter of German opinion in England. May I therefore ask him to reply, as fully and candidly as his official obligations allow, to one or two questions which are exercising the minds of many English friends of his country? I am thinking of course of the events of the past week.

No one denies the competence of a sovereign State to establish degrees of citizenship: to enact that Catholics (to take an example from our own history) may not vote, or that peers may not sit in the House of Commons. These are matters of internal policy; and any foreign criticism of such arrangements must be, or ought to be, subject to the consideration that every country has the right to order its domestic concerns as it deems best in its own interest. Knowing the intensity of family feeling among Jews, and their proficiency in the arts and sciences, I may think it unwise for the German State to say to a Jewish father: 'We cannot prevent your son from becoming a famous musician or physicist; we can only see to it that he does not become a famous German musician or physicist.' But it is for Germany to discover, not for me as a foreigner to point out, the unwisdom of such a proceeding. So far, I am entirely in agreement with those German statesmen who insist that the treatment of the Jews in Germany is a matter of domestic, and not international, concern.

I will go farther. I know that the Jewish question in Germany today has a history of generations or even centuries behind it. I know, too, that in the years of German misery after the war, very many Germans were most harshly dealt with, and suffered the most galling indignities, at the hands of individual Jews, of Jewish firms, and public authorities in which the Jewish element was dominant. I am not prepared to deny, what Germans have often represented to me, that the restoration of Germany to economic health, and therefore national independence, was most grievously impeded by false views urged in London, Paris, and New York by Jews who only saw in the German lands a promising field for international exploitation.

But, I say, those times are past and over. Germany today speaks with her own voice: is mistress in her own house. And surely, whatever appetite for revenge on the Jewish people may have subsisted must by now be sated? I ask Dr Fitz-Randolph: What are we, the friends in England of the German people, to think? Is the German State verging on bankruptcy, and so compelled, like an Eastern tyranny, to plunder? Is the German Government verging on collapse, and therefore obliged to stimulate its partizans with fresh intoxicants?

Dr FitzRandolph is an educated man, a member, I take it, of one of those universities which, in the days of their freedom, were the glory of his country. He knows that in these matters recrimination is folly: all great States have great sins on their conscience. But he knows, too, that no major transaction in the thought or practice of one country can be a matter of indifference to all others, because it is by such occurrences that the civilization of a country is assessed, its purposes divined, its strength and honour determined. Today Germany stands at the bar of human opinion, impeached for hideous cruelty and wrong inflicted on her own subjects, and I ask Dr FitzRandolph: What defence has he to offer? That Germany is so strong that she can defy the conscience of the world? And, if so, of what force are her promises? Or that Germany is so feeble that she cannot extend to her subjects impartially the protection which is the elementary right of every inhabitant of a civilized country? And, if so, of what value is her friendship? Of what worth is her civilization?

Yours, etc.,

G. M. YOUNG

[There was no reply to this letter]

The War against Germany ...

From Major H. N. Robertson   *5 October 1939*

Sir,

A correspondent asks in your columns today whether our Government are afraid to let us read neutral and even French newspapers. I crossed the Channel to France last week and returned today. On the outward journey my copy of *The Times* and other London papers and magazines which I had bought at Victoria for the journey were confiscated before I was allowed to embark. 'No printed books or newspapers may be exported or imported,' I was told. Twenty paces farther on and over the gangway the same newspapers were being freely sold on the boat! They were on sale also at the French port of disembarkation.

On my return today I threw overboard, before disembarking, my French, Dutch, and Belgian newspapers, and then, shining with conscious virtue, submitted myself to customs examination only to find that criminal tendencies are not easily suppressed even by the will to repentance. For there was discovered in my suitcase, where it had lain since I left home, an ordinary 7s 6d English novel, published in London and purchased there some weeks ago. This contraband of war was eagerly seized upon, to be forwarded, I was informed, to the Chief Censor at Liverpool, of whom any inquiries might be made.

From such blind and pompous folly of inflated functionaries not even P. G. Wodehouse, nor indeed The Book itself is exempt. Sir, will you not move to succour the shaken sanity of the censorship? By all means let our trembling rulers forbid us the neutral and allied Press. By all means let them forbid to Allies and to neutrals the indiscreet or treasonable columns of *The Times*; but surely there must be on the booksellers' shelves some harmless trifles which might be exempted and even prescribed for those like myself who, endeavouring to serve their country, must undertake the long and slow and most uncomfortable journeys of wartime.

Throughout my journey I had with me a briefcase containing eight or nine pounds of typewritten documents, but these apparently are without the ban. This, I suppose, is merely an oversight on the part of officialdom.

I am, Sir, your obedient servant,

H. N. ROBERTSON

[If the Wodehouse endangered was *Uncle Fred in the Springtime*, published in London on 25 August 1939, the censorship was wise. Frederick Altamont Cornwallis Twistleton, 5th Earl of Ickenham, was notoriously a subversive influence apt to subject his nephew Pongo Twistleton to soul-testing experiences]

... and the New Bureaucracy

From Mr G. L. Reid   *8 December 1939*

Sir,

My father, aged 81 and confined to his room the past two years, has been picked out by the Ministry of Agriculture as a fit person to be exhorted to 'Dig for Victory'. His garden is about one-eighth of an acre. The packet delivered by post 'On his Majesty's Service' contained 94 leaflets together with a typed slip informing him where further supplies may be obtained.

Yours faithfully,
GRAHAM L. REID

[Four days later intelligence reached Printing House Square concerning a grandmother, aged 90 and almost blind, who had been similarly approached by the department soon to become immortalized by the radio programme ITMA as the 'Min of Ag and Fish']

From Mrs H. M. Child   *11 July 1940*

Sir,

The Ministry of Aircraft Production has urgently appealed to the women of Britain to give up all their aluminium. Going this morning to buy enamel saucepans to replace the aluminium saucepans which I intend to give to the nation, I saw a woman buying a set of four large new aluminium steamers. What is the use of asking us householders to give up the aluminium we are using when the shops are full of aluminium goods which anyone can buy?

Yours &c.,
HELEN M. CHILD

From Mr H. Ashton-Hopper   *9 December 1940*

Sir,

For some months the Government has been urging the public to 'Keep a Pig'. I kept a pig. In due course I arranged, subject to a permit to slaughter from the Ministry of Food, for a bacon factory to kill and cure the said pig. Having sent it to the factory with the permit to slaughter for our own consumption, I now receive from the local food office (from whom the permit was obtained) a letter in which they say that 'in no circumstances' may the bacon factory cure the pig for me and that the carcass must be collected by me the day after it is killed.

In a household of two we could not possibly eat a whole pig, and we have no knowledge of or necessary equipment for curing; we may not sell any part of the carcass, and if we were allow it to waste through being unable to eat it before it went bad, we should, I have no doubt, be liable. What does 'A' do with the pig? Is this sensible in a time of food shortage or is it crass idiocy?

Yours truly,
H. ASHTON-HOPPER

[Apparently all the writer had to do was to join, or form, a pig club. If the latter, he would appoint himself chairman and secretary. However, to form a pig club, one required a permit, and it was uncertain whether this was granted before or after acquiring a pig. But the man or woman who belonged to a pig club could legally get his/ her carcass cured, before eating half and selling half to a butcher.

Sometimes, the tensions of war being what they were, one government department would disagree with another]

From Major-General R. H. Allen (retd)   *16 January 1943*

Sir,

The following extract from the files of a welfare officer in a munition factory may be of interest.

December 9 Write Welfare Officer of the Ministry of Labour asking for help to get razor blades. Point out that works are 10 miles from nearest large town and workers mostly live in villages where no blades are obtainable.

December 18 Local Welfare Officer replies he has no authority. Refers me to local Price Regulating Committee. Write this body same day.

December 28 Board of Trade replies! Refers me to H.M. Inspector Factories. Says latter has authority under Order 2149 to issue permit of razor blades.

December 29 Visit H.M. Inspector personally. He has never heard of Order 2149, but kindly rings Board of Trade. Discussion ensues on telephone. Board of Trade says order sanctions purchase of cutlery. Inspector says razor blades are not cutlery. Board of Trade says they are. Drawn battle, both sides maintain their position.

December 29 Write Board of Trade Headquarters in London asking for decision.

January 13 No reply. No decision. No razor blades.

Yours faithfully,
R. H. ALLEN

[Local Government naturally took the hint]

From Dr John Sainsbury   *9 April 1943*

Sir,

I have just received from the London County Council, Room 49, County Hall, a *questionnaire* – on the left the query, on the right my reply. It says 'I am unable to trace any record of local taxation licence duty having been paid by you this year in respect of your dog.'

It seems incredible that, when every man and woman is wanted to carry on the war, there are still some who have time to send out these ridiculous notices. The answer, of course, is that I have never had a dog in my life. Room 49 also asks me to put a penny stamp on my reply.

Yours faithfully,
JOHN SAINSBURY

[The war with Germany was successfully concluded on 7 May 1945; that with the new bureaucracy continues]

English Accents

From the Headmaster of Gainsborough Grammar School
23 December 1940

Sir,

In a leading article today you assume the truth of a recent announcement that I intend to teach my pupils 'the southern accent', and at the same time you comment upon the apparent absence of surprise and uneasiness on the part of the parents. I suggest that the parents' attitude is due to first-hand knowledge of what I said. Please allow me a little space in which to set other minds equally at rest before I regain the comfortable obscurity from which I have been rudely snatched.

At a recent meeting of parents I agreed, in response to a request, to encourage the use of 'standard', not 'southern' English. Standard English I have since roughly defined as a manner of speech which can be used in any part of the country without distracting the hearer's attention from what the speaker is saying to how he is saying it. What degree of local speech is compatible with this definition is probably a matter of opinion; without doubt, however, the affected drawl is excluded equally with the broad brogue.

Here I know I am on dangerous ground; but whether one likes it or not, a large number of grammar school boys will attempt to change their manner of speech on leaving school. They will take no pleasure in the accent which distant countries find so rich and attractive. If they desire vigorous speech they will prefer it to be the vigour of clear ideas forcibly expressed rather than that dependent on an accident of pronunciation. For them this interesting dialect may have been the cause of failing in an important interview, or may increase an undergraduate's natural shyness to the verge of misery. Why quote the cases of men whose accent has not been a bar to Cabinet rank? These men have generally seen to it that their sons are free from dialect.

Since all these considerations have urged, and will continue to urge, a number of boys to shed the broader forms of dialect, we propose to help them to do so by training them as early as possible. Those who wish it will alter their speech; those who disdain such things will ignore the training. This is the practice in most schools of the country. It would only be if we failed to fall in line that the parents might have cause for surprise or uneasiness.

Yours faithfully,
F. W. LOCKWOOD

[In 1940 boys had no thought of making a career as a television 'personality']

An 'Inverted Rainbow'

From Mr M. G. Micholls   **28 April 1941**

Sir,

At about 6.30 on the evening of 21 April I saw an inverted rainbow north-west of Wentworth. The arc was quite small. Perhaps one of your readers who also saw it may be able to give some explanation of this phenomenon.

Yours, etc.,
M. G. MICHOLLS

[In 1882 Charles Ashley Carus-Wilson, later Professor of Electrical Engineering at McGill University, had been sent to Bucharest to fit the King of Roumania's palace with electric light. Approaching – or perhaps approached by – *The Times*, he dealt with the 'inverted rainbow'.

'This appearance was part of a magnificent phenomenon called the Parhelia, and is caused by the sun shining through an atmosphere filled with minute crystals of ice. The sun is surrounded by two rings and flanked on each side by two cross-shaped masses of golden light.

'Above the inner ring is an inverted arc, crystal white, and above the outer ring another inverted arc brilliantly coloured like a rainbow. The whole is seldom seen in this country, but parts of it may sometimes be seen. Some years ago I saw it completely in Canada, and was able to identify it with the vision of Ezekiel, who gives a very accurate description of the whole phenomenon.']

The End of the 'Bismarck'

From Mr H. W. B. Joseph   *9 June 1941*

[Fellow of New College, Oxford]

Sir,

The hunting down of the *Bismarck* was a great feat of sea-manship and organization: her destruction a great service to this country. For this we must all rejoice. But the ordeal of her crew was horrible: to describe it for the satisfaction of the British public, as was done by the BBC tonight, was to minister to the more ignoble emotions which war lets loose; in essence it was no better than to entertain the public with an account of a bull-fight, and of the animal's sufferings when brought to bay.

Nor was a word said tonight, nor in previous accounts that I have heard of the battle from the BBC, of the magnificent courage with which her crew fought to the last. We expressed some scorn for the conduct of the *Graf Spee*; when an enemy ship shows the spirit lacking there, cannot we express any respect? It was an unworthy and ungenerous item in the news.

Yours, etc.,

H. W. B. JOSEPH

[The British film *Sink the Bismarck!* appeared in 1960]

Salvage and History

[The Minister of Supply, Lord Beaverbrook, had recently called for 100,000 tons of waste paper]

From Miss Vera Brittain   *30 October 1941*

Sir,

I write to deplore the present campaign for the indiscrimin-ate destruction of documents and records in the interests of salvage. While it is, of course, important to writers and pub-lishers, as well as to the direct war interests, that every scrap of waste paper should be retrieved, it is even more important to avoid exposing British culture to forms of vandalism com-parable to those which have destroyed the culture of Central Europe. This threat is especially alarming when so many valu-able books and documents have already been lost through air raids.

History and literature may well be deprived of collections similar in value to the Paston Letters and the Diaries of John Evelyn and Samuel Pepys, if the present injunctions to destroy ledgers, diaries, notebooks and letters continue unchecked. Had the campaign to save paper between 1914 and 1918 taken this particular form, many lasting records of the Great War could never have been compiled. Cannot something still be done to create a sense of proportion? The appointment of a local librarian or antiquarian to every salvage committee seems to be one expedient worthy of consideration.

Yours, etc.,

VERA BRITTAIN

[The public seemed to lose interest in Lord Beaverbrook's call when it became obvious that, for every ton they saved, government departments produced two tons of memoranda]

The Sex of Chicks

From Mr R. C. Punnett   *16 February 1942*

Sir,

The country is demanding eggs, and consequently the pullets to lay those eggs. The food supply for poultry is limited and likely to be more strictly so. Every bit of it should be devoted to the pullets that we want and none, if we can help it, to their brothers who, though welcome enough in times of peace, now consume the food that should go to their sisters. National policy demands that all cockerel chicks, save those required for breeding, should be destroyed at hatching; for in this way alone can we rear more pullets and obtain more eggs.

Centuries ago the Chinese discovered that by a minute examination of the conformation of the vent in the newly hatched chick they could determine the sex in over 90 per cent. The Japanese, with their quickness in imitation, seized their opportunity and developed the method, with the result that some of our great hatcheries, recognizing their skill, imported them over here. On the outbreak of war they were, of course, interned, but I am informed that as the result of a petition from the National Poultry Council to the Ministry of Agriculture the Home Office is likely to free them again. That *fas est et ab hoste docerie* I freely grant, in spite of the humiliation involved. But in this case it is not really necessary since in actual fact this country has gone one better than the Japanese.

For some years the Cambridge School has been developing auto-sexing breeds – breeds in which the sexes of the chicks declare themselves at hatching by the colour of their downs. By the use of such breeds the services of the sexer can be entirely dispensed with. Moreover, by the very nature of their constitution these breeds can be multiplied far more rapidly than ordinary ones. If we set our minds to it the bulk of our poultry population could, in three or four years, be made to consist of these auto-sexing breeds. How this can be done is shown in an article to be found in the January number of *Poultry Industry*. In this way we get rid of the unwanted cockerel at the source, we protect the would-be purchaser of pullet chicks, we check the waste of valuable food on cockerel chicks, and we spare ourselves the humiliation of being dependent on enemy subjects for knowledge vital to our wartime economy.

I remain, yours faithfully,
R. C. PUNNETT

Coloured Soldiers

From Mr D. Davie-Distin   *2 October 1942*

Sir,

I am the manager of a snack bar in Oxford, and have had a rather unfortunate state of affairs, which is beginning to exist in this country, brought very forcibly to my notice. The other night a coloured United States soldier came into our establishment and very diffidently presented me with an open letter from his commanding officer explaining that 'Pte —— is a soldier in the US Army, and it is necessary that he sometimes has a meal, which he has, on occasions, found difficult to obtain. I would be grateful if you would look after him.'

Naturally, we 'looked after' him to the best of our ability, but I could not help feeling ashamed that in a country where even stray dogs are 'looked after' by special societies a citizen of the world, who is fighting the world's battle for freedom and equality, should have found it necessary to place himself in this humiliating position. Had there been the slightest objection from other customers I should not have had any hesitation in asking them all to leave.

I should like to feel that everybody shared my views, as England's reputation for hospitality is in danger of being questioned. Incidentally, the gentleman in question showed his gratitude by a donation of just twice the amount of his bill in our blind box.

Yours faithfully,
D. DAVIE-DISTIN

Business Brevity

From the Reverend Basil Bennett   *29 November 1943*

Sir,

I have recently received a letter from a well-known firm with a large mail-order connexion with whom I have been dealing for some years. At the head of the letter appears the following:

'In reply please quote E/09881/GD E/1765/CD 0/8504/SD 0/6855/CD DW/TL.'

Yours faithfully,
BASIL E. BENNETT

H

From Miss G. W. Hughes   *2 December 1943*

Sir,

My maternal grandfather, John Becke, who was born in 1817, thought it illiterate to sound the 'H' in any word derived from the French. He always spoke of 'otels, 'ospitals, and 'umour; and declared that if you said *h*otel, you must say *h*onest.

Yours faithfully,
GLADYS W. HUGHES

[Sir John Gielgud, born 1904, prefers to read 'umour]

The Price of Hector

From the Bishop of Stepney   *15 December 1955*

Sir,

On D-Day the divisional headquarters of which I had the honour to be chaplain attended a special service in the parish church of Wye, Kent. Hector, the indefatigible organ blower, was at his best. A few days later I received his request for payment. It read: 'To blowing for the invasion . . . 7s 6d.'

I am, Sir, your obedient servant,

✠ JOOST STEPNEY

Doodle-Bug

[The first flying bomb fell on London 13 June 1944]

From Mr N. E. Odell   *9 October 1944*

Sir,

There is nothing new under the sun, not even the term 'doodle-bug', lately and widely applied to the flying bomb. For the sake of historical accuracy, and before the latter barbarous instrument be haply relegated to oblivion, it may not be amiss to record that the word 'doodle-bug' has been in use in Canada and America among mining men for some 20 years.

There it has been applied to certain geophysical instruments of a magnetic, electrical, or gravitational character which are used in prospecting for minerals. Some of these instruments (the magnetic kind) have, incidentally, been in use in Sweden for the purpose of locating iron ores since the beginning of the seventeenth century, and it is even possible that a colloquial term, equivalent to the American 'doodle-bug', may have been in current usage there. In any case the flying bomb cannot have it all its own way!

I am, Sir, your obedient servant,

N. E. ODELL

Hitler

From Dr R. Eisler   *7 May 1945*

Sir,

Two short footnotes to your obituary of the Führer. The often alleged change of name by Hitler's father amounts to this: Austrian peasants have regularly two names, one derived from the name of their freehold – the 'house name' (*Hausname*) – transmitted from owner to owner in case of inheritance or sale of the property, the other the family name a man signs on documents (*Schreibname*). A man is 'called' (*heisst*) by his house-name as long as he dwells there and owns his place; he signs himself (*schreibt sich*) with his family name. The change from the one to the other is evidence of the sale or cession of property-rights to a new owner. '*Hitler*' (from *Hütte, Hitten*, diminutive *Hittel*) means 'small cottager' or 'little cotman', and is originally an expression of contempt on the part of the bigger landowners in the neighbourhood. So is *Schicklgruber*, 'the owner', a, 'the man of the chequered pit' – i.e., a low-lying patch of land, piebald with sandy patches and dark scrub.

Hitler 'drank in the pan-Germanism of' Georg von Schoenerer, not 'of Luege'. Dr Karl Lueger was the great leader of the Christian-Socialist Party, a fervent Austrian, and an enemy of Pan-Germanism.

I am, Sir, your obedient servant,
ROBERT EISLER, late of Dachau and Buchenwald

An Airman's Grave

From Mr H. Wentworth Clubb   *13 June 1945*

Sir,

My son, Sergeant Pilot Osward Lindsay Clubb, of 111 Squadron, was killed in action over Northern France in April 1942 while engaged in defending our heavily attacked bombers. He was buried at Pihen, near Calais, and I append a translation of an extract from a letter received from the Curé of Pihen:

'. . . The grave is in good condition and well cared for. The Germans (a thing they never did before) gave a solemn funeral with a military band and guard of honour.

They even offered a magnificent wreath in admiration of the courage showed in the combat . . .'

It is some consolation to know that the bravery of our men was so honoured by the enemy.

Yours faithfully,
H. WENTWORTH CLUBB

Provisions at Potsdam

[The Allied leaders Truman, Stalin and Churchill (replaced by Attlee after the general election results announced on 26 July) met for the last time from 17 July to 2 August 1945]

From Mr C. B. Acworth   *20 July 1945*

Sir,
One of the avowed aims of the Potsdam meeting is the parcelling out of the world's food supply to avoid Europe facing famine this winter. That being so one can only marvel at the tastelessness of the propaganda which announces that delegates will be fed on 'every luxury' in the way of food, that air transport has been given to wines from France, angostura from the West Indies, &c. Concern about the supply of game and strawberries-and-cream hardly seems worthy of a conference concerned with providing wheat for the elementary need of bread, nor does it make an agreeable pendant to the fact that our troops in Berlin have up till now been subsisting on compo rations.

Yours faithfully,
C. B. ACWORTH

[On 17 July the evening meal consisted of caviare, cold meat, turkeys, partridges, salads of all kinds, vodka and wines. Sir Alexander Cadogan, Permanent Under-Secretary at the Foreign Office, thought it 'rather disgusting in the midst of a starving country']

Cheese . . .

From Mr Ivor Back   *24 December 1945*

Sir,

I want to ask a simple question. In what way did the substitution of the monotonous 'mousetrap' cheese for the
splendid native cheeses of this country help us to win the war?
In what way does it now help our return to prosperity? Whenever I have had the opportunity I have put this question to
economists, but not one of them has been able to give me a
satisfactory answer. More than anything else the people of this
country are crying out for variety in their diet. It is understandable that in the case of food imported from abroad this
cannot be readily achieved; but native products like cheese
could surely be made accessible to them.

Good cheeses like the Stilton and the Wensleydale and the
lesser known Blue Vinney (whose véry names now make one's
mouth water) are not luxuries; they are within the reach of
even a modest purse and they are also an important item in a
balanced diet. I do not know whether their manufacture has
been suppressed by some high authority, but, if this is the case,
I do earnestly hope that they will soon be restored to us.

I have the honour to be, Sir, your obedient servant,

IVOR BACK

. . . and Chianti

From Mr John Longrigg   *28 January 1947*

Sir,

The other day I bought half a pound of Blue Danish cheese
and some white Chianti. The purity and intensity of the pleasure they produced were so disproportionate to the simplicity
of the arrangements involved that I am almost led to believe
that it is worth being confined for months to mousetrap and
beer. Are chocolate biscuits only exciting when they are produced only occasionally? And are we to sympathize with the
man who beat his head against the wall because it was so nice
when he stopped?

I remain, Sir, your obedient servant,

JOHN LONGRIGG

[On 25 February 1947 Dr Edith, later Baroness, Summers-kill, Parliamentary Secretary, Ministry of Food, informed the House of Commons it was not the function of her Ministry to pander to acquired tastes but to ensure that those who had had no time to acquire those tastes had suitable food; the nation liked mousetrap cheese. For the Conservative Opposition Mr Lennox-Boyd said the lady had brought class consciousness into cheese]

The Scholar in the Scullery

From Mr C. V. Davidge   *27 February 1946*

Sir,

Many people must have voted for the present Government thinking that it would have the interests of education at heart. But has it? The complete lack of domestic servants has struck a blow at education such as has not been seen for centuries. Every married don here, and I suppose in other universities and schools, spends his time washing up in the scullery. We do not object to the work; we are proud of it. We find, as we always knew, that a good classical education fits a man for anything. Common Room conversation scintillates with hints on how to clean dirty saucepans and our wives declare that the washing up has never been done so well. But the more time we have to spend in the scullery the less time there is for the reading and teaching that is demanded of us The same must be true in all other walks of life.

What is the remedy? There must be thousands of women in Europe who would make excellent domestic servants and would give anything to come to this country. Instead of sending food to them where they are struggling in deplorable conditions, let us bring them here where they would be useful. Think of the effect of the headlines: 'Great Britain offers a home to 500,000 women, victims of the war'.

Moreover, there appear to be many Irish women willing to come to this country as domestic servants. Instead of doing anything to help, the Ministry of Labour puts the greatest difficulties in the way of anybody wishing to employ them. I have tried, and am still trying. Perhaps, Sir, you may be able to move the Ministry.

Yours faithfully,
C. V. DAVIDGE

[The remedy in 1946 was for dons of Keble College to remain single – or get divorced and live in college]

Palestine

[On 29 June 1946, after much violence, 2,000 Jews were detained in Palestine]

From Colonel Walter Elliot   6 July 1946

[a former Conservative minister whose life could eventually be summed up, in part, by the initials after his name – PC, CH, MC, FRS, FRCP]

Sir,

Recent events in Palestine, culminating in the action of Saturday 29 June, are the worst news received in this country for many a long day. The House of Commons rightly demanded and obtained a debate at the earliest possible moment, but even the closest study of the debate does not give much relief or illumination.

The Governmment case seems to be that the government action arose out of 'a long series of terrorist and illegal actions'. 'What is the alternative?' asked the Prime Minister. Let us look for an answer. The long series of terrorist and illegal actions is undeniable and deplorable. The question at issue, however, is whether the recent actions of the Government are likely to bring it to a close.

It is not as though we were without experience in such matters. The long series of terrorist and illegal actions in Palestine is short indeed, compared with the long series of terrorist and illegal actions with which we were familiar in Ireland. These were not brought to an end by government violence. They were brought to an end by free negotiations with those at whose hands we had suffered those very injuries (and they many, from ours). Also by a policy clearly thought out and resolutely followed. It should be added, by a policy possible of fulfilment.

The rooting out of 600,000 Jewish settlers is impossible. So is the rooting out of 1,600,000 Arabs. So is today, and it may be for a long time to come, the changing of hearts. But it is also impossible for the two peoples to inhabit peacefully together the same country so long as one or the other has, by the obscurity of government policy, ceaselessly to jockey for position. It is also impossible, after recent events, to look forward to an long period during which Britain can carry on the detailed, intricate, day-to-day government of the country, which requires the consent, or at least the acquiescence, of both sides. The house is burning down; it is not a question of its economy but of its salvage. Because today other things are burning down, more vital than most of us had ever believed could be thus consumed; among them a great deal of Britain's good name.

In Ireland the crisis was settled by partition – rough surgery, but effective. In Palestine much the most authoritative review of the position, that of the Peel Commission, recommended the same remedy. I supported it then. I support it now. I do not believe that the admission of 100,000 Jews will solve the problem, even the present problem; though it would do much to palliate the lot of those who are still, a year and more after V Day, living in the slaughter camps in which we found them.

The problem will not be finally solved without a policy which the two sides can understand, and which the world can accept. Such a policy has been enunciated by as distinguished and authoritative a Royal Commission as is ever likely to survey this field. Such a policy is certainly physically possible. Here is the alternative for which the Prime Minister asks. What is needed is not a search for further alternatives, but an end to the endless delays. Meanwhile it is impossible to emphasize too strongly the injury which is being caused by the present position; caused not only in Palestine, not only elsewhere abroad, but here at home, where a feeling of nausea, of incredulity like that of nightmare, spreads, as people listen to the news, or read descriptions or, still worse, justifications, of what the days are bringing forth, in the Holy Land.

I am, yours sincerely,

WALTER ELLIOT

[In due course, Britain announced the mandate would end on 15 May 1948. On that date the Jewish Agency declared the state of Israel established. The first Arab-Israeli war followed]

Army Nicknames

From Mr Reginald Bosanquet　　　　　　*1 August 1977*

Sir,

Thinking about the film *A Bridge Too Far* can any of your readers explain why World War Two generals had such incredibly childish nicknames?

'Jumbo', 'Squeaker', 'Pip', 'Boy' and 'Bubbles' come to mind.

Yours faithfully,
REGINALD BOSANQUET

From Major-General Sir Alec Bishop　　　　*3 August 1977*

Sir,

The reasons underlying the nicknames 'Jumbo', 'Squeaker' and 'Boy' referred to by Mr Reginald Bosanquet in his letter are that the first general possessed a large and impressive stature, the second a voice which would rise to a high pitch when under excitement, and the third because of his youthful appearance.

I have never understood the reasons underlying the conferment of 'Pip' and 'Bubbles' on the other two.

Yours faithfully,
ALEC BISHOP

From Mr Gregory Blaxland　　　　　　*3 August 1977*

Sir,

The answer to Mr Bosanquet's query is that generals of the Second World War acquired their childish nicknames, not through anything they did in that war, but through the clubby nature of regimental life at the time of their joining, which in most cases was before the Great War of 1914.

Some were purely descriptive, as in the cases of 'Jumbo' Wilson, who looked like an elephant, and 'Squeaker' Curtis, who had a high-pitched voice. Some stem from an episode, such as the emission of bubbles by Evelyn Barker on his first attempt at pipe-smoking. (Another 'Bubbles' was the infant model for the famous advertisement.)

But the most childish and most numerous nicknames are those automatically linked to a name, and these can be misleading. 'Strafer' Gott affords a good example. It occurred to me while I was writing a book on the North African campaign (recently published with title *The Plain Cook and the Great Showman*) that 'Strafer' ill described this humane and well loved general. Then I recalled the words attributed to the Kaiser, *'Gott strafe England'*. There could be no escape thereafter for any soldier with the surname of Gott from the nickname of 'Strafer'.

Yours faithfully,
GREGORY BLAXLAND

From Mrs Primrose Feuchtwanger　　　　　*3 August 1977*

Sir,

Mr Reginald Bosanquet might be interested to know that my late father, Major-General H. Essame, to whom Ronald Lewin generously referred in his review of *Corps Commander* last week, had slightly turned in feet and took shorter than normal strides. He was known to his troops as 'Twinkletoes'.

Yours faithfully,
PRIMROSE FEUCHTWANGER

From Mrs Derek Oulton　　　　　*3 August 1977*

Sir,

Mr Bosanquet refers in his letter to some unusual military nicknames. I once heard the son of one of the generals he mentions introduce himself to my husband by saying 'I'm Squeaker's boy, the Oat's godson and the Burglar's nephew'.

Yours faithfully,
THE OAT'S DAUGHTER

From Mr K. R. Simpson　　　　　*4 August 1977*

[Department of War Studies and International Affairs, RMA Sandhurst]

Sir,

Reggie Bosanquet queries why it was that British generals in World War Two had such incredibly childish nicknames as

'Jumbo', 'Squeaker' and 'Boy'. Surely this reflects nothing more than the preparatory school background of these generals. Equally childish nicknames can be found amongst the literary and artistic talent of that generation. Types of nickname have a lot to do with national characteristics.

For instance, the Germans in the Second World War preferred to give generals nicknames which were a play on words. Thus Field-Marshal Keitel was known as 'Lakeitel', a play on the German word *lakai*, meaning lackey, and Field-Marshal Hans Kluge was known as 'Kluge' Hans, a play on the German word *klug*, meaning clever. More sinister was the nickname 'Strength through Fear', derived from the Nazi leisure organization 'Strength through Joy', given to Field-Marshal Schörner, an officer not noted for his sense of humour.

Yours truly,
K. R. SIMPSON ('Whacko' Simpson)

From Mrs Hilary Aggett   *4 August 1977*

Sir,
The incredibly childish nicknames given to World War Two generals surely derived from the fact that most of their contemporaries, both senior and junior officers, went to public schools where witty nicknames were the order of the day.

I served on the staffs of 'Monkey' Morgan, 'Dolly' de Fonblanque, 'Windy' Gale, 'Pug' Ismay, 'Jorrocks' Horrocks and, lower down the ranks, with 'Poppy' Flanders and 'Fairy' Fairhurst.

Yours faithfully,
HILARY AGGETT (Captain, retired)

From Brigadier J. H. P. Curtis   *4 August 1977*

Sir,
The answer to Reginald Bosanquet's question is simple. The last war generals acquired their 'childish' nicknames at the outset of their Service careers, often while still in their 'teens.

In the early nineteen hundreds Christian names were resorted to only after a suitable period of acquaintance had elapsed. As an alternative a ready form of identification was needed amongst the junior officers who invented nicknames for each other based usually on a personal idiosyncrasy or physical feature.

By the late nineteen-thrties when I joined the Army, the

invention of new nicknames had become less necessary since Christian names were used at once.

Which is why, Sir, I can but sign myself

Yours faithfully,
SQUEAKER'S BOY

[Brigadier Curtis points out that 'Squeaker's' (Major-General H. O. Curtis) nickname had nothing to do with his voice. 'Origin TOP SECRET' – see also Sir Evelyn Barker's letter, 8 August 1977]

From Mr Oliver Everett   *5 August 1977*

Sir,

Followers of the Bosanquet nicknames correspondence (admirable for August) might also like to know that the present day Indian Army has inherited the nickname habit (and much else) from their British forbears.

Examples include Major 'Pickles' Sodhi of the 61st Cavalry; Majors 'Binny' and 'Mao' Sherghill of the 7th Light Cavalry and the Deccan Horse respectively, and, of course, Colonel 'Bubbles' Jaipur.

Yours faithfully,
OLIVER EVERETT

From Mr G. T. St J. Sanders   *5 August 1977*

Sir,

Were not Army nicknames immortalized after the first World War in Sapper's stories? I call to mind Spud Trevor of the Red Hussars, Dog-face (Major Chilham), Pumpkin (twice), Hatchet-face, Tiny Tim (twice), Bimbo Charteris and, of course, Captain Bulldog Drummond.

In Gilbert Frankau's *Royal Regiment* the two principal characters were 'the Hawk' (Colonel Sir Guy Wethered) and 'Rusty' (Major Thomas Rockingham).

Yours faithfully,
G. T. St J. SANDERS

From Mr Donald Wilson   *5 August 1977*

Sir,

General Urquhart's nickname was 'Tiger' and General Sir Ivor Thomas, who commanded respect not unmixed with apprehension from his staff, was usually known as 'Von Thoma'. Nothing boyish about either of those two, I do assure you.

Yours faithfully,
DONALD WILSON

[But was General Ritter von Thoma, who surrendered to Montgomery on 4 November 1942, known as Ivor Thomas?]

From Wing Commander Bentley Beauman   5 *August 1977*

Sir,
The generals are given these strange nicknames mainly for security reasons so that the enemy (and most other people) cannot possibly tell who they really are.

Yours, etc.,
E. BENTLEY BEAUMAN

From Sir Alan Lascelles   6 *August 1977*

Sir,
Army nicknames were not always affectionate. In 1915, my divisional commander, who had been christened Richard, was Dirty Dick to his friends, and Filthy Richard to all the rest of us.

Yours faithfully,
ALAN LASCELLES

From General Sir Evelyn Barker   8 *August 1977*

Sir,
I have delayed my answer to Mr Bosanquet's letter just to see what reaction it got. It has certainly produced much information on the subject but mostly inaccurate. None of the nicknames so far mentioned had anything to do with a private or public school background. They all (I'm not sure about Pip Roberts) came into being during the owner's early days in the Army and originated from some inherent characteristic.

The 60th Rifles when I joined before World War I had a number of officers with nicknames given them after they joined such as Loony, Tripe, Oxo, Squeaker, The Oat and many others, and I know the reasons for all of them. Often on marriage their wives inherited their nicknames, and Loony's wife took exception to it. Luckily Tripe never married. As regards my own, I regret to say I have no connexion with Sir John Millais' delightful painting of his grandson (later Admiral Sir William James) who naturally was called Bubbles. He died in 1974. For many years it was used as an advertisement for Pear's Soap. Nor in any case has it anything to do with pipe smoking as Mr Blaxland declares (3 August). The reason for it is Top Secret and only divulged to my closest friends. However, I will give Mr Blaxland the clue that it has some connexion with a camel and not with a pipe. Actually I only smoked a pipe during World War II.

Yours faithfully,
EVELYN H. BARKER, 'BUBBLES'

From Mr L. G. Scales   *9 August 1977*

Sir,
To me, a ranker who served throughout the war at the sharper end of the Army, the chumminess of nicknames seems quite out of keeping with the recognized aloofness of generals. Apart from Wilson's 'Jumbo' and Montgomery's 'Monty', I never got to know what their nicknames were. Moreover, had I been able to get that close and dared to have asked them, my chances of escaping charges for insolence would have been very slender indeed.

Yours truly,
L. G. SCALES

Eleanor Rathbone

[At the time of her death on 2 January 1946, Eleanor Rathbone was Independent MP for Combined English Universities]

From Mr H. Redlich   *14 October 1946*

Sir,
June 1940. At Huyton, the large central camp for civilian internees, thousands of men are idling, deeply depressed and full of anxiety about their fate and that of their families from whom they were taken away without notice. Barbed wire all round reminds them of the Nazi concentration camps where most of them had suffered before. Wild rumours are spreading. Suddenly, news is going round that two MPs are in the

camp to talk to the camp-father and perhaps to the internees. They flock to the hut where discussions are in progress between the two visitors and the British commander. The camp-father is patiently walking up and down in front of the hut that is almost besieged, well guarded by soldiers. In pouring rain he and the internees wait for a long time. Everybody keeps inside a small spark of hope that cannot be deadened by the rain.

At last the doors open. A woman appears, behind her a man's face, both flanked by soldiers with fixed bayonets. The woman begins to address the men: 'You are not forgotten.' They hardly discern her words, many do not understand. But what they feel is: This is democracy! They feel the warmth of her motherly voice. The woman's face in the open door is beaten by the pouring rain. Her face, her voice are nursing the gleam of hope left in their hears. Then they disperse and carry the message round among those thousands, most of whom have taken their part in the fight against Nazism; many are still taking it now.

What Eleanor Rathbone has done in those dark days both for the honour of Britain and the spirits of the internees cannot be measured by words. Every one has now a chance of honouring her great human deeds by contributing to the memorial sponsored by the greatest British names.

Yours, etc.,

H. REDLICH

[Eleanor Rathbone's abiding legacy was the Family Allowances Act]

Golden Eagles

From Mr Seton Gordon   17 August 1946

Sir,

I have read with much interest the article in *The Times* on the status of the golden eagle in the Scottish Highlands. The writer is to be congratulated in drawing attention to a state of affairs which every lover of nature must deplore.

As he rightly observes, there are two ways in which the eagle can be protected. (1) By preventing the shooting and trapping of the bird. (2) By protecting the eggs. Unfortunately for itself, the golden eagle is so large a bird that there is no chance of a pair taking up their quarters in a district without

151

their presence being at once known. At a time when grouse are everywhere scarce, it is only natural that the tenant or owner of a moor should be anxious to destroy those birds and animals injurious to Lagopus Scoticus.

Fox and grey crow (both have greatly increased during the war years) must be kept down, but what of the eagle? This great bird does take grouse, but it prefers hares and rabbits. It also preys on the grouse's enemies. I have on several occasions found a stoat brought as prey to the eyrie. The grey crow is also taken, and a friend one day found no fewer than seven grey crows at an eyrie. The golden eagle also brings fox cubs to the nest as food for the young. I am confident that, if every eagle in Scotland were killed, there would follow no visible increase in the number of grouse.

It is true, as your Correspondent says, that the eagle is being killed on Highland estates, but I think he is wrong to place the blame and responsibility for this on the gamekeepers and stalkers. He should blame rather the owners of the estates and their factors or land agents. I know that the keepers and stalkers on a good many Highland estates have received orders during the past year that enemies of grouse, including the golden eagle, are to be destroyed whenever possible. The Highland gamekeeper is usually a keen lover of nature, and such an order is often (I do not say always) unpopular, and may even be evaded.

The remedy is that the owner of the ground should give orders that he wishes the golden eagle protected. One has only to see the result of such protection when it is given to realize what a difference it would make. The Duke of Sutherland, for instance, strictly protects the eagle on his Sutherland estates, and I have yet to meet one of his deerstalkers or gamekeepers who wishes to molest the bird, even on grouse ground.

To protect the eagle is easy: to protect the eggs is more difficult. The Society of Bird Watchers and Bird Wardens has done good work in offering rewards to gamekeepers and shepherds who guard an eyrie on their ground. When an egg collector is willing to pay the sum of £10 for a clutch of golden eagle's eggs, a considerable temptation is placed in the way of a poor man. How this can be prevented it is difficult to say, but the golden eagle is so long-lived a bird that, even if the eggs of a given pair were taken for 20 or 30 years each season, the birds themselves would remain in full vigour. Therefore it seems to me that the most urgent problem is now to prevent the eagle from being killed. In most Highland counties the golden eagle is protected by law: what is needed is that the law should be backed by moral opinion, for only thus can it be enforced.

I am very doubtful whether marking an eagle's eggs with indelible pencil will render them safe from egg collectors. A well-known collector once told me that if he found in an eyrie eagle's eggs thus marked 'he would stick a pin through them'. That was a good many years ago, and I have little doubt that science could now find some means of removing the marks of an indelible pencil from an egg-shell.

> I am, etc.,
> SETON GORDON

Message from Germany

From Herr Paul Zimmermann   18 *January 1947*

Sir,

May I beg you to forward to all the British and American prisoners of war who have been in the camps of Heydekrug, Bankau, and Moosburg in 1943–5, and who remember me, my kindest regards and best wishes for a bright and happy new year? I hope that they have all returned home and are in good health.

> Yours very sincerely,
> PAUL FR. ZIMMERMANN, Camp Officer

[More than three weeks elapsed between the writing of this letter and its publication. Censorship? Postal service? Decoding?]

Historical Sense

From Mr John Boyd-Carpenter, MP   3 *January 1948*

[Conservative Member for Kingston-upon-Thames; since 1972 Lord Boyd-Carpenter]

Sir,

I have just received a letter postmarked Omaha, Nebraska, originally addressed to me at 'British Parliament, Oxford, England'. This duly reached me with the following comment written on by some Post Office official, 'Not since Charles I.' Even though historically this does involve a slight inaccuracy, I do not believe that there is any other country in the world in which the public services are conducted with such a sense of history.

Yours, etc.,
JOHN BOYD-CARPENTER

[Parliament met at Oxford on 28 March 1681 during the reign of Charles II]

A Plea for Thatchers

From Sir Alfred Munnings, PPRA   *15 January 1948*

Sir,

Thatching, like all skilled country crafts, is dying out. In our wide district, one solitary thatcher lives at Thorington Street, Stoke-by-Nayland. This quiet, wonderful man leaves his mark in villages for miles around, covering stacks and preserving the life and beauty of many a stalwart barn and cottage. Wherever you may go in his area, his work, embellished often with true traditional decoration, is a joy to behold.

After many calls, catching him at home only in the evenings, I at last got him to do a job for me, and, having seen him at work, I am convinced that it would take a strong and wiry woman to accomplish the clipping of the lengthened line at the eaves, 'straight as a die', as the saying is. Centuries ago, one or two skilled villagers, working with such a man, must have taken less time than we imagine to build one of those warm and lasting cottages with steeply pitched roof and white-washed walls.

When talking with this craftsman about our countryside, which once had sheep and stock on every farm and where children once gathered acorns, I suggested that every child, rich or poor, rural or urban, should be taught the meaning of the soil. His reply was, 'Yes. It would fill their minds and give them something to think about, and if they lived 500 years they then wouldn't have learned all there is to know.'

I am, Sir, yours obediently,
ALFRED MUNNINGS

University Seats

[Of 615 MPs after the general election of 1935, some 12 represented universities: Oxford 2, Cambridge 2, London 1,

Combined English 2, Scottish 3, Wales 1 and Northern Ireland 1. The smallest 'constituency' was Queen's University, Belfast, with fewer than 4,000 voters; the largest, the Scottish Universities with more than 50,000 – so proving what Scots had long maintained, that they were the best educated of all Britons]

From the Master of Trinity College, Cambridge
10 February 1948

Sir,

It seems a pity that, for the purpose of abolishing the anomaly of the plural or alternative vote, a valuable institution like university representation should be abolished. The two things are separable. A machinery would no doubt have to be set up to prevent anyone from voting both for a university and for another constituency, under heavy penalties.

Whether this were done or not, there are strong reasons, as you have pointed out, for retaining university representation. It is a time-honoured peculiarity of our constitution, more than three centuries old. It enabled Isaac Newton to sit in two Parliaments. It still supplies the House with a number of men most of whom are not attached to either party and who bring an element of which both parties stand in need. Men like Herbert Fisher and John Buchan were university members who added a fine contribution to the higher aspect of parliamentary life. During the late war Professor A. V. Hill, for Cambridge, represented not a party but science, with valuable results.

To abolish the university members will be taken as a sign of indifference to higher education. It is possible to sacrifice too much to the desire for absolute uniformity everywhere and in everything.

Yours, etc.,
G. M. TREVELYAN

From Mr A. J. P. Taylor and Mr G. D. N. Worswick
9 February 1948

[Fellows of Magdalen College, Oxford]

Sir,

The Hebdomadal Council is elected to control the administrative affairs of Oxford University; it has no authority to speak for university opinion in political matters, and we regret that it should have entrusted Dr Stallybrass, Principal of Brasenose College, with the task of defending the university constituencies. The voters in the university constituency are scattered all over the country; and no one can know their opinions on this question. We can only record that many resident graduates would welcome the abolition of plural voting. Others would like to see alternative possibilities considered, such as university representation in a reformed House of Lords; but these, too, would prefer abolition to the retention of the present system.

The universities have certainly often elected members who would never have succeeded in any normal constituency; the same could be urged with greater weight in favour of the rotten boroughs. These produced a Pitt, a Canning and a Gladstone; the universities have Ramsay MacDonald to boast of.

Yours faithfully,
A. J. P. TAYLOR
G. D. N. WORSWICK

[In 1948 A. P. Herbert was MP for Oxford University. The university franchise ended in 1950]

The Lass of Richmond Hill

From Mr Leonard Humphrey Razzall   *6 August 1948*

Sir,

Your leading article of today (4 August) complains of the litter left in Richmond Park by descendants of the Lass of Richmond Hill. As a Yorkshireman exiled in London may I point out that the lady in question, who was, as you say, both neat and sweet, never lived in Richmond, Surrey, but was born and bred in Richmond, Yorkshire. She was, however, wooed and wed by a Londoner, which may explain the bad behaviour of her descendants.

I am, Sir, yours faithfully,
LEONARD HUMPHREY RAZZALL

[The lady was Frances l'Anson, the Londoner Leonard McNally, a barrister who wrote *The Lass of Richmond Hill* – set to music by James Hook.

Mr Razzall's letter had the unusual distinction of appearing twice in *The Times*: in 1948, and in August 1973 under the heading *25 years ago*]

Cricketers' Initials

From Mr J. C. H. Hadfield   *8 July 1950*

Sir,
   No amount of over-familiar allusions to 'Len', 'Bill' or 'Roley' in the descriptive cricket reports can make up for insensitive treatment of the score sheet, which is, after all, the true poetry of the game. The popular Press today (*The Times* is an honourable exception) grants initials indiscriminately to amateurs and professionals alike, but has apparently decided that a ration of only one initial a player can be allowed. How can Mr N. W. D. Yardley, who was so richly endowed by his godparents, maintain his moral authority as England's captain when the penny papers either 'Norman' him or write him down in the score sheet as a mere 'N. Yardley'? Meanwhile his team-mate, Wardle, is allotted a wholly superfluous initial 'J', though he was blessed at birth with a surname which, without adornment, expresses the quintessence of Yorkshire slow left-arm spin and guile.
   I do not wish to appear undemocratic or a mere *laudator temporis acti*, but I admit some nostalgia for the Arcadian days when the score of the recent leaders in the county championship (though they were then lowlier placed) glowed with the lyrical simplicity of such names as Quaife or Lilley, or glittered with the baroque splendour of the Honourable F. S. G. Calthorpe (who possessed even more initials than that, I believe, but modestly discarded some of them on the cricket field). At a time when London has a superb exhibition of the literature of cricket it is surely fitting to make a plea for a higher aesthetic approach to the nomenclature of players.

Yours faithfully,
J. C. H. HADFIELD

[The 'Len', 'Bill' and 'Roley' were Hutton, Edrich and Jenkins. *Debrett* limits the former Warwickshire captain Calthorpe to three initials, but insists he was really F. S. Gough-Calthorpe – perhaps too cumbersome to fit any score sheet]

A Station Harmonium

From Mrs J. Calvert   2 *June 1951*

Sir,

Is there a station in England which provides a harmonium in the waiting-room for the amusement of passengers, other than Troutbeck in the Lake District? Yet British Railways are considering closing it as unremunerative.

I am, Sir, yours, etc.,
JANE CALVERT

[Perhaps because the locals used it mainly for playing the harmonium]

The Stymie Defended

[A golfer was stymied when his opponent's ball lay in a line between his and the hole, the two balls more than 6 inches apart. The stymie was abolished in 1951]

From Lieutenant-General Sir Alexander Hood   2 *June 1951*

[Governor and C-in-C Bermuda 1949–55]

Sir,

As a golfer of more than 50 years standing who played in the days of the gutty ball, and a Scot, may I protest most strongly at the proposal to abolish the stymie? What is the reason for the proposal? As I understand it, it is that it is considered unfair. Surely there are many other unfair things in golf – the bad lie off the straight drive, the kick off the line of that perfect approach, the sudden rain storm catching some of the competitors in a medal round? None of these can be prevented: they probably lose more strokes and holes than stymies. But no one, I hope, would wish to alter them. All these unfair things can be overcome by the good golfer, and the stymie in particular often affords an opportunity of surmounting it by delicate touch or proper appreciation of the situation. Is this the start of a campaign to eliminate all the so-called unfair things? Will a straight driver of over 200 yards be allowed to 'prefer' his lie, and so on?

There has been far too much meddling with a great game. Let us stand up for the pure rigour of the game as played by our fathers. The very word 'stymie' has entered into our language, and although its origin remains obscure, it may well have been coined by some Greek scholar and golfer of long ago, and deserves to be retained. By all means go back to stroke and distance for out of bounds and lost ball, and if some people prefer to putt with an abbreviated polo stick – well, let them, but hands off the stymie. Let it stand.

I have the honour to be, Sir, yours faithfully,
ALEX HOOD

[In the fourth round of the British Amateur at St Andrews in 1930, Cyril Tolley left himself with an un-negotiable stymie at the 19th hole. His conqueror, Bobby Jones, went on to win not only the Championship but the British Open, the US Open, and the US Amateur: the only Grand Slam in history]

Period Voices

[A *Times* fourth leader, in this Festival of Britain year, remarked that to summon up memories of 1851 the BBC had our ancestors sounding like 'very accomplished but rather imaginative actors . . . waspish men and arch women']

From Mr G. M. Young   9 May 1951

Sir,

To make up for a very bad visual memory I have a good aural memory, and I can call up voices which have been silent for 50 years. I am quite certain from my own recollection that the private, domestic, conversational voice of the Victorians (and their predecessors) was very much like our own. But for public purposes – reading aloud, quoting poetry, reciting some favourite passage of parliamentary eloquence – they did use a voice which would strike us as histrionic, though to them it was quite natural. In my youth I knew an old man who had heard Macaulay speak and could imitate his cadences. 'For me the good old cause is still the good old cause' was chanted rather than spoken. And I can remember the High Master of St Paul's, Frederick Walker, chanting, rather than speaking:

'Tot congesta manu praeruptis oppida saxis': which, I

suppose, is how Pitt delivered the greatest of all Virgilian quotations:

'Nosque ubi primus equis Oriens adflavit anhelis. . . .'

If the BBC speakers would observe this distinction we should be spared much of the misleading, misplaced waspishness and unction which you deplore in their renderings of Victorian conversation. In the House, Peel could be as unctuous as any of them, and Goschen was charged with Sadler's Wells Sarcasm in a Budget speech.

Yours faithfully,

G. M. YOUNG

[author of *Victorian England, Portrait of an Age*]

'Thermal Heating'

From Mr Henry Strauss, KC, MP   *9 May 1951*

[Conservative Member for Norwich South]

Sir,

Why 'thermal heating'? What heating is not 'thermal'? We shall next have round circles, wet water, unfriendly hate, and globular spheres.

I am, Sir, your obedient servant,

HENRY STRAUSS

From Mr Robert Sinclair   *16 May 1951*

Sir,

What is your learned correspondent going to do about 'the truth, the whole truth, and nothing but the truth'?

Yours, etc.,

ROBERT SINCLAIR

Origin of the Blazer

From Mr H. M. Stewart   *15 May 1951*

[of Lady Margaret Boat Club]

Sir,

The Oxford Dictionary and the author of your leading article have by no means traced the blazer back to its origin.

The earliest reference I have been able to locate – see the *Cambridge Review* of 8 June 1950 – is in *The Cambridge University Almanack and Register*. The first issue, referring to the season 1851–2, gives the uniform of the Lady Margaret Boat Club alone as consisting of '. . . a red guernsey or "blazer" . . .'. The fact that the word is in inverted commas shows that it was still slang, while its red colour gives the origin of the word. We still do not know how early it originated, and another problem is set. What was the garment like? For a guernsey should be knitted, while Walter Wren, who was at Christ's College, Cambridge, in 1852, said in a letter to the *Daily News* in 1889 that, in his time, the blazer was the 'red flannel boating jacket' of the Lady Margaret Boat Club.

I am, Sir, your obedient servant,
H. M. STEWART

Ordeal for Sentries

From Mr Henry Maxwell   *9 May 1951*

Sir,

While it is natural that tourists and visitors to London should take an interest in the sentries at Buckingham Palace, it is surely unnecessary for them to gather in groups in front of these boxes to gape and stare at them at the range of a few feet, as though they were wild animals. Not infrequently visitors come right up to a sentry and proceed to photograph him at point blank range, while sometimes, amidst much amusement, the girl friends of the visitors will station themselves at either side of the sentry to be photographed with him.

All of this must be extremely embarrassing and annoying to the sentries, though they bear the bad manners of the visitors with exemplary patience. I cannot help thinking that they are entitled to a little more consideration, and that the police should be instructed to move people on when their attentions are likely to prove an embarrassment to soldiers on duty.

Yours faithfully,
HENRY MAXWELL

Tax on Dollar Earnings

From Mr Evelyn Waugh   *6 February 1952*

Sir,

In the heyday of our parliamentary institutions a candidate could often secure election by dispensing a few guineas in beer-money at his own charge. In their decline the bribes are enormous and paid by the taxpayer. Members of Parliament, of all parties, admit in private that there are many measures which would be beneficial to the kingdom at large, but which they dare not advocate for fear of losing popularity with the labourers.

The present Chancellor of the Exchequer [R. A. Butler] has suggested that we are at a turning-point in our economic history. May I, therefore, make a modest proposal: that all dollars individually earned in the United States and changed into pounds, should be exempt of all tax? I think he would be surprised at the amount of relief this would give him in his chief task, turning dollars into pounds. Actors, lecturers, dancers, writers – those who most uphold our prestige abroad; more even, let it be said, than politicians – are not tempted to save their dollars and bring them home, if the result is confiscation.

To give an example from my own profession. It is not unusual for ~~~~~~ ~riter to be offered £20,000 to £50,000 for the film rights of his work. ~~~~ ~ writer, presumably, is already paying a high rate of supertax. The re~~~~~ ~f his film rights is the only possible way of saving for his old age – ~~~~ ~ ~ as many deplorable examples show, may fall on a writer at a time of life which is youthful for a politician. Surely it is expecting a fanatical patriotism to ask him to sacrifice all but a trifle of this sum, to the production of ground nuts and Gambian eggs. Successful writers are constantly refusing generous offers from American editors simply because their rewards would be nugatory. Let them have their money to spend in this kingdom; they will work harder and the kingdom will benefit with them. Of course, such a concession would be unpopular with the labourers. It would be a gravely needed proof that the present Government are seriously concerned with their financial predicament, and not merely with the purchase of votes.

I am, Sir, your obedient servant,

EVELYN WAUGH

Lords Debate on the BBC

[The BBC monopoly was under discussion]

From Mr Andrew Cruickshank   *9 June 1952*

Sir,

I am an actor and a writer who occasionally works for the BBC both in television and in radio. When a play of mine is accepted for either medium I am delighted. When it is rejected I am prompted to debate the matter, and even to consider matters normally outside my sphere, such as the House of Lords debate on sponsored television. Unlike Lord Moran my conclusions are these. The noble lords who favour the continuation of the BBC in its present form bear an extraordinary resemblance to a Jacobin club which regards itself as the repository of the people's will, with this difference that instead of encouraging the destruction of the BBC so that the people's will may be more effective, they desire its continuity in order that what they consider 'good' may be advanced. Their resemblance to the Jacobins does not end there. Like Jacobins they favour a restricted mercantilism which is the system on which the BBC with its modest fees and autocratic selection works. Indeed, my conclusions lead me to believe that these noble lords have given the first demonstration in this land of Marxist analysis in the field of culture.

If there is a moral to be drawn from the House of Lords debate it is that, instead of concentrating on man, a little attention might be devoted to the rights of Englishmen. If there is a hope to be expressed it is that when the debate is resumed, since Lord Moran mentions Plato, some voice will approach the matter on the lines of Aristotle and St Thomas and that what is at present considered 'ideal' might be reviewed in the light of what is still 'practical'. A little attention and thought might be given to the conditions from which arise a Shakespeare and Burbage, a Shaw and Granville-Barker, an O'Casey and Yeats. These combintions may have arisen arbitrarily, but the faith which created the conditions in which they could combine was clear. Can the air whose conditions the BBC controls be so described?

I am, Sir, yours faithfully,
ANDREW CRUICKSHANK

Difficult Nomenclature

From Sir Carleton Allen, QC   *19 December 1952*

[Warden of Rhodes House, Oxford, 1931–52]

Sir,

The Commonwealth maintains remarkable unity in diversity, but it seems to have great difficulty with its nomenclature. We must not speak of the 'British' Commonwealth – that is too nationalistic; nor of 'empire' – that is too imperialistic; nor of 'colony', 'dependency' or 'colonial' – that is too superior; nor, certainly, of 'possession' – that is too possessive. And now, since the recent resolutions of the Prime Ministers, we must not speak of 'Dominion' – that is too dominating, though it is difficult to see why it suggests that a Dominion is dominated by anybody but itself.

What advantage has 'realm' over 'dominion'? 'Dominion status' was a very convenient and, surely, an inoffensive term. 'Independent status', on which Ceylon was apparently the first to insist, does not denote membership of the Commonwealth, and might be applied equally well to any sovereign foreign State. Or are we in future to speak of 'realm status'? Since colonies are now, it seems, 'territories', are their inhabitants to be known as 'territorials'? And shall we some day be told that 'Commonwealth' is inappropriate because we have not enough wealth (or weal) in common? It is all very confusing to simple minds.

Yours faithfully,
C. K. ALLEN

From Mr T. S. Page   *30 December 1952*

Sir,

If precedent is followed, the *mot juste* for Head of the Commonwealth is Protector.

Your obedient servant,
T. S. PAGE

164

The Siren's Note

From Lord Broughshane   *6 February 1952*

Sir,

The Home Secretary, Sir David Maxwell Fyfe, has announced that large supplies of new sirens have been ordered by the Government for the purpose of giving warning of approaching air raids. May I express the hope that in the specification for these sirens it will be provided that they should sound a strong and defiant note, and not the wailing catcalls which chilled our marrows in the 1939–45 war?

I am, Sir, your obedient servant,

BROUGHSHANE

[Perhaps marrows were meant to be chilled]

* Te ripi o te rarangi kai

From Mr A. J. Brown   *19 September 1953*

Sir,

I am completely in agreement with the remarks passed by Sir Alexander Maxwell, chairman of the British Travel and Holiday Association, concerning the printing of menus in French, and think this practice is an insult to intelligent British people. As a visitor from New Zealand (they do it there, too) I feel that whoever is responsible for preparing the menu is not giving the hotel tone, but is doing it an injustice by inflicting on at least 80 per cent of the guests a crossword puzzle without any clues, at a time when they are feeling more hungry than playful. The embarrassment caused when the waiter says 'I'll try and find out' need not be described, and I do not think that a lack of knowledge of the French language puts the guest on a lower social stratum, any more than would a Frenchman's ignorance of the Maori language.

What an uproar there would be in France if their menus were to be printed in English. Aren't we sufficiently proud of our language to aver that it is fluent enough to do justice to even the best British cooking? With all respect to the French culinary art, this idea was inflicted upon us many years ago, and I think it is well past the time when our leading hotels should set an example, and, if they cannot print a wholly English menu, at least they could show an English interpretation of their 'cooking French'.

Yours faithfully,
A. J. BROWN

[*The above letter was originally headed 'Reading the Menu'. Asked to provide a Maori translation, the New Zealand High Commission gently pointed out that the Maori language is not a written one, nor is there an exact word for 'menu'. However, they did suggest 'The Reading of the Food', a phrase which may come in useful to the next French rugby team to visit New Zealand]

Misplaced Stresses

From Miss Athene Seyler   *6 June 1953*

Sir,

The Church and the stage have sometimes been called the guardians of the English language. This charge now surely falls on the BBC. In yesterday's otherwise beautiful commentary on the Coronation service we heard the peeresses described as peer-*esses*. This is as incorrect as it would be to refer to host-*esses* or even act-*resses*.

I beg to remain, yours faithfully,
ATHENE SEYLER

[Miss Seyler was playing Lady Hunstanton in Oscar Wilde's *A Woman Of No Importance* at the Savoy Theatre and being even wittier than the author]

Litter in the Streets

From Mr Philip Carr   *14 October 1953*

Sir,

At the very beginning of this century, M. Lépine, that most famous and efficient Parisian prefect of police, abolished the then prevalent litter in three days. He announced that the police, including plain-clothes men, would be mobilized to take out a summons against any and every person who was seen to

166

drop a paper, or any rubbish in the street, and the maximum penalty would be imposed; and he did what he announced that he would do.

Yours faithfully,
PHILIP CARR

Counter-Tenor Voices

From Mr Albert Pengelly   *13 January 1954*

Sir,

In his review of Rimsky-Korsakov's *Le Coq d'Or* at Covent Garden your Music Critic touched on a notable void in present-day musical knowledge when he posed the query as to whether the tenor-altino voice of M Cuenod is the same as that of a counter-tenor or an alto. None of the standard works of reference, however, makes a distinction between the counter-tenor and the alto voice, and even *Grove* identifies one with the other. The counter-tenor voice is, I submit, one of tenor quality pitched exceptionally high, free from any falsetto quality and having a ringing tone not found in the alto voice, which is usually the falsetto overtone of a bass voice.

Purcell made the distinction when he used trumpets against the virile counter-tenors and flutes with the soft altos. Might we not encourage the use of this traditionally English voice by recognizing the counter-tenor voice in its own right without having its terminology appropriated by altos, no matter how great their range and facility?

I am, Sir, your obedient servant,
ALBERT PENGELLY

'How Many Civil Servants.'

From Colonel H. de Watteville   *21 October 1954*

Sir,

If a retired Army officer be permitted to offer a few remarks on this subject, might he record certain impressions derived from General Staff service which entailed a close contact with the civil administration of the country, first between 1916 and 1922, then again during 1943 and 1944?

These impressions remain very definite. During the 1914–18 war, secretaries, stenographers, and typists were scarce; establishments did not provide any large number. So there arose a perpetual rush – and some competition, too – in all lower administrative grades, civil, naval, and military alike, to obtain such assistance. The output of documents of all kinds was consequently kept down; still the administrative machinery functioned without undue shortcomings.

In the 1939–45 war this clerical personnel had risen to enormous proportions – possibly owing to the intake of women; much of it was perhaps not of the highest quality. The direct result of this growth was undoubtedly that even from the lowest grades of officials there was being produced a mass of directives, instructions, regulations, and memoranda that would have baffled, if not demoralized, participants in the First World War.

Such a spate of documents, and of 'paper' generally, threw an increasing burden on all executive personnel at the base of the pyramid. Often it might complicate their labours; not infrequently it might stultify their best efforts. Once a very minor official, when reproached with the futility of the instructions which he was passing downwards, at least to certain recipients, could only reply: 'Well, Sir, what else can I do? If I didn't pass on these new regulations in this way, I might get the sack!' How often did higher authority seriously study the quandaries, the anomalies that might occur in the wake of that torrent of 'paper'? Too often, so it might appear, the remedy involved more supplementary or explanatory memoranda, i.e. more clerical labour.

One more serious consequence of this increase of 'paper' seemed to be the inevitable tendency to throw more work on all the higher authorities involved. It followed that, in order to meet the heavy 'upward' influx of documents, ...onal assistants' might be appointed, who ... their own myrmidons, had to be call... ...o ease the strain thus thrown on the chi... ...uorities. And in addition to this increase, the multiplication of 'specialist' branches – an unavoidable aspect of the case in these days – still further expanded all staffs from their original size in 1939.

Now wireless telegraphy has contributed further to the clerical work to be dealt with. Alas! that it should be contributing to the obvious risk of over-centralization and the suppression of individual thought and action. On the other hand, the arrival of the aeroplane may be restoring an element of personal contact between the highest authorities and the lower 'executive' personnel – a welcome tendency.

But here, again, is this process not bringing about a virtual duplication of the highest administrative and executive grades; will these substitutes require their own personal assistants and clerical staffs? We trust not. The recent Korean conference held at Geneva at least proved an object lesson as to the fashion in which this process could extend.

I am, Sir, yours, &c.,

H. DE WATTEVILLE

[Professor C. Northcote Parkinson gave his law to the world in 1958: a Civil Service expands by an inexorable rule of growth, irrespective of the work, if any, which has to be done]

A Matter of Tempo

[Two London concerts by the Berlin Philharmonic Orchestra in January 1955 were cancelled on the death of Wilhelm Furtwängler. However, Sir Thomas Beecham agreed to conduct the Royal Philharmonic Orchestra in the same programmes as a tribute to his old friend. The work referred to in the letter below was the third Brandenburg concerto; Sir Thomas's affable tone was doubtless due to the rave notice accorded his performances of Strauss's *Don Juan* and Brahms's C minor symphony. What he did with the *Eroica* symphony and *Till Eulenspiegel* in the second concert seems to have been even more remarkable]

From Sir Thomas Beecham, CH   *25 January 1955*

Sir,

I believe that it is generally well known that I have much respect for and sympathy with those brave fellows who attempt the hazardous task of musical criticism. More particularly does this partiality of mine apply to *The Times*, which alone among London journals of the present day devotes adequate space to the consideration of music in its various aspects. For these good reasons I refrain from uttering a word of reproach when I read something that strikes me as being unusually inexplicable.

But last Tuesday, 18 January, I played with my orchestra at Festival Hall a minor work of Johann Sebastian Bach, by no means representative either of his greatness or of his period. The following morning I was positively dazzled to read in one of your esteemed columns that my performance of this trifle was a positive travesty, and that the nature of the crime was to be discovered in the headlong speed adopted by me; comparable, according to the genial writer of the critique, with the famous ride of John Gilpin or it might have been Richard Turpin, Esq.

Now, Sir, I hope that you will agree with me that 'travesty' is a mighty word to use when belabouring an executive artist in respect of some alleged offence. I therefore am emboldened to enter a modest defence against such a grave charge. What is the truth of the matter? It is that my tempi on this occasion differed in no way from those adopted by 19 out of 20 conductors throughout the world during the past 50 years. All my concert programmes are tape recorded and each one is played to me the day after the event. On this occasion I was able to verify that the respective tempi employed by me in the two movements of this concerto were – in metronomic language – 92 and 80. Since then I have obtained the gramophone records of four other orchestras playing under their regular conductors the same piece, and what do I find? (Incidentally these other records were played in the presence of four skilled and grimly independent witnesses.) They are:

1	Boston Symphony Orchestra	92 and 76
2	Danish Orchestra	92 and 76
3	Boyd Neel Orchestra	92 and 84
4	Stuttgart Chamber Orchestra	88 and 80

From this it will be seen that four of us adopted exactly the same tempo in the first of the two movements, three likewise in the second movement, and where there was any difference it did not exceed one point of metronomic indication. (In the metronomic calculation there is nothing between 76 and 80, this slight difference being hardly distinguishable.) I think then, if I am to be convicted of the misdemeanour of 'travesty', there must stand in the dock beside me the vast majority of my colleagues and their orchestras over the long period of time to which I have referred.

What is the explanation of this apparent mystification? I think, if I may so suggest, that it lies in the comparative inability of nearly all listeners to distinguish correctly between the three separate entities of speed, rhythm and accent. I freely admit that I play this particular piece with a great deal more vigour and emphasis than any of my distinguished colleagues,

170

and it is possible that there are those that do not care for this treatment of it. But their complaint, if they make it, cannot be directed against me on the ground of excessive speed. Long ago I commented in a book of mine upon the tendency of so many persons to imagine that I was an apostle of rapid tempi, although I was able through the evidence of gramophone records to establish that the majority of my interpretations might have erred in the contrary direction.

I trust that both you and the writer of the notice in question will look upon this little remonstrance of mine as having been uttered in a spirit of friendliness and respect.

I am your obedient servant,
THOMAS BEECHAM

Gloves for Greasy Rugby Balls

From Dr Thomas Bodkin   *20 January 1955*

Sir,

As one who, 50 years ago, often watched closely Basil Maclear playing rugby at Lansdowne Road, I am most positive that he never wore mittens. He did wear fine white kid gloves, such as all the young men of his day wore at dances. Not only was this the admirably dandiacal habit of one who always appeared well turned out on the field but it was also a calculated practical procedure. Gloves of that sort are the best of all integuments for the handling of a greasy ball.

I am, Sir, your obedient servant,
THOMAS BODKIN

The Defence Dilemma: Three Types of Modern War

From Major-General J. F. C. Fuller   *8 July 1955*

Sir,

I agree with your Defence Correspondent, whose articles you printed yesterday and on Monday, that it is time we decided on what kind of war we should organize, arm, and train for. But in the second of his articles on 'The Dilemma of Defence Planning', he confuses rather than clarifies this question, first, by making use of the catch-penny terms 'hot' and 'cold' war,

171

and, secondly, by defining cold war 'as anything from the Mau Mau rising in Kenya to another Korea'.

Let us drop these ridiculous terms and revert to military nomenclature. Today we are faced with three types of war, of which two are in nature physical, and the third dominantly psychological. The physical types are unlimited and limited war. In the first no limitation is set to the weapons used and the tactics resorted to – its aim is the annihilation of the enemy. Such was the Second World War, which we based on the asinine slogans of 'unconditional surrender' and 'victory at all costs'. In the second, which may be divided into major and minor limited wars, policy, aim, means employed, &c., are limited. The recent war in Korea is an example of a major limited war, and the present operations in Kenya of a minor limited war, which in former days would have been called a 'small war'.

Your Defence Correspondent confuses the issue when he calls limited wars 'cold wars'. They are nothing of the sort, and can be extremely hot. If any type of war is to be defined as 'cold', then it is war by treason and subversion, in which the emotions of men replace the bullets and bombs of unlimited and limited war. Its aim is to rot an enemy internally by revolution instead of compelling him by external physical means to accept the will of his antagonist. This type of war is sometimes called 'psychological war', a better name would be 'subversive war'. It was the type decided upon by Lenin and was raised to a fine art by Stalin; it is the most deadly type which faces us today.

On this question M. Raymond Aron observes in his illuminating book *The Century of Total War*: Western military experts are not sufficiently freed from traditional conceptions to realize that the cold war is the real war which is raging all the time. Therefore that the battle against propaganda and subversion must be waged indefatigably; 'the elimination by trade unions of Stalinist ringleaders', he writes, 'often signalizes a victory comparable with the formation of an additional army division'. Herein the key of economy should be sought.

Yours faithfully,

J. F. C. FULLER

Station-Masters

From Mr Edwin Haward   *7 September 1956*

Sir,

When I was last in Japan – 16 years ago – the station-master, equipped with curved sword and spotless in white cotton gloves, stood to attention, facing outwards by the side of the departing engine, till the train had cleared the platform and, indeed, passed out of sight. It would be pleasant to know that this picturesque symbol of punctilious observance of railway discipline had survived. If memory serves aright the ceremony was rounded off by a deep bow.

Yours, &c.,
EDWIN HAWARD

From the Reverend H. W. R. Elsey *11 September 1956*

Sir,

The station-master at Turnham Green station at the beginning of this century was a dignified, bearded figure. He signalized the approach of a train by a stately march along the platform, announcing in an authoritative tone: 'Hammersmith, Earls Court, Victoria, Westminster, Charing Cross, Blackfriars, and Mansion House train!' This, to a boy, made the journey to the City seem at least 100 miles. When he was not available this duty was performed by a porter, who rang a bell as he peregrinated the platform. I noticed, however, that the station-master himself never condescended to the bell.

I am, Sir, yours very faithfully,
H. W. R. ELSEY

From Sir George McRobert   *4 September 1956*

Sir,

It is not in Britain only that station-masters are special. In *Khaki and Gown* the first Lord Birdwood recorded the well known tale of Rivett-Carnac, the pompous and dignified opium agent of Ghazipur. While parading the platform of an Indian railway junction he was asked by a Bengali clerk the time and platform of departure of the next train to Calcutta. The official's furious 'How the devil should I know; why don't you ask the station-master?' earned the classic rebuke 'Sir! If you are not station-master why you thus so proudly walk?'

I am yours faithfully,
GEORGE R. MCROBERT

Hip Baths

[THAMES HARE AND HOUNDS desire to purchase silver running figure for trophy; also Victorian hip baths. – Secretary, 48 Pont Street, SW1]

From Mr A. Fletcher   *21 February 1957*

Sir,

As the unwilling author of the advertisement for hip baths that appeared in the Personal Column last week, I must make plain the fact that this outmoded form of ablution is retained in Thames Hare and Hounds by members who know of none other. Those of us who yearn for the trickling warmth of the modern shower-bath are not comforted; there is a shower but it is cold.

The snug and soothing picture described in your leading article of 18 February is but a sop to reaction, for while our seniors find the hip bath scandalously enjoyable, the younger members think only of the bathrooms in their homes. The hip bath is good for wallowing, not for washing, and after it one remains all spattered with dirt. Tom Brown and his friends thought hare-and-hounds the most delightful of games, but they had buttered toast in the housekeeper's room; for us the only reward is a second bath at home.

Yours faithfully,
ANTHONY FLETCHER

Concert Hall Acoustics

[In June 1957 Stokowski conducted the LSO in two concerts at the Royal Festival Hall – one devoted to Berlioz, Ravel, Debussy, Prokofiev and Stravinsky, the other to an unusual programme: Schubert's *Rosamunde* overture, the second symphony of Schumann and the eighth of Vaughan Williams]

174

Sir,

After conducting recently the splendid London Symphony Orchestra in the Royal Festival Hall, which in so many ways is well planned, I have the impression that it is a pity that the children and adolescents now growing up in London, and who are interested in the compositions of the great masters and also in contemporary music, often hear these either with too much reverberation, as in the Albert Hall, or with little, as in the Royal Festival Hall.

Such conditions are far from ideal for the future of English music, both for the listeners and for the English contemporary composers when they hear their music performed for the first time in either of these halls. Because of the great amount of absorption in the Royal Festival Hall the high tones sound thin and metallic and the low tones of the cellos and basses are correspondingly weak, so that the music is distorted and the tonal balance intended by the composer is not achieved.

The great violin-makers, such as Amati, Stradivari, and Guarneri, have clearly shown the ideal resonant and reflectant qualities of wood. If the walls and ceiling at the stage end of the hall were sheathed with good, simple wood at reflective angles so as to diffuse equally the sounds from the stage, and if the end of the hall farthest from the stage remained as absorbent as it is at present, thereby still avoiding echo but lengthening the reverberation, this hall could be greatly improved so that the acoustics could be of the same high quality as its other well-planned characteristics.

I write this letter not in a spirit of criticism but in the hope of being constructive, and with the thought in mind of composers, listeners, performers, and the art of Music.

Sincerely,
LEOPOLD STOKOWSKI

Teddy Boys

Sir,

I would wholeheartedly endorse the refusal of Miss Dickinson and Mr Paul, expressed in their letters on 8 and 9 May, to equate the problem of juvenile delinquency with that of the Teddy boy, while admitting that the two do, to a certain extent, overlap. The first problem I would not attempt to discuss here; on the second I would endeavour to make two points:

First, that in this country, for the first time since the industrial revolution, we have in these Teddy children, both boys and girls, a highly solvent, semi-articulate working-class youth with a strong sense of corporate identity, albeit in part the result of commercial exploitation and of constant attention in the Press. This group has the independence – I would almost say the arrogance – born of having money to spend; it has its own idols drawn from its own ranks, who do not for a moment attempt to repudiate their Bermondsey or Elephant and Castle origins; it has, I would submit, Sir, the beginnings of its own simple but tremendously vigorous culture. These young people do not spend their evenings watching television nor, with a few exceptions, fighting one another with bicycle chains; the ambition of the greater number of them is to play a musical instrument, even if it is only a washboard in a skiffle group.

Second, that in a time of considerable material prosperity the class war has very largely abated. Where bitterness still exists it is with the older generation of working people; certainly it is not with the Teddy children. Where the group does feel a corporate resentment it is towards the older generation as a whole; it is as if the age war had succeeded the old class struggle.

I cannot attempt, Sir, to propound a solution to the problem, but I would submit that it would be one of the tragedies of our age if this great source of energy and potential talent were allowed to run to waste. These young people deserve a dignified and sympathetic hearing; unreasoned condemnation is as much out of place as soup-kitchen charity.

I am, Sir, your obedient servant,
NEMONE LETHBRIDGE

A Horror Dated?

From Lady Holt-Wilson   *27 December 1958*

Sir,

Is there any way by which the High Court of Parliament, the Lords of Appeal, Scotland Yard, or even the Goons, can stop the insidious horror which is creeping upon us?

First it was 'Rock 'n' Roll', then I was offered 'Snakes 'n'

Ladders' in an otherwise respectable toy shop; and now I see the name of 'Jones 'n' Son' painted over a shop in a town near by.

I can only suppose that, despite the ever-increasing millions which we spend each year on education, we are still, as a nation, only concerned with Bread 'n' Circuses.

Yours faithfully,
A. HOLT-WILSON

[The eye rejects what the ear takes for granted?]

Living Language

From Mr Robin Hull   *23 October 1959*

Sir,
'Yeah', 'yep', 'yip' and now 'yup'. All these substitutes for plain 'yes' are objectionable and unnecessary, but 'yup' (usually delivered with an aggressive smack of the lips) strikes one as particularly repellent.

The idea of this variant finding a permanent place in English speech is horrifying. But who knows? 'Yup' may yet be displaced, in its turn, by 'yop' or even 'yap'.

Yours faithfully,
ROBIN HULL

A Lesson from the French

[1,400 foreign students of French literature in 55 countries had been asked to write an essay on the French book, ancient or modern, which had impressed them most. The most favoured authors – Saint-Exupéry, Corneille and Camus – also topped the lists in French *lycées*; Proust was a poor also-ran, Balzac more or less ignored]

From Mr Cedric Burton   *1 January 1959*

Sir,
Your leading article of 27 December on 'The Thread of Thought' provides food for thought for all those who are interested on the difficulties which beset would-be undergraduates and which you state so admirably in an adjacent column under the title 'Too Much Cramming'.

If young Frenchmen and young students of French can proclaim the influence of St-Exupéry, Corneille, and Camus on their lives – precisely these three authors, as you point out – it is because they have read and thought about enough books to make the confession of such an influence possible. Too many schoolboys in this country have no time for this sort of reading. They cannot read books; they must study them. Books are a necessary obstacle on the road to examination success and, together with the notes and commentaries which accompany them, something to be learnt, written down, and, very frequently, forgotten.

Under modern conditions of specialization the cramming of the two set books for Eng. Lit. is often the only contact which the prospective scientist has with the literature and thought of his own or any other country. It is the good fortune of the French schoolboy that he does not have to spend time in mastering the intricacies of sterling money sums, or in learning the fractional identities of rods, poles, and perches. His syllabus, too, gives him far greater encouragement to read widely at the lower levels. As a result the French schoolboy can be given at least an introduction to disciplined thought, as distinct from the mere acquisition of fact, before he enters a university.

The need for students who can think analytically or speculatively is no less urgent in the Sciences than in the Arts. Those who can only memorize are not likely to become more than expert technicians, and for them the technical college, from which an equalitarian society will surely not 'long withhold parity of esteem with the universities, would provide a more suitable training. By limiting admission to the universities to those who have shown that they can think the present pressure would almost certainly be relieved and the universities would be able to fulfil their proper function.

For this to become a practical reality three things are needed. First, a syllabus for schools which encourages wide reading and intellectual initiative. Secondly, an effective recognition by the universities of the value of objective thought and idea in candidates for admission. Thirdly, teachers who are not content with an equipment of facts learnt long ago and added to haphazardly with the passing years, but who are willing and capable guides, stimulating by their own thought the thought of their pupils.

I am, Sir, your obedient servant,

CEDRIC BURTON

'Not for Joe'

From Mr D. B. Hague   *19 October 1960*

[of the Royal Commission on Ancient Monuments in Wales and Monmouthshire]

Sir,
One of the unstratified finds encountered this summer during the excavation of a medieval monastery on a tiny Welsh island was a stem of a nineteenth-century clay pipe. On it was stamped the inscription 'Not for Joe'. I am mildly curious about Joe and would appreciate any enlightenment.

Yours faithfully,
D. B. HAGUE

From Mr J. C. Trewin   *21 October 1960*

Sir,
I imagine that the inscription, to which he refers in his letter today, on Mr D. B. Hague's excavated clay pipe stem derives from a comic song written, composed, and sung by Arthur Lloyd in the 1860s. Its chorus ran:

> Not for Joe! Not for Joe!
> Not for Joseph, if he knows it!
> No, no, no! Not for Joe!
> Not for Joseph, oh dear, no!

Apparently Joseph Baxter was a London bus-driver whose favourite catch-phrase was 'Not for Joe!' The song, triumphant on the halls, had a very large sale.

Yours faithfully,
J. C. TREWIN

From Mr M. M. Chisholm   *22 October 1960*

Sir,
My father's (born 1857) favourite joke was about a little church which had a kind of barrel-organ for a limited number of hymn tunes.

One day it had to be carried out playing 'Not for Joe', having come to the end of the sacred music. That pipe must have been engraved with the song title.

Yours faithfully,
M. M. CHISHOLM

Farewell to the Farthing

From Mr W. McG. Eagar   *13 January 1961*

As the farthing becomes no more than a numismatist's specimen you may care to put on record one use of it contained in an account of his childhood given me a few days ago by a friend who was a member of a boys' club in Bermondsey at the time of the First World War. His father, a decorator in more or less regular work, earned 6½d an hour, and every Saturday gave his wife 'a golden sovereign' to pay the rent (which was 7s 6d a week) and to buy food and clothing for parents and four little but growing boys. The baker at the end of the street changed the sovereign, deducted the amount of the mother's weekly bill for bread, and added to the change one penny, which he obliged her by changing into four farthings. Each child was given one farthing as pocket money and invariably spent it on sweets. Whether the weekly indulgence in sweets or general dietetic deficiency had more to do with the children's bad teeth could be a nice question.

I am, Sir, yours, &c.,
M. McG. EAGAR

[It may be necessary to remind younger readers that whereas the present ½p coin is worth £1/200th, the farthing (¼d) was worth £1/960th]

By Degrees

From Mr E. J. Le Fevre   *9 December 1961*

[writing from Queen Mary College, University of London]

Sir,

The news that the Meteorological Office proposes to adopt for its published forecasts the scale of temperature preferred by all scientists and most technologists and used internationally is most welcome. On reaching your fourth leader of 6 December, I was amused until I noted that you also had a fifth leader and that the fourth was presumably to be taken seriously.

The population of the countries using the international

scale vastly outnumbers our own and it is high time that our 50 million should be 'put out' slightly for the greater convenience not only of our numerous technologists but also of 500 million people in other lands.

In 1934 irresponsible attacks deprived us of the 24-hour clock. It is indeed shocking that so serious a paper as *The Times* should fail at this present time warmly to support the move away from our archaic Fahrenheit scale, which not only causes international confusion but also hampers technology at home.

If, Sir, you do not wish the body-temperature of all right-thinking people rapidly to rise above 36·99°C please treat this long overdue reform in a less insular manner.

Yours faithfully,

E. J. LE FEVRE

From Mr P. L. C. Richards   *18 December 1961*

Sir,

Mr Le Fevre's letter in your issue of 9 December draws attention to yet another example of our wicked insularity. When one thinks of all those poor Germans and Italians wearing themselves out trying to translate the probable mid-day temperature in East Anglia into their own centigrade, just because the selfish English expect the weather service, for which they pay, to use a scale they understand, it makes the heart bleed.

But Mr Le Fevre and his friends at the Meteorological Office have overlooked a worse scandal. Not only are the forecast temperatures given in the Fahrenheit scale, which is not used outside the Commonwealth and the United States, but the forecasts are written in English, a language also only used in the Commonwealth and the United States. It is time we gave up this 'confusing' habit of insisting upon English and had our forecasts in German (or is it French?) with perhaps the regional bits in Flemish, Dutch and Walloon.

Everybody knows that the only people who matter are the Western Europeans; or have the Common Marketeers been overplaying their hands?

Yours, &c.,

P. L. C. RICHARDS

[And not a word to remind us of Réaumur]

Where the Prince Died

From Dame Rebecca West   *18 December 1961*

Sir,

The article on 'Where the Prince Consort died' in your issue of 13 December raises a mystery over which I had often brooded. I have never been able to understand why Mr Lytton Strachey or Dr Randall Davidson [appointed Dean of Windsor in 1883; later Archbishop of Canterbury], much less two of the Queen's pages, should have regarded it as singular of Queen Victoria to preserve the Prince Consort's bedroom after his death in the same state as it had been during his lifetime.

The writer of that article gives an instance of a similar memorial action at the Court of Hanover; but surely the custom was followed not only by royalty but by all sorts of people who had such large houses that they could afford to sacrifice a room.

I have been told half a dozen times in my life of families who had observed this custom; and the last instance was recent. Only about four years ago the father of an American friend of mine died in the state of Kentucky, aged 92; his wife had died 20 years before him, and until his death her bedroom was kept exactly as it had been when she was alive. Her clothes hung in the wardrobe, her brushes and hand-mirrors were on her dressing-table, and the bed was turned down every night. The old gentleman was of German origin.

Yours faithfully,
REBECCA WEST

Looking Back on 1961

From Mr Thomas Richard Oliver   *10 January 1962*

[writing from Connecticut]

Sir,

I may be influenced somewhat by local attitudes but it does seem odd that your 'Year in Retrospect' (30 December) omits John F. Kennedy's Inauguration as President of the United States of America on 20 January. From over here it seems to be of at least as much importance as the fact that 'Scouts

were permitted to wear long trousers' on 1 November –
although that sounds like a good idea.

Yours faithfully,
THOMAS RICHARD OLIVER

Sampling the Public

From Professor D. W. Brogan   *11 June 1962*

[Sir Denis Brogan was Professor of Political Science at
Cambridge 1939–67]

Sir,
I find it very difficult to understand the indignation at the
effect of polls expressed by Mr Aidan Crawley, MP, and others.
The wish not to 'lose your vote' may be a very foolish one,
but it is very widespread. I don't share it myself (a Liberal,
I have only once voted for a successful candidate in a non-
university election, and that candidate was Duff Cooper, not
a Liberal). But the fact remains that people want to know
whether, between two candidates, one is more likely to win
than the other. The public opinion poll serves the function, in
an imperfect way, of the first ballot in France, and the pri-
mary in the United States.

In any event there is, in the attack on the polls, a con-
temptuous view of the electorate as a merely passive body
which follows the trend of voting in a sheeplike fashion. Is
there any reason to believe that this is true? I can remember
the late Sam Rayburn, who served as Speaker of the House
of Representatives of the United States for longer than anyone
else in history, expressing his views on polls.

He told me that the Democrats high command paid a great
deal of attention to polls. It bought all of them. But what the
pollsters did not know was what the politicians did with the
information they paid for. He said that in the past presidential
election (he was speaking in 1944) the Democrats were told
they could carry state X.* They did not believe the pollster
and did not spend men, money or effort in that state. Yet
they did nearly carry the state and would have done so if
they had made an effort. 'Because we didn't believe the poll,
the poll was wrong. If we had believed it, it would have been
right.' Is there not a lesson here for the present panic-stricken
enemies of public opinion polls during elections?

Yours, &c.,
D. W. BROGAN

[*Probably Wyoming, which the Republicans carried by a mere 2,502 votes; possibly Ohio, where the majority was 11,530]

Ho, Clo, &c

From Mr W. P. Scott   *3 April 1962*

Sir,

When I lived in the Mill House, the telephone directory said that I lived in The Mill ho; now that I live in Long Close it says (although there is an inch of space to spare) that I live in Long clo. These abominable abbreviations are, I am told, 'standard practice' and 'an exception cannot be made'. What *is* the financial saving, I wonder, from such horrors?

(A typist in a London store now tells me that I live in 'Love' Close, but such a pleasant propinquity would certainly not be considered practice by a Telephone Manager.)

Yours faithfully,

W. P. SCOTT

From Dr H. W. Swann   *6 April 1962*

Sir,

I sympathise with your correspondent of Long Clo. If it is true that exceptions cannot be made in the Tel Dir, there is at least favouritism for while someone is allowed to live in a 'glade', I am forbidden a smaller 'wood'.

If there are to be economies in space and printing why not start with exchanges? Abolish that cumbersome roundabout 'SHEphrds Bsh' and the long 'MINcng La' and let us hear no more of that strange 'SWIss Cotge'. Give us simply SHE, MIN, SWI, HOP, KIP, JUN, &c!

Yours faithfully,

H. W. SWANN

From Mr Michael Bishop   *7 April 1962*

Sir,

When my name appeared in the telephone directory as Bishop Michl, I wrote to the Telephone mngr saying that I objected to having my vowels cut off. My name has appeared in full ever since, though I still live in a gro.

Yours faithfully,
MICHAEL BISHOP

From Miss Margaret Prideaux   *10 April 1962*

Sir,

How much worse to live in a mws.

Yours faithfully,
MARGARET PRIDEAUX

Sharing the Cup

From Mrs Dora Haley   *14 April 1973*

Sir,

It seems that the rules of hygiene are paradoxical – to say the least. Nowadays, a shop assistant who licks her finger in order to facilitate the picking up of a paper bag in which to put cakes, or similar items of food, risks dismissal. Yet, during Eucharist Services in church, the chalice is passed from mouth to mouth along a row of a large number of communicants, usually without even a wipe (not that this would make much difference, as generally the same small piece of cloth is used. I saw this in a cathedral recently.)

Is there some magic, some mystical element? Because the chalice is a sacred vessel, is it considered to be immune to germs? One only asks where is the sense or reason in preaching hygiene when such anomalies prevail?

No wonder that the common cold develops into a widespread influenza epidemic – not to mention other diseases. I know that many folk will disagree with my viewpoint on this subject, but during a recent sermon on Radio 4 it was stated that we must not be afraid to speak out against something which we consider to be wrong, and I think that this is definitely wrong. I heard of a woman who contracted a lip infection.

However, it must be mentioned that in the majority of Nonconformist churches tiny individual communion glasses are now being used. Why not in Anglican churches, and cathedrals, too? Surely, prevention is better than cure?

Your sincere reader,

DORA HALEY

From Mrs M. Fletcher   *18 April 1973*

Sir,

I write at once to endorse most heartily every word of Mrs Haley's letter today (14 April). This is a subject dear to my heart, as in 40 years of regular church attendance there has

187

not been a single occasion when I have approached the altar rails with anything but a heart full of dread of the ordeal that lies ahead of me. If coughs and sneezes abound among the congregation then my anxiety to be first in the queue far outweighs any other emotion, and totally obscures for me the true meaning, purpose and beauty of the Sacrament.

If in a restaurant one is handed a cup with traces of lipstick upon it one does not hesitate indignantly to return it and demand a clean one. Why then should I, in church, be expected to place my lips upon not one but many fresh and fruity impressions with never a qualm? I know for a fact that many old people, living alone and dependent upon good health to look after themselves, eschew the service of Holy Communion for dread of infection picked up from the chalice, greatly though this goes against the grain for them – it is a very real fear. My daughter once took a Roman Catholic friend to Sung Eucharist in York Minster at the height of the tourist season. When he saw the four-deep queue of communicants and the chalice passing from mouth to mouth with never so much as a token wipe he confessed that he was so revolted that he felt he could never attend an Anglican service of Communion again.

I have sincerely tried, over the years, to overcome my revulsion and distaste and have failed utterly. To me there is only one change necessary in our church service in this day of so many and such seemingly unnecessary changes, and that is the archaic practice of having to take wine from a communal chalice.

Yours sincerely,
MONICA FLETCHER

From the Reverend Maurice C. Garton   *18 April 1973*

Sir,

I fully agree that from a practical point of view Mrs Haley has a strong case, but the fact is that millions of people of all races, all over the world, use the common chalice regularly, and have done for centuries; and yet there is no strong evidence that there has been an epidemic as a result. The Church has many enemies, and if there was conclusive proof that disease has been spread by this means, the enemies would have published it abroad. Moreover at the end of the service the priest usually consumes what is left, and therefore would be most liable to be infected, but the life insurance companies give the clergy a 'good life'. The one instance Mrs Haley adduces is irrelevant, as there may have been other causes of infection. You cannot argue from a particular to a general.

I agree that the use of a purificator is useless from a hygienic point of view. I use it in case some other matter gets on to the chalice. It has been argued that as wine is alcoholic the alcohol will kill any germ, and therefore the Free Churchmen who use non-alcoholic wine are wise to use the individual cup. I leave this point to the scientists as I am not competent to give an opinion. What seems to me important is that the priest repeats the words of Our Lord 'This is my Blood', and by this he understands 'Blood' to means 'Life', and if we receive Christ's Life then that will not result in physical death. In a materialistic world it is well to remember that spiritual values are more important than material ones, and the Communion Service is a constant reminder that Christ's values overturn material ones.

Yours, etc.,
MAURICE C. GARTON

From the Reverend T. J. Marshall   *18 April 1973*

Sir,

With reference to the complaint of Mrs Dora Haley, all that is required is for the General Synod of the Church of England to pass a Measure rescinding the Act of Parliament of 1547 (1 Edw VI c 1) which introduced Communion in two kinds into the Church of England.

If Holy Communion were given in one kind only, not only would it be more hygienic, but it would restore the practice of our national church for a thousand years and bring the Church of England into line with the greater part of Christendom and so promote the cause of Christian unity.

Yours faithfully,
T. J. MARSHALL

From Mrs Patricia Collins   18 April 1973

Sir,

As an Anglican and a bacteriologist I share Mrs Haley's doubts about the common Communion cup.

However, would not the Church of England Rubric preclude the use of individual cups?

Why not Intinction?

Yours faithfully,
PATRICIA COLLINS

From Bishop Thomas S. Garrett   17 April 1973

Sir,

Our commendable, if sometimes excessive, concern with hygiene needs to be counter-balanced by the reflection that every time one comes in contact with infection and gets away with it one builds up one's resistance.

Most worshippers accustomed to share one cup in Holy Communion would be loth to give up its symbolism, particularly when that of the one loaf advocated by many would-be reformers of worship has largely failed to oust the individual wafer. But why not experiment with the use of a spoon in administering the cup, as is the custom in some Eastern churches, and as is recommended (though by no means universally practised) in the Church of South India? The wine is poured from the spoon into the mouth of the communicant without touching the lips. It needs some practice by both clergy and their congregations: but once they are used to it they might well agree that it is the best way. The inkwell-sized individual Communion glasses to which Mrs Haley refers involve an enormous amount of washing up in large congregations.

Yours faithfully,
T. S. GARRETT
Bishop in Tirunelveli, Church of South India

From Mrs Pamela Vandyke Price   17 April 1973

Sir,

Mrs Dora Haley is right to be concerned about hygiene. Would that – as she supposes – the finger-licking shop assistant did risk dismissal! Also those who handle food and money at the same time, who wear long hair while serving in food shops

– and would that the customers who bring in animals and who smoke in these shops were asked to leave.

But Mrs Haley's fears about hygiene at Holy Communion can be allayed. It is wine, fermented liquor, which is used in the Anglican Eucharist. Wine is one of the very oldest disinfectants in the world, which is why wounds were washed with it. Others in authority will be able to answer Mrs Haley as to the exact role and significance of the wine at Communion, but any layman reading the New Testament should be in no doubt that Our Lord took a cup of wine at the Last Supper and that this cup was shared among those present.

In the world of wine, it is routine for glasses to be shared and sometimes a number of people will taste along a line of wines, each using the same single glass. I have never known anyone contract any infection by doing this, although naturally anyone with a cold or any kind of mouth infection would not taste in this way. It is to be supposed that anyone with a communicant's sense of responsibility would take thought and either decline to take the chalice or, if merely in doubt, arrange to take it last. But in any case and in a wholly material sense, the wine itself is a safeguard.

> Yours truly,
> PAMELA VANDYKE PRICE

From Commnder E. Astley-Jones (RN, Retired) 17 April 1973

Sir,

Mrs Haley's letter prompts me to suggest that celebrants could follow the practice of Bishop James, who, when he administered this sacrament at his church in Basil Street in London in the 1930s, dipped the wafer into the wine and then put it into the mouth of the communicant.

> Yours faithfully,
> E. ASTLEY-JONES

From the Reverend Sydney Linton   *17 April 1973*

Sir,

Mrs Dora Haley appears to over-estimate the risk of germs in the use of the common cup at Holy Communion. The clergy, whose duty is to consume what remains after all have communicated, far from being more infected than the laity, have an above-average expectation of life.

> Yours faithfully,
> SYDNEY LINTON

Sir,

I am afraid it is impossible to deny that sharing the cup at Holy Communion is an unhygienic procedure. For instance, smears of lipstick can be very unpleasant and many priests fail to wipe the rim of the chalice. Even this practice does little to lessen the risk of infection, which is undoubtedly a theoretical possibility and I doubt whether any bacteriologist would share Mrs Vandyke Price's faith in the very low antiseptic properties of wine.

At the Brompton Hospital, during the years when it was the 'Hospital for Consumption' and the danger of infection with tuberculosis was greatly feared, Holy Communion was always administered by intinction (dipping the wafer in the wine, as described by Commander Astley-Jones; the words of administration being modified to include both elements). The wider use of this simple practice deserves serious consideration by the Church authorities. It is much easier than employing a spoon and there is no danger of spillage because the wine is absorbed into the wafer. Also it has the advantage of speed and this can be a blessing in these days of large parish Communion services.

Yours faithfully,
A. F. FOSTER-CARTER

From Mr H. D. F. Taylor   *17 April 1973*

Sir,

The true believer at the Eucharist is not concerned with hygiene but trusts in God.

Faithfully yours,
H. D. F. TAYLOR

Ignore the Poet

From Mr Robert Graves   *30 March 1962*

Sir,

At the risk of offending my friend Cecil Day-Lewis, let me offer 'Ignore the Poet!' as more salutary advice to public-spirited organizations than 'Don't Forget the Poet!'

A true poet writes because he must, not because he hopes

to make a living from his poems. Obsession with principle keeps him out of literary gang-warfare, commerce and patronage. He never considers himself affronted by neglect, and treats whatever money comes from the sale of his poems as laughably irrelevant to their making. If neglected enough and obsessed enough, he buys a hand-press and publishes his own work, despising any form of whipped-up public charity. He knows that 'who pays the piper, calls the tune'. How to reconcile poetic principle with earning a livelihood is for him to settle, and no one else.

A pretended poet with nothing urgent to say, joins a movement, studies fashion, courts publishers, badgers elder poets for testimonials and expects the nation to support him. I beg the directors of all public-spirited organizations to ignore him. He is one of many idle thousands. There are never more than four or five poets in any country at the same time who are worth reading, and all tend to be fanatically independent. It is far better for a poet to starve than to be pampered. If he remains true to his obsession, then the older he is when fashions change and money suddenly pours in (often with a rush that would have made Alfred Lord Tennyson gasp) the less self-reproach will he feel, and laugh the louder.

Yours, &c.,
ROBERT GRAVES

[And what if the directors of Lloyds Bank had ignored T. S. Eliot?]

Education for the Army

From Lieutenant-General J. W. Hackett　　　　*21 April 1962*

Sir,

A pamphlet has recently been published by the Army League entitled *A Challenge to Leadership*. It is described as 'an examination of the problem of officer recruitment for the British Army'.

Any serving officer would agree that the purpose of this paper is admirable. Nevertheless it is just possible that some of what it has to say about academic standards may not make the happiest of impressions upon schoolmasters, parents, and young men, and might even prove misleading. I hope, therefore, you will permit me, as a serving officer expressing entirely personal and unofficial views, a few short observations designed to correct some of the misapprehensions it might cause.

The pamphlet refers to the observation in the Grigg report that the present educational requirement for entry into the Royal Military Academy 'carries with it the implication that the Services are a suitable career for the duller boy'. Whatever else the pamphlet may do it does regrettably little to refute this suggestion.

It goes on to report: 'We rejected any radical alteration in the present academic standards.' The League has fortunately no power here either to accept or reject, but it takes up a position which will, I hope, command no very wide support.

The academic standards which the Army continues to accept in candidates for training as officers are lower than those required for entry into a university. They are also lower, on the whole, than those required for acceptance into management training in industry.

As a senior serving officer I am aware of the considerable dissatisfaction with which this position is regarded by many in the Service. I am also keenly aware of most of the difficulties which face the War Office in trying to improve it. The complacency of the Army League pamphlet on the point is not exactly helpful.

The pamphlet goes on to refer to the need for more university candidates. A leading Sunday newspaper comments: 'Why should a university man want to join the Army? The pamphlet put out by the Army League last week does not answer the question, though it asks for more graduates. . . . Universities exist mainly to train men in the exercise of critical intelligence; the Army demands implicit obedience. . . .'

There is a clear need for critical intellects in the Armed Forces. Whatever may be thought of the ethical basis of the Nuremberg trials there is no doubt at all that unquestioning obedience is in some circumstances quite wrong. In British military practice it is in fact upon occasion expressly forbidden. The identification of the occasion, however, is not easy. It might sometimes prove impossible for anyone inadequately trained to think.

We are also faced with new and terrifying problems in warfare. Military minds flounder nowadays among abstracts which perilously few of us are equipped to handle. The requirement for higher education among officers is far indeed from resting solely on the need for men to direct the operation of complex and sophisticated equipment. This is by no means clear from the pamphlet. Reference is made to increasingly complex assignments, 'demanding high initiative and wide general knowledge'. But knowledge, whether general or specific, may turn out to be of secondary importance. What is certain to be wanted is a critical intelligence.

'University education is now open to all classes', says the pamphlet, 'but only a handful of graduates now take commissions annually in contrast to about 70 in pre-war years.' The writing in this passage is typical of a pamphlet which is scarcely likely to increase the flow. There is no doubt at all that we need in the Armed Forces today many more men who have been subjected to the severer university disciplines. There is also no doubt that the Forces of the Crown have much to offer them. But I intend no disrespect to some old friends no longer serving when I say that it might be safest to keep out of the hands of any undergraduate who is thinking of applying for a commission the dismal little documents they have sponsored.

I am, Sir, yours faithfully,
J. W. HACKETT

[Hackett, General Sir John, DSO, MC, MA, B Litt. (Oxon); successively Commander-in-Chief, BAOR, and Principal of King's College, London]

From an Express Train

From Mr H. C. B. Mynors   *18 October 1963*

Sir,

An article in today's (16 October) issue discusses how to send a message from an express train. Faced with this same problem on the same line, I consulted the steward in charge of the dining-car. He provided me with pencil and paper, made an incision in a large potato, and himself lobbed the potato to the feet of a porter as we ran through Peterborough, with my message wedged in it but clearly visible. The station-master did what was necessary.

The steward would not take anything: he was glad to be of service.

Yours faithfully,
H. C. B. MYNORS

Sir,

Your recent article, and the letter from Mr H. C. B. Mynors, dealt with the subject of passing a message from an express train. May I suggest that they are still tackling the 'nursery slopes'? The real problem is how to get a message *on* to an express train.

On Wednesday of this week a friend of mine travelled to Plymouth on the crack Cornish Riviera Express. Unfortunately he left Hanwell too early for the morning post and was anxious to have a particular letter. By prior arrangement, therefore, I placed myself on the main down platform at Hanwell and Elthorne station. I rolled two newspapers (yours) up tightly and constructed a loop of about 1ft diameter to which I pinned the letter. The express train came through at an alarming speed and catching a glimpse of an outstretched arm, I was able to place the loop over this protrusion.

Alas, Sir, your newspapers broke into many pieces and I suffered the indignity of having to retrieve the letter from the permanent way some 100 yards down the line. More satisfactory exchange equipment is in the design stage and I hope to be able to report quite soon on the successful test of a prototype.

Yours faithfully,
H. M. JENKINS

Sir,

I once had to send a message from a boat train travelling from London to Southampton. Advised by the Cunard representative to weight my plea with a half-crown, and to wrap both in a clean handkerchief, I watched him catch an erect Coldstream Guardsman in the small of the back as we passed through Woking station. Sure enough, my American visa reached me by the very last boat train.

Yours, &c.,
A. R. D. WRIGHT

From Dr W. D. McIntyre   *24 October 1963*

Sir,

Your correspondent, Mr H. M. Jenkins, who had such an unfortunate experience trying to get a letter on to the Cornish Riviera express, should have used the standard American method of the bow stick.

All that is needed is a long flexible stick with a Y-shaped end. In each of the points of the Y there should be slits, through which cotton, or light string, is looped to form a bow. In the centre of this bow the rolled-up message should be tied. Provided that the stick is held at just the right height, the passenger merely has to grab into the gap between the arms of the Y, pulling the string, and with it the message, from the stick.

At a wayside station, on the route of one of the great expresses from Chicago to the West, I have seen as many as five of these sticks, arranged fan-like in a frame, for various members of the train crew to collect their messages.

Yours faithfully,

W. D. McINTYRE

Comprehensive Schools: an American View

From Mr L. R. Sterling   *18 January 1965*

Sir,

May an American who has now taught in an English school for two years comment on one of your current educational controversies?

For the sake of your schools, England, please examine thoroughly the American experience with comprehensive schools. After years of teaching in American state and independent schools I have no doubt that schooling is less effective for the bright in a comprehensive school, if the goal is to provide a rigorous academic education. The bright who are stable and motivated will work well almost anywhere; but the bright who are weak and/or lazy and/or who come from homes where learning is not greatly valued often suffer in a comprehensive school, where a high intellectual tone simply cannot be maintained and where the anti-school elements among the less able often include colourful youths who can exert great influence over the weaker of their bright peers.

My two years here have confirmed my opinion that the

British as a whole are the soundest people on earth, in education and other fields. But I am most disappointed to see a strong movement afoot to destroy the supreme grammar school aspect of your school system in favour of a barely tested (in England) comprehensive plan. Why the haste? Have the advocates of comprehensivism clearly examined America's disappointments? And why have not national leaders pointed out more clearly that strict internal selectivity will be necessary in comprehensive schools if academic excellence is even to be attempted? Most American schools have learnt this lesson now, after 30 years of experience with non-selectivity, and its most unhappy results (the tide turned in the late 1950s). And even at that a student in an ordinary English grammar school is well ahead of a selected student of the same age in an ordinary American comprehensive school. You have something good here, worth being very proud of; do not throw it away.

This whole situation is a bit tragic, as an educational issue becomes lost in the swift, changing currents of politics and social reform (and, more specifically, there will be the personal tragedies of those many bright youngsters from all classes – the nation's future leaders – who will not develop as well in a comprehensive as in a grammar school). That the major public schools – those inbred bastions of class consciousness – might be attacked can be understood; that the excellent direct grant or maintained grammar schools, based on selection by merit, should be attacked is not understandable to this American.

My faith is in that standard that has so often guided the English: the common sense of the calm, balanced, intelligent, educated, experienced man. And I think all such men would agree that the selection of youngsters having the most ability, in a pretty reliable way, without regard to class, for the purpose of providing them with the fullest possible schooling, is in the finest traditions of democratic belief. I hope that British common sense will determine that a rush to comprehensive schools is not to the advantage of the English people.

Most sincerely,

L. R. STERLING

[In March 1967 a UNESCO survey stated that a selective system tends to succeed relatively well in bringing a small number of students to outstanding accomplishments, but a more comprehensive system can bring a larger group of students up to fairly high levels of performance]

They shall have music?

From Mr Arthur Swinson   *28 April 1965*

Sir,

I'd be glad if someone could explain to me how it has come about recently that if one has workmen in the house one is compelled to endure their transistor radios. In the last few months my family and myself have experienced this nuisance from plasterers, bricklayers, carpenters, glaziers, and electricians. In fact, the only craftsmen who seem to find enough stimulus in their job are the plumbers.

The attitude of the building trade seems to be one of resigned acceptance. Architects smile wanly and change the subject. Foremen suggest none too politely that one should wake up and realize which decade one is living in. And the men react indignantly, as if one was depriving them of a basic human right.

It would be interesting to know how widespread this nuisance is, and if anyone has dealt with it successfully. Can one, for example, put a 'no transistor radios' clause in the contract?

Yours faithfully,
ARTHUR SWINSON

[The BBC invariably state that one per cent of radio listeners are tuned to Radio 3]

Rum Running

From Mr. F. C. Anderson   *15 January 1966*

Sir,

It beats me how anyone can really think that sanctions will bring down the Smith regime in Rhodesia in a matter of months.

During the war we completely blockaded Madagascar for two whole years because of their pro-Vichy loyalties, yet when our troops arrived there in 1942 they found life going on quite serenely.

The cars were running more or less happily on rum, of which Madagascar is a large producer.

Yours faithfully,
F. C. ANDERSON

Intellectuals

From Mr John Moore   *15 April 1966*

Sir,

Ten years ago, at a luncheon in honour of Shaw's centenary, I sat next to the Russian Chargé d'Affaires. He was a taciturn fellow. After our initial exchange of pleasantries a silence fell. He seemed lost in thought. Five or 10 minutes went by. Then he said to me suddenly:

'You are an intellectual?'

Like any Englishman worthy of the name I hotly denied the distasteful accusation.

Another silence fell. The saddle of lamb came and went. The Russian brooded darkly. I could see he was deeply troubled. At last he turned to me and demanded:

'If you are *not* an intellectual, why are you here?'

I had no answer.

I am, Sir, your obedient servant,
JOHN MOORE

Voice for de Gaulle

[On 24 July 1967 the General had roused Montreal with a cry of 'Vive le Québec libre!', so uniting *The Times*, the BBC, the Canadian Prime Minister Lester Pearson, *Le Monde* and *L'Humanité*]

From Dr A. L. Rowse   *12 August 1967*

Sir,

Since it is clear that no one is going to speak up for de Gaulle, perhaps an historian may – it would be a pretty poor show if there were no one in this country to understand his point of view. Isn't it desirable, even important, that it should be understood?

De Gaulle is the most historically minded of statesmen, along with Churchill, and he has an historian's memory. Neither the United States nor Britain, after liberating France, showed any interest in supporting or maintaining the French Empire. Why should he show any interest in maintaining what is left of the British Commonwealth?

Thrown back on France, what he has achieved for France is nothing short of miraculous – the transformation of a defeated country into the most potent power in Western Europe, with a decisive voice in its construction and shaping. If only we had had a de Gaulle in the postwar period to take the right options! But there has been nobody up to the level of our needs since Churchill.

Any fool can spend, any party can whittle away a country's resources, weaken it by endlessly outbidding each other for the support of an electorate that cares for neither and can never understand the country's long-term interests. I am sure politicians do not understand the contempt serious-minded people feel for both their parties and for what they have brought the country to. The sinister dialectic of political parties is ruining this country as it ruined France. De Gaulle put a stop to that.

I do not suppose that he wishes to disrupt Canada, merely to underline and draw international attention to the Frenchness of French Canada. In that he has certainly succeeded as usual, and accomplished precisely what he intended in going there, nothing more and nothing less. It will be interesting to watch the reverberating effects of the emphasis he has given into the 1970s.

Yours, &c.,
A. L. ROWSE

No Soup for the General

From Mr W. R. Sellar　　　　　　　　　*16 February 1968*

Sir,

Your Cookery Editor, with all the authority of *The Times* behind her, advises us to make cream of asparagus soup by opening a tin (10 February).

No wonder, Sir, that General de Gaulle considers that we are not yet ripe to enter Europe.

Yours faithfully,
W. R. SELLAR

Before it is too late – case for higher standards

From Dr S. E. Ellison　　　　　　　　　*11 October 1969*

Sir,

Is it not about time that a group or association was formed to resist the destructive and demoralizing trends in our present community? There is increasing evidence that the stability of the traditional British way of life is threatened. Venereal disease is increasing. Termination of pregnancy is increasing. Drug addiction is increasing. Hooliganism is increasing. Smoking is increasing. Gambling is increasing. All being examples of anti-social behaviour.

There are, of course, many reasons given for these changes, but not least is the apparent need of the national press, the BBC (both sound and television), and the live theatre, to depict the behaviour of the 'sick' members of our community in a way which suggests that they are to be admired. In recent weeks we have had front page photographs of unmarried ladies with their respective babies, pornographic films on television, and nude actors and actresses. I am cynical enough to believe that this pandering to the baser instincts in human beings is carried on purely for financial gain and in no way can be argued to be an educative exercise.

The developing child is inevitably naughty in his attempt to challenge the authority of his parents or teachers. With increasing age there is increasing challenge. In previous times this challenge was handled more or less effectively by both parents and teachers. Today however we have reached a situation in which not only children but also young adults desire to rebel and throw down established order. Only the senior citizens are left to join together to resist this gathering destructive force.

This tide of immorality, self-deception, and insatiable appetite for all that is worthless must be resisted by an even stronger group in the community who do not wish to see this country destroyed by a sickness as dangerous and as virulent as the plague.

Public opinion, if one believes our newspapers, is still a force to be reckoned with. But can one rely on our newspapers to play fair? Have they not a vested interest in stimulating the appetite of the public for all that is degrading? Make it more spicy and sell more newspapers. People are just not interested in good clean healthy living – or so it seems.

I throw out a challenge. Men and women who believe in the decent way of life step forward and say so. Provoke the newspapers and the BBC to show where they stand. Let it clearly be seen that all that is immoral and 'sick' in our society is not to be tolerated, let our leaders in all walks of life speak out before it is too late.

Yours faithfully,
S. E. ELLISON

Immigration

From Mr C. A. Prince   *23 October 1969*

Sir,

On 11 October my son broke his ankle playing rugby at school. I took him to the local hospital casualty department where we were received at 7.15 p.m. by an Irish receptionist. He was X-rayed at 10 p.m. by an Indian radiographer. At 11.30 p.m. a doctor from Pakistan examined him and looked at the X-rays. The leg was then manipulated and set in plaster of paris by an Australian. At 12.30 a.m. he was put to bed for the night by a West Indian nurse. It was, of course, the weekend.

Let no one try to impress me with their claptrap about immigrants.

Yours faithfully,
C. ANTHONY PRINCE

Those Who Write

From Mr Richard Usborne   *18 January 1969*

Sir,

Someone has counted the Yours faithfully, Yours sincerely, Yours, &c., &c., valedictions in letters to you over a six-week period. Someone else has, of course, given the count of girls' and boys' Christian names in your Births for last year. And today you publish another correspondent's survey of the kinds of people who wrote to you last year, from dons and schoolmasters down to captains of industry.

May I warn your correspondents that I have started a count for 1969 of people whose first paragraphs start 'It has been drawn to my attention' and of those who start a subsequent paragraph 'Of course', and of those whose last paragraph starts 'Surely'.

Up to the time of his death Monsignor Ronald Knox was hoping one day to get you to publish a letter from him answering all the correspondents on all the subjects of a single day . . . all in one letter. May 1969 be the *annus mirabilis* in which someone manages that.

Yours, &c.,
RICHARD USBORNE

[Alas! But perhaps no one tried]

Pinpointed

From Mr J. D. L. Drower   *29 January 1969*

Sir,

I have just received my quarterly account from the South East Gas Board. I notice that although it now deprives me of my right to have three initials and only allows me the first two, by way of compensation I am given a reference number of 21 figures. Therefore, Sir, instead of signing myself J. D. L. Drower,

> I proudly beg to remain,
> Your obedient servant,

One hundred and forty trillion,
Three hundred and forty-two thousand five hundred and seventy billion,
Eighteen thousand million,
Twenty-three thousand, eight hundred and twenty-five.

[One of those rare instances when *The Times* did not print a signature in capitals]

The Agonies a Comedian Bears

From Mr Tommy Steele   *8 February 1969*

Sir,

Having just read the wonderful article in your paper (Saturday Review, 1 February), I feel that perhaps a little more could be said concerning the profession, the environment, the very existence of a comedian.

The big difference between a dramatic actor and a comedian is basically one of 'sound'. They both thrive in creating emotions in their audience, but it is the lot of the comedian also to create a sound – laughter. It is not enough for him to feel the moment is amusing, he must *hear* the audience feel it. This can, and quite often does, cause deep anxiety to the man whose task it is to make an audience forget their anxieties.

Throughout the theatrical profession you will find it is the funny man who is the worrier, the crier, the creator of difficulties. He dreads the day his timing goes; he fears his audience; he thrives on laughs and dies with silence.

The comedian is never off stage. He has to prove 25 hours

a day that he still has control over his listeners. He always has new material to test. He has his act which he protects like a tigress guards her young. He lives in constant fear that his 'gems' will be stolen, and they often are.

It is said that when the end of a comedian is at hand, he 'dies from the eyes'. Sit in an audience long enough and you have to see it at least once in your life. He stares transfixed. You will feel his animosity with every line. He loved you once, but now you frighten him. He knows you will never laugh for him again.

Such a comedian is not unlike Manolete. He faces the same dangers, he is tortured into risking all to please his audience and, alas, as in the case of the great Tony Hancock, he comes to the same end for the same reason.

Yours,
TOMMY STEELE

[The article which so moved Mr Steele had been written by Michael Wale, scriptwriter to Tony Hancock towards the end of the comedian's life]

Top Tonsils

From Mr G. Reichardt   *12 February 1969*
Sir,

In at least four consecutive bulletins on Saturday 8 February, the BBC not only made news, but headline news, out of the momentous fact that one of the Beatles had had his tonsils removed. This inevitably prompts the question: whose are the Top Ten Tonsils in the England of 1969?

Yours, &c.,
G. REICHARDT

Caught in the Machine at HMSO

From Mr R. N. Pepper   *22 February 1969*
Sir,

There is an interesting machine at HM Stationery Office, as will be seen from the following diary:

Jan. 7   I ordered one copy of the Theft Act, 1968; no reply.

    15   I wrote asking for the copy before the end of the

week when it would be required for the Court of Quarter Sessions to begin on 20 January: no reply.

29 Postcard saying 'the item is being reprinted'. I wrote to the Controller stating the facts, mentioning the absurdity of legislation being brought into force without adequate copies available, and asking his explanation.

Feb. 5 Postcard acknowledgement of my first order.

7 Received copy of the Theft Act with invoice.

10 Received second copy of the Theft Act with compliments.

11 Received third copy of the Theft Act with invoice. Returned third copy and invoice to the Controller again asking for explanation: no reply.

17 Received fourth copy of Theft Act with invoice.

Yours faithfully,
R. N. PEPPER

This Is It, Folks

[On 17 November 1969 Mr Rupert Murdoch launched the *Sun* whose sports editor began his address to readers 'THIS IS IT, FOLKS'. After a *Times* leading article had commented on the *Sun*, and in particular on the above-mentioned phrase, an American reader pointed out that 'folks' is used in the best transatlantic circles . . .]

From Mr T. F. Higham   *1 December 1969*

[Fellow Emeritus of Trinity College, Oxford, and former Public Orator]

Sir,

I doubt whether the United States Air Force in the Second World War 'originated' the phrase 'this is it' as stated by Mr Rosenthal (22 November), though they may well have made it popular.

Early in this century, when ancient Greek was more widely studied than now, the phrase had some little currency. It exactly translates a colloquial idiom τοοτ εκεῖνο found in two of the most frequently read comedies of Aristophanes, the Birds and the Frogs. In its simplest form it is used when something previously spoken of or foreboded has come to pass, as in Birds 354 and Frogs 318, 1342. Professor W. B.

206

Stanford in his commentary on the Frogs, first published in 1958, translates 318 by 'this is it' and 1342 by 'that's it'. In 1908 the latter expression was used also by Gilbert Murray (v. 318); but I have not found the exact form 'this is it' in any translation prior to Stanford's. Very likely the United States Air Force had by then made its use more natural.

I myself, when lecturing on Aristophanes in the twenties, sometimes illustrated the idiom by a story brought from British India over 60 years ago. It told of a bishop who lived in great fear of a paralytic stroke and was constantly pinching one leg or the other to test their sensitivity. Once when dining out in formal episcopal dress he alarmed the company by struggling to rise from the table and saying tragically 'This is it! All feeling's gone.' But it was not his own leg he had been pinching – as was explained with some asperity, by the lady on his right.

(It has been said that any story gains 10 per cent if attached to a bishop. I used to preface mine with words to that effect until approached one year by a member of the audience who assured me that the story was true and told of a bishop in his family. I regret that I have now no record of the name.)

Yours faithfully,
T. F. HIGHAM

[In February 1981 Mr Rupert Murdoch bought *The Times*]

Unfair Differentials

From Mr James Thomson   *7 September 1970*

Sir,

You have had a lot of letters about people being bloody-minded. You have not had any that I have seen about why people like me are what you would call bloody-minded.

I read your paper in the public library – I can't afford to purchase it every day. It is the same for a lot of ordinary working people like me. So you don't get much of what we think.

I am 50 years of age. I started work at 15 years of age. I will work, if I am lucky, until I am 65 years of age. I might live to 70, but I will be lucky if I can work to 70 because, even if I am able, and willing, the bosses don't want us. So I shall have the old-age pension. I have not been able to save.

In all my working life the money I have got will amount to about £60,000. That is the highest it could be.

I saw in your paper that the Chairman of Bowring's insurance gets £57,000 a year. And of course he gets a free car, free drinks, trips abroad with his wife, etc. He gets in a year as much as I get in all my working life. The differential is a bit wrong somewhere. Or what about your reports about wills. Often you see someone, a stockbroker, for example, leaving £500,000. That is his savings, not what he lived on. It would take me 500 years to earn that little lot. Something wrong with the differential there too.

The Tory Party goes on about competition. How much competition was there when Brooke Bond put up their prices and all the others did the same. They didn't want to, they said. But they did it. Beer, petrol, milk, it all goes up the same . . . what price competition?

Then we get a lot of talk about the law of supply and demand. Well, this affluent society produces a lot of effluent. So dustmen are in short supply. So they ask for more money. What a howl from the papers, TV, radio, the lot. No howls about Brooke Bond or the others. Why? If you ask 99 people out of a hundred they can manage all right without stockbrokers. But they don't like being without dustmen. The law of supply and demand is fine for some, but not for others. Why?

We get lectured about our duty to the country through exports. Well, more and more we work for international firms. What country are they loyal to? Dividends and profits is the answer. The people who lecture us spend a lot of time, with the help of newspapers like yours, finding out how to miss paying taxes. We help to earn the money they should be paying taxes on . . . but we can't dodge by insurances or going abroad to live.

You talk about equality of opportunity. What was the first thing Mrs Thatcher did but help those with money to stay at grammar schools? And what about BOAC having some of its routes taken away to give them to a private company, private shareholders and bankers. It was some of my money through the taxes that built up BOAC. Nice social justice this is.

I am not a communist or an anarchist. I believe there must be differentials. But the trouble is the differentials are all wrong, and there's too much fiddling at the top. Where I work there are lavatories for bosses . . . you can only get in with a key, hot and cold, air conditioning, nice soap, individual towels. Then there are lavatories for senior staff . . . hot and cold, not so good soap, a few individual towels, but good rollers. Then there is ours . . . no hot and cold, rough towels, cheesecake soap. And no splash plates in the urinals. How do you think we feel about things like that in the twentieth century? Waving Union Jacks doesn't help.

Well, if ever we get a government in this country that will pay and play fair, you will get an end of strikes. When profits matter more than people you will get trouble. It didn't need Barbara Castle to tell us that power lies on the shop floor, in the drawing-room and the typing pool. We know that power is what matters. The Government is going to change the rules of the game to try to beat us down. That won't work either. Starving our wives and kids if we strike is just going to get what it deserves. But give us a deal that we can see is fair, and the trouble will end.

It's no good economists and financial experts preaching. You can use the telly, radio, papers the lot to try to convince us that we have got to be the first to suffer. That's useless. We know the papers and the telly and radio give one side of the story. We know the other. You don't. Or you don't want to. So there will be a fight. We might lose a round or two. But we will win in the end. And if we have to fight to win instead of being sensible on both sides, the losers are going to suffer a lot.

You can call this bloody-minded. Try bringing up three kids on my pay and see how you like it. There's plenty for every-body if it's shared reasonably. And if, as my mate says, we want to try to have the bridge and beaujolais as well as beer and bingo, what's wrong with that?

Yours faithfully,
. JAMES THOMSON

[The above letter appeared during the eleventh week of Mr Edward Heath's Conservative administration]

Division by Brow

From Mr Geoffrey Grigson   *16 January 1970*

Sir,

One of many unencouraging things about the murder of the Third Programme has been the cant of the bulletins which covered it. A change was for our good: we mustn't be divided by brow, in the seventies. The victim would soon be in better shape and was only having his name enlarged to Three and Four.

Perhaps it is true that we are losing less a substance than a recollection. But that is only because the Third Programme has been run down in the last few years. Administering the arsenic had begun; and what has now been murdered – what has now 'passed over', as the bulletins might say – was far from being the programme of intellectual energy (and world influence) shaped by the late George Barnes.

The proper remedy wasn't murder, but a brisk rejuvenation. Meanwhile, though the hide of the murderers is evidently too thick to be pierced, there are two rejoinders to be made. What does Mr Ian Trethowan, who smoothly says that division by brows is too old-fashioned, believe to be the proper description of Radio One (which is the only English offering easily heard by listeners in France, Germany, &c.)? To go on with his terminology, isn't Radio One lowbrow, or lowest brow, unrelievedly, in a spaniel-like way? Isn't this stratification by brow? Wouldn't a stratification at one extreme level justify another at the opposite extreme?

Of course one is sceptical about the spoken content of Radio Four. The Third Programme was – or was once, or was meant to be – an identity, a corporeal idea, a vehicle of the arts and thought, to which many of us in the BBC and out of it worked with zeal and thankfulness. Destroy the identity and the name, and you destroy the will, the duty, the possibility of focused enthusiasm. On today's evidence (Mr Trethowan having let slip a few remarks) I prophesy cant-cum-mediocrity as the content of Radio Four.

Yours faithfully,
GEOFFREY GRIGSON

Etymolomania

From Miss Joyce Grenfell   *16 January 1971*

Sir,

Last October I had my hair done in a glamorama in the state of North Carolina.

Yours faithfully,
JOYCE GRENFELL

Britain's Sovereignty and the EEC

From Mr Kenneth Tynan   *27 July 1971*

Sir,

Is it for fear of driving undecided Tories into the pro-Market lobby that the left in this country has thus far soft-pedalled the strongest single argument against our joining the EEC – namely, that entry will do enormous and possibly irreparable harm to the chances of socialism in Britain? (I mean, of course, genuine socialism, and not the sort of coalition-caretaker-capitalism which your editorials have been holding out as bait for hesitant leftists.) Sir Tufton Beamish is one of the few Tories who have openly admitted that the tremendous threat it poses to the left is among the Market's most enticing features.

The EEC is a capitalist power-block dedicated to the perpetuation of the post-war schism of Europe. Its face is set firmly against the Warsaw Pact countries, so much so that Dubcek's Czechoslovakia – the finest flower of European socialism since the war – would have stood no chance at all of being considered for admission to the EEC. The Market is essentially the economic arm of NATO, and it deplores any backsliding towards neutralism, let alone socialism and its dread concomitants, the public ownership of land and the means of production.

One sees why the Labour right are so eager for entry: it would mean that they would never again have to worry overmuch about placating their left. Yet it is sad that a wing of the party so rich in historians should not have reflected that the Common Market in its fullest state of development will be the most blatant historical vulgarity since the Thousand Year Reich. Hitler's blueprint for the salvation of Europe was a vision in which the western powers – Germany, Britain, France, Italy, Spain and the Low Countries – led the world in a crusade against communism. He failed to realize his dream. The Market could come close to fulfilling it for him.

Not long ago the Swedes, after careful thought, withdrew their application on the grounds that it would be incompatible with their tradition of political neutrality. They are quite content with associate membership, which has all the economic advantages and none of the political fetters of full membership. Perhaps we should learn from their example. Recent history has spelled out a message we would be foolish to ignore. It is that small countries are flexible and capable of change, while large power groups (the USA, the USSR) are musclebound dinosaurs, inherently conservative and equipped with enough repressive strength to resist any internal pressures for change.

A politically and economically unified Western Europe would be a capitalist fortress in which this country would have lost its manoeuvrability and above all its freedom to choose the socialist path.

Yours sincerely,
KENNETH TYNAN

English Attitudes to Irish Crisis

From Mr P. G. B. Wills   *9 February 1972*

Sir,

The real tragedy of the Ulster problem is not, hard though it may be for the relatives and friends of those involved to understand, the dead and injured, whether in Londonderry or elsewhere, but the real and deep division between the people of Great Britain and those of Ireland which neither side seems prepared to understand, or if they do, unable to admit.

It is difficult for any Englishman, though probably less so for the Scots and Welsh, to understand the almost appalling depth of irrational feeling the Irish have about their country. If the International Court of Justice was to find unanimously that every person killed in Londonderry had been shot in the back by the IRA there would still be three million Irishmen who would believe, and ensure that their children and grandchildren believed, that the British were responsible, and that Ireland had gained another 13 martyrs to oppression.

The English are not great brooders on martyrdom. Ask any hundred people in London who was Nurse Cavell and it is doubtful if 10 could answer. Ask any hundred people in Dublin who was Kevin Barry and it is doubtful if fewer than 90 would tell you, and at great length.

This is not to decry the temperament of the Irish, that is their way of life. It is simply to point out that it is almost impossible for the English to come to terms with a people that, for example, insist on holding illegal marches, on which they have in the past demanded a ban, to express a political feeling, which they refuse to express by constitutional means,

212

that the British Government should take 'Political Initiatives', which they refuse to discuss except on their own terms.

I am afraid, therefore, that just as we are incapable of understanding this type of logic, there will be a backlash in Britain by people who will no longer be willing to see their soldiers shot, or their policemen injured, in the interests of a turbulent and seemingly irrational people who rely on us for their economic existence, whether in Ulster or Eire, whose citizens have free access to our country, and liberty of expression here, and who are treated by our laws better than our relatives in Australia or New Zealand or Canada.

There are as many solutions to the Irish problem as there are Irishmen, and many of these – a revision of the border, economic sanctions, withdrawal of troops, etc. – have been ably aired in your columns. Any of these are possible, and all would be unpopular in some quarters, but what is essential, if the Irish people are to be preserved from a British backlash that could destroy them, is that the British Government should lay down a long-term policy for the country, and insist, under the threat of the many sanctions available to it, that it will implement these policies within two years. If the Irish, whether from the North or South, wish to have these policies modified, then we should accept these modifications if they are mutually agreed. If not, we should go ahead and carry them out.

If nothing else, such a policy would lead to talks of some sort.

Yours faithfully,
P. G. B. WILLS

[Edith Cavell, a 50-year-old nurse, helped British troops to escape over the Dutch frontier from Belgium. For this she was shot by the Germans in 1915. Kevin Barry, an 18-year-old student at the National University and member of the IRA, was captured after an ambush of British soldiers in which some were killed. For this he was hanged by the British in 1920]

Shetland Islands and Oil

From Dr W. R. P. Bourne   *14 August 1972*

[Director of Research, The Seabird Group]

Sir,
Shell show remarkable sensitivity and taste in their selection of names for oilfields. While the first in the North Sea, Auk, was named after birds which are normally pure white below, and the second, Brent, after a bird which has a race with an unusually dark breast wintering in the North Sea area, we are told that the third, Cormorant, will be named after a bird which is normally almost entirely black. The author of *Paradise Lost*, moreover, reports that Lucifer looked like a cormorant when he settled on the Tree of Life.

Could the oil companies perhaps tell us whether they are taking any other measures to ensure that the names of sea-birds are not forgotten around the North Sea, apart from investigations into how to wash them after they become oiled?

Yours faithfully,

W. R. P. BOURNE

Britain in Europe

From Mr Arthur Koestler   *4 January 1973*

Sir,
After the greatest anti-climax in British history – joining Europe not with a bang but a whimper – may I propose two suitably modest and painless steps on the hard road to Europeanization?

On 1.6.1972 I wrote to an American friend asking for some information. He supplied it in his answer dated 6.5.1972. This looks like precognition, unless one knows that Americans date their letters by putting the number of the month before that of the day, which causes frequent confusion, particularly to third parties on the European continent. Continentals use Arabic numerals for the day, and Roman numerals for the month, so that the above dates would read 1.vi.1972 and 5.vi.1972. Would it be insulting national pride to adopt this simple and sensible system?

My second proposal is prompted by the harrowing experience of being introduced to strangers at cocktail parties. 'Meet

Mrs (name inaudible); and this is Mr (name slurred).' Hostess vanishes and you are trapped in a game of blind man's buff. On the Continent this is forestalled by the introducees clicking their heels and bellowing their names (females don't click but bow). Couldn't we try it?

Please note the moderation of these proposals: hand-kissing may be postponed until a later stage.

Yours sincerely,
A. KOESTLER

From Mr P.-H. de Rigaud   *4 January 1973*

Sir,

On only the second day of Britain's membership of the EEC it is unfortunate that, on the front page of Tuesday's *Times* and boldly printed for all good Europeans to see, you should have the headline 'Thousands of workers take French leave'. How ironic, too, that this outmoded military idiom should be used in the very issue of your newspaper containing the special report 'Forward into Europe'.

While you might suppose, Sir, that your headline would find its French equivalent in *Des milliers d'ouvriers filent à l'anglaise*, I would assure you that we rarely use the expression. And only rarely (and then, like ourselves, for humorous effect) do the Spanish use their equivalent: *despedirse a la francesa*. You would certainly not find the French form used as a headline in *Le Monde*, for example. You would be much more likely to read: *1er janvier; jour de congé pour des milliers d'ouvriers britanniques* or *1er janvier: jour de chômage en Angleterre*. But *filer à l'anglaise*? Never.

Yours truly,
PIERRE-HENRIE DE RIGAUD

From Mr Peter Black   *4 January 1973*

Sir,

Yesterday I helped to drink a bottle of Graves negociated, as it said on the label, by Burton Père & Fils of the Gironde. The label added:

'mis en bouteille par Burton Sheen Ltd., Dorking.'

Is this the earliest recorded fruit of Britain's entry?

Yours faithfully,
PETER BLACK

Oarswomen's Dress

From Miss Phyllis Hartnoll   *19 March 1973*

Sir,

I do not know where Mr Philip Howard got his information about women's rowing in Oxford in 1927 (article, 13 March), but I can assure him that 'long skirts with elastic at the bottoms to prevent their ankles being exposed' were not worn. Apart from the impossibility of rowing on sliding seats in such garments, women's dresses at this time, both for day and evening, were up to and even above the knee, and ankles had long been 'exposed'.

As a member of the Oxford crew until a few days before the race with Cambridge – which I was forbidden to take part in by the Principal of my college – I wore navy-blue shorts, woollen ankle-socks and suitable shoes, a short-sleeved open-necked cotton blouse, and a heavy white woollen polo-necked pull-over which could quickly be discarded when necessary.

And it was not 'to avoid shocking the men' that we rowed before breakfast, but because it was the most convenient time, the river being comparatively empty then and our days already overfull from 9 a.m. onwards. We certainly rowed also in the afternoons as soon as we had achieved a certain degree of competence, as I remember to my shame that on one occasion while coxing the women's boat I inadvertently committed the heinous crime of holding up the university eight.

Yours sincerely,
PHYLLIS HARTNOLL

From Miss Rosamund Essex   *21 March 1973*

Sir,

I go back further than Miss Phyllis Hartnoll in rowing at Oxford. In 1919, at St Hilda's College, we wore our ordinary skirts and slipped a loop of black elastic over them just above the knee. This had nothing to do with showing ankles (which were visible anyhow under mid-shin-length skirts). The elastic was to keep the skirt from catching in the sliding seat, throwing the boat into confusion and causing someone to catch a crab. We did not use elastic for fixed-seats training crews.

The elastic was a perfect pest, and made for hard work when you came forward and opened your knees to pull. So annoying was it that in 1920 it was abandoned. I was one who advocated shorts: but they were thought too 'forward', and were not allowed. So we graduated into short 'divided skirts', which were the next best thing and did not catch in the slide. We wore long black stockings and white sailor blouses with regulation square collars and black scarves.

Yours sincerely,
ROSAMUND ESSEX

From Mrs I. S. Jacobs   *21 March 1973*

Sir,

In London not all of us were so up-to-date as Oxford in 1927. I sculled for Bedford College on Regent's Park lake in that year, wearing a white cotton blouse, black shoes, black woollen stockings, and navy blue bloomers beneath a short navy blue skirt, which, to prevent it catching in the sliding seat, was held together between the thighs by a large safety pin.

Yours truly,
ISABEL S. JACOBS

From Mrs Mary King   *22 March 1973*

Sir,

To correct the statements of Mr Philip Howard (13 March) and of Miss Phyllis Hartnoll (19 March) I brave the potential sneers of Radio 4 to write that it was Newnham College, not Cambridge against which Oxford rowed in the twenties. I was No. 5 in that VIII in 1929 wearing dark brown shorts, stockings to match and a blazer of the same colour with mustard facings. Girton rowed in skiffs only. We had a competition in style and speed for one mile on the Thames and were judged equal.

My pale-blue blazer was awarded for swimming for members of both colleges were included in that team.

Yours faithfully,
MARY KING

From Mrs Eleanor Price   *26 March 1973*

Sir,

Miss Hartnoll may have rowed in shorts at Oxford in 1927 but at Cambridge in 1918 we rowed in gym tunics. I stroked the first women's eight on the Cam, a very amateurish affair as we had no proper coaching. There were four oars from

Newnham (my college) and four from Girton, and Newnham provided the cox.

'Our tunics came just over our knees, and to prevent them catching in the slide we did have a piece of elastic, which we buttoned, not round our ankles of course, but round our thighs. The college authorities insisted on our wearing skirts to bicycle down to the boathouse, and a dressing-room had to be provided where we could take these off before getting in the boat. I went down in 1918 so I do not know when shorts were first permitted.

Yours faithfully,
ELEANOR PRICE (née Marshall)

How They Spoke

From the Editor of Debrett   *22 January 1973*

Sir,

Why is it that when Queen Victoria or King Edward VII are portrayed they are usually, but quite inaccurately, made to speak with a strong Teutonic accent? This was very noticeable in *Darling Daisy*, one of BBC 2's *The Edwardian* series, when King Edward's heavy broken English was twice punctuated with 'ja'.

Lady Longford, in her *Victoria RI*, states that the Queen spoke 'without a trace of German accent'. Two people who conversed with King Edward told me that only his 'r' was slightly guttural, which Sir Philip Magnus mentions in his biography of that king.

Yours faithfully,
PATRICK W. MONTAGUE-SMITH

[Helen Hayes played Queen Victoria on Broadway, Anna Neagle, Fay Compton and Irene Dunne, among others, in movies – all without a Teutonic accent. Edward VII's fate may be due to Max Beerbohm's caricatures, which certainly made the king sound Teutonic]

Flowers for the Queen

From Mr Laurens van der Post   *23 March 1973*

[Knighted 1981]

Sir,

I would be most grateful if I could pass on the following to you and your readers before the bloom goes from it.

I have just stepped out of a cab in which I travelled through London with a starry-eyed taxi driver. I had hardly got into the cab when he looked at me and said: 'D'you mind guvnor if I tell you something? I have just been at the airport at Heathrow and there, suddenly, this Frenchman comes up to me carrying a magnificent bunch of flowers in his hand. Gosh, you should have seen it guvnor, and he hands it to me and says "Taxi, if I pay you double fare, will you take these flowers and give them to your Queen?" And I looks at him as if he was mad and he says to me: "Now look taxi, I am serious; are you on or are you not?" And what do you think I did?'

'What did you do?' I asked him.

'Cor, I couldn't let 'im and 'er down, so I just come from the bleeding Palace.'

Yours truly,
LAURENS VAN DER POST

National Crisis

From Mrs Frances Stewart   *18 December 1973*

[Institute of Commonwealth Studies, University of Oxford]

Sir,

Today (14 December), the front page of *The Times* announces 'that to ensure industrial and economic survival many areas of industry and commerce will go on a three-day week', and records the Prime Minister's appeal for national unity. In your leader you support the Government's policy of rigid and inflexible resistance to the miners' claim.

In the same issue Sheila Black provides further guidance to *Times* readers on buying Christmas presents. She recommends a new range of watches, for those who 'like a wardrobe of the

219

things', costing £120–£139; an 18-carat gold toenail cover (only, unfortunately, made in big toe sizes so 'the other eight nails have to go naked'), at £88 a pair; a ballpoint pen (18-carat, £200).

Miners, after seven hours underground, take home £31 a week after deductions. Train-drivers' top rate is £33 a week. (Reported in the same issue of *The Times*.)

How can the Government expect a sense of national unity, and that workers should hold back from palpably justified claims, for the sake of the national interest, in a society where inequalities are so huge and so glaringly illustrated?

Yours faithfully,
FRANCES STEWART

[A General Election was called for 28 February 1974]

From Mr R. S. Levy   *23 February 1974*

Sir,
Conversation overheard on my station platform:
Small boy: 'I hope Harold Wilson wins.'
Commuter: 'Why?'
Small boy: ''cos my dad says we're going to Australia if he does.'

Yours faithfully,
R. S. LEVY

[Mr Wilson did win and formed a minority Labour Government with Mr Michael Foot as Secretary of State for Employment]

From Mrs Peter Fleming   *27 April 1974*

[later, as Celia Johnson, a Dame of the British Empire]

Sir,
In the Welsh tradition of referring to people by the names of their jobs, as Jones the Post or Davis the Bread, would it not be in order to speak of the Rt. Hon. Member for Ebbw Vale as Foot the Bill?

Yours faithfully,
CELIA FLEMING

Why the Crow is Bran

From Dr Dafydd Evans   *24 February 1973*

[writing from Queen Mary College, London]

Sir,

The article on British dialect bird-names in your issue of 17 February raised a host of questions and problems, in answer to which I propose to make only a few points.

Some local names reveal the complex linguistic history of a given area. Thus the answer to the query as to why the crow is called 'bran' in Cornwall is that this name is, not surprisingly, of Celtic origin. Some bird-names, e.g. of the falcons, were introduced with the Norman Conquest. The name 'kestrel' clearly derives from French *cresserelle*, but what of 'windhover' and 'flutterer'? Such names, clearly descriptive, are unlikely to be older, Anglo-Saxon, ones; they are probably of comparatively recent origin, replacing perhaps an older name which has become 'opaque'.

Chaffinches never stop calling themselves 'pinks', 'spinks' or 'twinks' . . . 'wincs' in Wales. Such names, apparently pure onomatopoeias, are probably deformations of an older opaque name. It is not difficult to trace these names back to the basic English name 'finch', Old English *finc*, compare German *fink*, Old High German *fincho*. This last name is related to French *pinson*, which seems to derive from a Gallo-roman *pincio/pincionem*. It is interesting to note that French dialects show a common variant of this name which changes the initial *p* to *k*, e.g. *quinson* in the east and south-east. There also occur sporadic variants especially in the border zones between *pinson* and *quinson* regions, e.g. the monosyllabic *tuin* and *tchui* and numerous reduplicative types, e.g. *tuintuin, kuikui, puipui, pinpin*, for reduplication is common in onomatopoeic reformations.

The giving of proper names to birds is an ancient usage and the explanations are complex, linguistic opacity and lexical confusion being two main causes. It is familiar birds that most frequently receive these appellations. The Londoner's 'Philip' for the sparrow has its parallel in the French *Pierrot*, of Parisian origin, which has here and there replaced *moineau*, i.e. 'little monk', itself a lively substitution for the earlier *passe/paisse* from the Latin *passer*.

221

Popular descriptive names in English dialects often have their parallels in the popular names found in France. The wagtails (incidentally often termed *hoche-queue*, etc., in French dialects) bearing the English names 'cow-bird', 'dish-washer' and 'washer-woman', referring to their fondness for following farm animals and for frequenting water, are called in French and Provençal *bergeronnette*, *bergère* and *pastourela* 'shepherdess', *louraire* 'ploughman', *vatseirouna* 'cow-girl', and *lapandière* 'washer-woman'.

Yours,
DAFYDD EVANS

Culture and Schools

From Mr Brian Jackson   *6 March 1973*

[writing from the Advisory Centre for Education, Cambridge]

Sir,

Most children come from working-class homes and inherit a distinctly working-class culture. Most of the education budget is funded by working-class taxes.

Nevertheless, school overwhelmingly matches the social needs of middle-class parents. So it was inevitable that we should see pressures for reform – such as the end of eleven plus and the collapse of the streaming system; together with pilot ventures such as the Open University and the Education Priority Area programme.

In my article in *The Times*, which has drawn such a strong response, I am trying to raise the next question. It is not enough to achieve structural reform if we wish schools to offer equal opportunities to all children. There is also a cultural challenge.

Most schools do not know what working-class culture is, or if they do, dislike it. It is as if the children came to school with nothing behind them. Inevitably, school cannot then convince many pupils that it offers a genuine educational dialogue. Inevitably it still breeds elites who are not so much hostile or friendly, but who are uncomprehending when they meet working-class life in action. Leaving aside rights and wrongs, observe the quality of bewilderment in the face of trade union firmness.

The traditional culture of the British working-class is something of which an educated nation should be proud. Consider the part it has played in the rise of Nonconformism, of the Co-operative movement, of trade unions, of sport, of brass and choral music. Look at the rich soil it provided for artists like Henry Moore, D. H. Lawrence, L. S. Lowry. Simply listen to the vitality of so much working-class speech. But above all note how, over so many generations, it has bred a habit of asking questions, of opening perspectives that are relevant for most people – but unusual for teachers.

Now visit a characteristic school. Depressingly often, it offers a social and intellectual entry into Janet and Johnland. School ultimately fails because it does not ordinarily recognize the vaidity of any other life style than that of the lower middle class – whose officers staff the institution.

None of this suggests that middle-class life styles are bad. I don't think that. Nor that children should be denied Shakespeare, Mozart or Newtonian physics. Nothing I have written implies that, or is likely to.

What I do insist on is that – if you observe the day-to-day reality of schools – it is clear that much of it is fundamentally irrelevant. School, instead of acting as a critical centre in society, is usually a *pax scholastica*: a buffer state defending the labour market.

If we want school to play some part in creating a multicultural society, then not only do we have to learn to see, accept and creatively deploy the cultures of the 3·3 per cent of immigrant pupils. We have to accept that of the 70 per cent working-class pupils.

Yours faithfully,
BRIAN JACKSON

223

Manners and Men

[On 19 May 1982 The Queen visited Winchester College on the 600th anniversary of its foundation. The next day a *Times* third leader discussed 'The Shameless Elite', and related the story of a lady entering a room which contained a Wykehamist, an Etonian and a Harrovian – the Wykehamist calls for someone to fetch a chair, the Etonian fetches one, and the Harrovian sits on it himself]

From Sir Charles Gordon   *22 May 1982*

[Clerk of the House of Commons]

Sir,

As a Wykehamist, I am happy to own a number of the soft impeachments contained in your leading article; but I cannot refrain from protesting at your shameless reconstruction of the well-known story of the chair.

It was, of course, the imperious and patrician Etonian who commanded that a chair be brought for the fainting lady; it was the unobtrusive, efficient and – dare I say it? – well-mannered Wykehamist who provided it.

Yours faithfully,
CHARLES GORDON

From Mr F. R. Salmon   *22 May 1982*

Sir,

The Wykehamist did not 'call out for somebody to fetch a chair'; he asked the lady, very politely, whether she would like one. That, surely, makes all the difference.

Yours politely,
F. R. SALMON

From Mr Thomas Morton   25 *May 1982*

Sir,

As a past inhabitant of both Harrow and New College (and therefore strictly neutral) I cannot allow the inaccurate story in the third leader today to go unchallenged). (Is your leader writer perhaps an Old Etonian?)

In the correct version an attractive girl enters a room containing an Etonian, a Wykehamist (of the junior foundation) and an Harrovian. The Etonian says, 'This lady needs a chair', the Wykehamist fetches one and the Harrovian sits down with the girl on his knee.

Yours faithfully,
TOM MORTON

From Mr T. J. Allison   26 *May 1982*

Sir,

Your editorial today has got it wrong! It is Etonians who notice that ladies have no chairs, Wykehamists who fetch them. That is why the latter make good civil servants: they assess and follow up creative thinking.

Yours very truly,
T. J. ALLISON

From Mrs Peter Spring   26 *May 1982*

Sir,

Am I, at 48, yesterday's woman? I am not surprised when any man, Wykehamist or not, opens a door for me (but then, my school motto was *In Fide Vade*). Certainly I thank him.

Yours in courtesy,
CLARE SPRING

From Mr James Palmes   27 *May 1982*

Sir,

Some fifteen years ago I was interviewing candidates for a vacant post. One was a Wykehamist, who made a poor impression on me and my colleagues. He seemed to us obtuse and conceited. Anyway, he did not get the job.

A few days later I received a letter from the frustrated

applicant, abusing me roundly for turning him down, pointing out that it was bad manners to reject Wykehamists and that I must mend my ways.

Yours faithfully,
JAMES PALMES

From Mr James Johnstone   *27 May 1982*

Sir,

The gentlemen's actions indicate that the attractive young lady can only have been a Marlburienne – anyone else would have been left standing.

Yours faithfully,
JAMES JOHNSTONE

From Professor P. V. Danckwerts   *28 May 1982*

Sir,

I suggest that the comparison between Wykehamists and Etonians should be extended beyond the question of manners to that of pragmatism.

During the first Atoms for Peace conference at Geneva in 1955 the Mr Big of the international energy scene was confined, raging, to his room by a cold. He instructed me and a fellow delegate to go to a pharmacy and get him some black currant syrup. My colleague (an Etonian) demanded 'courants noirs'. I (a Wykehamist) waited for the pharmacist to ask us (in English) what we required.

Yours, etc.,
PETER DANCKWERTS

[The absence of two initials after Professor Danckwerts's name suggests that the Letters Editor was being modest on behalf of this Wykehamist]

. . . and Women

From Miss Imogen Clout   *29 May 1982*

Sir,

The tale of the Wykehamist and the chair calls to mind the anecdote illustrating the distinguishing characteristics of the five Oxford 'women's' colleges.

Five girls, one from each college, meet. Their conversation concerns a young man of their mutual acquaintance:

The girl from Lady Margaret Hall asks, 'Who are his parents?'

The girl from Somerville asks, 'What is he reading?'

The girl from St Hugh's asks, 'What sport does he play?'

The girl from St Hilda's asks, 'Who is he going out with?'

And the girl from St Anne's says 'Me'.

At least, that is the version which I was told, when I was at St Anne's.

Yours faithfully,
IMOGEN CLOUT

From Mrs Hal Wilson   *4 June 1982*

Sir,

I too remember the story of the five Oxford women undergraduates discussing the young man.

I am sorry to have to tell Miss Clout, however, that in my day at Lady Margaret Hall the young lady from St Anne's was reputed simply to have said *'Where is he?'*

Yours faithfully,
GILLIAN WILSON

From Mr Max Taylor   *31 May 1982*

Sir,

In my untypical experience, the Cheltenham girl says, 'Gosh you look pale', the Wycombe Abbey girl says, 'I'll get you a glass of champagne', and the Heathfield girl drinks it.

Yours faithlessly,
MAX TAYLOR

[While Mr Taylor pays?]

From Mr Paul Stewart   *2 June 1982*

Sir,

The story as I understood it was that a pretty girl came into a room containing three ex-public schoolboys who provided her with a chair to sit upon and then proceeded to argue amongst themselves as to which of them should receive the credit for this deed.

The girl stifled a yawn, made her excuses and left the room.

Yours faithfully,
PAUL STEWART

From Mr Nicholas Freeland   2 June 1982

Sir,

I seem to remember that at Charterhouse we had enough chairs for everyone to be able to sit down.

Yours faithfully,
NICHOLAS FREELAND

From Dr John Herbert   2 June 1982

Sir,

The young gentlemen of Harrow, Eton and Winchester may indulge themselves in idle banter about who does what with a chair, but their fathers have arranged matters so that old Lliswerrians can no longer hew the wood to make the chair.

Yours faithfully,
JOHN HERBERT

From Mrs Douce Forty   8 June 1982

Sir,

At St Hugh's in 1947, I was told: The young man stood outside the college.

Somerville said: 'What does he read?'
L.M.H. said: 'Who are his people?'
St Hilda's said: 'What does he play?'
St Hugh's said: 'Bring him up.'

Yours nostalgically,
DOUCE FORTY

From Dr Jennifer Orchard   8 June 1982

Sir,

In the version which reached us at St Hugh's, the St Anne's girl concludes the conversation with: 'He's my husband, actually.'

Yours faithfully,
JENNIFER ORCHARD

From Mr P. A. Gascoin   *8 June 1982*

Sir,

Had the 'girl from St Hilda's' who asked 'Who is he going out with?' been a girl from University College, London, she would have asked 'With whom is he going out?'

Yours faithfully,
P. A. GASCOIN

Concorde

[Pan Am and TWA had cancelled their options to buy Concorde]

From Professor J. K. Galbraith   *3 February 1973*

Sir,

In telling today that the British Government wish to exercise closer control over the costs of the Concorde you say that: 'Crew seats (*sic*) developed under a contract for £45,000 were unsuitable and a consequent cost charge was first put at £216,000 and then raised to £409,000.' (Later the Government got the figure down to £325,000.)

I do not wish to comment on the high cost of furniture these days; and one wants the men who pilot planes to be seated in the greatest comfort and security. But my chauvinist instincts were stirred by the magnitudes involved. As an American I associate this sort of thing with our aircraft industry. Are your people being imitative? Or, another thought, was the sub-contractor in question one of our experts in the design of imaginative cost over-runs? If the last is the case you should swallow national pride and, in a manly way, give us credit. These were only chairs after all.

Faithfully,
JOHN KENNETH GALBRAITH

Coach and Concorde

From Mr Philip Short   *19 January 1978*

[of the Department of Electrical and Electronic Engineering, The University, Newcastle Upon Tyne]

Sir,

How delightful it was to see your photograph of a Concorde aircraft together with an East Anglian mail coach this morning.

By consulting a recent reprint of a 1831 Newcastle guide one can see that the present postal service to London from here is about the same now as it was then. Except on Fridays the mail coach departed every night at 9.30, arriving in London at 6 a.m. on the morning after next.

How agreeable it would be if, inspired by your illustration, the Post Office were to return to the use of horses to improve the postal connection with London in these more distant regions. With improved roads, pneumatic tyres and a better class of horse, much could be done. Maybe we could then catch the night mail even if we did post after 5.30 p.m.?

Yours faithfully,
P. SHORT

Cleopatra as the Dark Lady

From Dame Agatha Christie   *3 February 1973*

Sir,

I have read with great interest the article written by Dr A. L. Rowse and published by you on 29 January, on his discovery of the identity of Shakespeare's Dark Lady of the Sonnets. She has always had a peculiar fascination for me, particularly in connexion with Shakespeare's *Antony and Cleopatra*.

I have no pretension to be in any way a historian – but I am one of those who claim to belong to the group for whom Shakespeare wrote. I have gone to plays from an early age and am a great believer that that is the way one should approach Shakespeare. He wrote to entertain and he wrote for playgoers.

I took my daughter and some friends to Stratford when she was twelve years old and later my grandson at about the same age and also some nephews. One young schoolboy gave an immediate criticism after seeing *Macbeth* – 'I never would have believed that was Shakespeare. It was wonderful, all about gangsters, so exciting and so real.' Shakespeare was clearly associated in the boy's mind with a school-room lesson of extreme boredom, but the real thing thrilled him. He also murmured after seeing *Julius Caesar* – 'What a wonderful speech. That Mark Antony was a clever man.'

231

To me Cleopatra has always been a most interesting problem. Is *Antony and Cleopatra* a great love story? I do not think so. Shakespeare in his Sonnets shows clearly two opposing emotions. One, an overwhelming sexual bondage to a woman who clearly enjoyed torturing him. The other was an equally passionate hatred. She was to him a personification of evil. His description of her physical attributes – such as 'hair like black wire' – was all he could do at that time (1593–4) to express his rancour.

I think, perhaps, that as writers do he pondered and planned a play to be written some day in the future; a study of an evil woman who would be a gorgeous courtesan and who would bring about the ruin of a great soldier who loved her.

Is not that the real story of *Antony and Cleopatra*? Did Cleopatra kill herself by means of an asp for love of Antony? Did she not, after Antony's defeat at the battle of Actium, almost at once make approaches to the conqueror Octavian so as to enslave him with her charms and so retain her power and her kingdom? She was possibly by then tired of Antony, anxious to become instead the mistress of the most powerful leader of the time. But Octavian, the Augustus of the future, rebuffed her. And she – what would be her future? To be taken in chains to Rome? That humiliation for the great Cleopatra – never! Never would she submit; better call for Charmian to bring the fatal asp.

Oh! how I have longed to see a production of *Antony and Cleopatra* where a great actress shall play the part of Cleopatra as an evil destroyer who brings about the ruin of Antony, the great warrior. She has finished with Antony.

Dr Rowse has shown in his article that Emilia Bassano, the Dark Lady, described by one of her lovers as an incuba – an evil spirit – became the mistress of the elderly Lord Chamberlain, the first Lord Hunsdon who had control of the Burbage Players. Presumably she abandoned the gifted playwright for a rich and power-wielding admirer. Unlike Octavian he did not rebuff her. In his mind Shakespeare kept that memory until the day that he wrote, with enjoyment and a pleasurable feeling of revenge, the first words of *Antony and Cleopatra*.

Shakespeare was probably not a good actor, though one feels that is what he originally wanted to be. All his works show a passion for the stage and for comparisons with actors.

How odd is it that a first disappointment in his ambition forced him to a second choice – the writing of plays – and so gave to England a great poet and a great genius. Let us admit

that his Dark Lady, his incuba, played her part in his career.
Who but she taught him suffering and all the different aspects
of jealousy, including the 'green-eyed monster'?

Yours faithfully,
AGATHA CHRISTIE

[Had Verdi turned his attention to *Antony and Cleopatra*,
and awaited Maria Callas . . .]

Say No More

From Mr M. L. Charlesworth   *11 October 1973*

Sir,
Amongst the memorable notices displayed by London Transport and recently reported by your readers, let this one find
a place:

Gents and lift out of order
Please use the stairs.

Yours faithfully,
M. L. CHARLESWORTH

The Age of Euphemism

From Mr James Bowker   *3 September 1973*

Sir,
How much longer must we endure the use of 'common-law
wife' to describe any woman who just happens to be living with
a man without recourse to the formalities of matrimony?
A common-law marriage is one in which the parties may
avail themselves of their common law rights only where there
is no local form of marriage, or where the local form is non-
Christian, by agreeing to take each other as man and wife
before an episcopally ordained priest or, in a country in which
the presence of an episcopally ordained priest is unsuitable,
before a priest not episcopally ordained.
To what extent, if any, is this definition relevant to the use
by the BBC of the euphemism that a convict in Albany Prison
was holding a warder at knife-point until he could see his
'common-law wife'?

Yours faithfully,
JAMES BOWKER

[When Raimunda de Nascimento gave birth to a child in August 1974, *The Times* referred to her as the mistress of Mr Ronald Biggs, the British train robber; BBC Radio 3 spoke of her as his 'girl friend']

Unearned Fortunes

From Mr E. C. Cade   *23 February 1974*

Sir,

If it is 'obscene' for banks to make 'windfall' profits, for property speculators to reap 'unearned' fortunes, and for other hypothetical figures to benefit equally from 'pushing pieces of paper around' in the City, why is it seemingly 'all right' for someone else to win £680,967 as a reward for filling in a few lucky Xs on a football coupon (*The Times*, Thursday, 21 February)? Will the moralists please explain their deafening silence or their double standard?

Yours faithfully,

E. C. CADE

The Sovereign's Duties

From the High Sheriff of Hallamshire   *20 March 1974*

Sir,

God save our gracious Queen, from all the politicians, historians and contributors to the media who during this last fortnight have continuously and publicly advised Her Majesty and all of us on her constitutional rights and duties – about which the Monarch is probably much better informed and aware than anyone in the realm. What no one has remarked or publicly acclaimed is Her Majesty's heroic dedication to duty.

On general election day in Britain the Queen of Australia, then about half-way through a strenuous royal tour, formally opened Parliament in Canberra. Less than thirty hours later the Queen of England was in Buckingham Palace ready to receive her Prime Minister and to exercise her most important constitutional responsibility in, probably, unprecedented circumstances.

No board of directors would expect or indeed allow one of their colleagues to discuss, let alone decide, matters of great importance so soon after such a long and exhausting journey. Mercifully, as it happened, there was a weekend's respite for Her Majesty. But after holding Britain steady for 12 days through the change of government, she set forth to resume the royal tour, in Indonesia where trouble threatened, knowing well the possibility of being called back within a week to exercise again her constitutional and royal prerogative. Long live our Noble Queen!

Yours faithfully,
GERARD YOUNG

Wrong Number

From Mr Michael Mason   *5 February 1974*

[writing from *Gay News*]

Sir,

I have discovered the reason for last year's marked decline in industrial harmony, and can account for the popular belief that the trades union movement is becoming increasingly dominated by communists.

The 1973 edition of *Whitaker's Almanack* gives the telephone number 01-639 9239 for the National Industrial Relations Court. Phone this number and you will find yourself talking to the manager of a Chinese take-away restaurant.

Yours faithfully,
MICHAEL MASON

Miners' Wages: Pay for Casual Work

From the Headmaster, Lliswerry High School, Newport, Monmouthshire   *22 January 1974*

Sir,

My work has been entirely in schools within a mining community for twenty years. During that time, I cannot recall a single entrant into the mining industry from my schools. In the early part of that period when apprenticeships were offered only to grammar school boys and for the whole of the time when good students might have taken up mining engineering, no pupils from my schools took up mining as an occupation or a career.

The reason is that all our fathers and grandfathers said to their sons with emphasis that they would never go down the pits. The unemployment and short time, the massive injuries and frequent tragedies, the dust and the water and the danger have stamped themselves on the race mind in South Wales. You don't have to argue that the miners are a special case; you feel it in the blood.

The miners up to this moment in the present crisis have broken no law and no agreement. They have simply ceased to work overtime and they draw for a week's work their basic £29.80.

Many of my sixth formers in the interval between A levels and university take casual jobs in local industry. They are untrained, unskilled and inexperienced. Several of them earned up to £28 a week. One of these because his birthday happened to fall in his work period, received a rise of £10 in his final month's pay. One fine young man netted £50 in one week as a teaboy (admittedly with overtime).

They told me of a man working in the same place who regularly took his bed to work with him. A boy earned £29 a week for cycling six times a day a distance of three-quarters of a mile with a sample of the furnace's melt to the laboratory. These boys tell me of even higher wages earned on building sites and motor-road construction. I am also familiar with some caretakers who earn £30 (with a house) for only and quite literally locking and unlocking premises.

The present government is intent upon inflicting defeat on the miners and thereby a psychological blow at every union who might push as far. The Prime Minister rejects appeasement. This might have been good psychology in the sixties. But in the present world crisis and in the economic state of the country, who is going to rally the nation, urge us to tighten our belts, face austerity and work harder?

It will be good for us all to do so. But what fool's paradise are we living in when, faced with the frightening problems of the day, we respond by working less? We deserve what faces us. Those of us who have clamoured against the permissive society and the throw-away life style are at last vindicated. 'We have told you so!' But we are also as a result becoming ungovernable.

Yours sincerely,
JOHN HERBERT

Selection Principle in Education

[Mr Reginald Prentice was a Labour MP 1957–77, Secretary of State for Education and Science 1974–5, thereafter a Conservative MP]

From Miss Iris Murdoch   *19 April 1974*

Sir,

I hear on my radio Mr Reg Prentice, of the party which I support, saying to a gathering on education the following: 'The eleven plus must go, so must selection at twelve plus, at sixteen plus, and any other age.' What can this mean? How are universities to continue? Are we to have engineers without selection of those who understand mathematics, linguists without selection of those who understand grammar?

To many teachers such declarations of policy must seem obscure and astonishing, and to imply the adoption of some quite new philosophy of education which has not, so far as I know, been in this context discussed. It is certainly odd that the Labour Party should wish to promote a process of natural unplanned sorting which will favour the children of the rich and educated people, leaving other children at a disadvantage.

I thought socialism was concerned with the removal of unfair disadvantages. Surely what we need is a careful reconsideration of how to select, not the radical and dangerous abandonment of the principle of selection.

Yours faithfully,
IRIS MURDOCH

The Artist and His Levels

From Mr John Bratby, RA   *22 April 1974*

Sir,

For some time to obtain entry to an art school a student has needed O and A levels – the equivalent of five O levels. As a result many embryo artists, with real dynamic creative powers and talent, do not go to art school, and will not develop. How can this misunderstanding of the nature of an artist exist? The ability to obtain O levels and A levels, and artistic ability, are different things.

Other educational establishments are concerned with students assimilating information, like blotting paper, but art schools are concerned with the development of creative abilities, the finding of an identity that is so important to an artist – nothing to do with O and A level abilities.

An artist can be a totally unintelligent person in the sense that he cannot pass examinations, but he has the creative personality.

Students of definite artistic talent and learning ability wishing to go to art school, who, for example, obtain four O levels, have to remain at school to obtain the requisite passes to qualify them for art school.

The Leonardo da Vinci type of artist, highly intellectual, is not what an artist is oftentimes. Painting does not spring only from the intellect, but primarily from spring sources of creative drives. Picasso, for example, like Soutine and van Gogh, was a creative animal, driven to make pictures compulsively. Like Leonardo he had ideas, the result of the creative personality.

The receptive personality, who can pass examinations, O and A levels, is another kind of human being, a robot fed with knowledge.

Yours sincerely,
JOHN BRATBY

Unsolicited Advice

From Mr David H. Hall   *22 February 1975*

Sir,

One has remarked the proliferation of bodies seeking to give advice (frequently unsolicited) upon various matters.

The nadir was reached this morning by the delivery to my bachelor establishment of a circular (issued by the Ministry of Agriculture, Fisheries and Food) entitled 'National Wild Oat Advisory Programme'.

Sir, is nothing sacred – or should I say profane?

I am Sir, yours etc.,
DAVID HALL

VIPs at the Academy

[Mr Jeremy Thorpe was leader of the Liberal Party 1967–76]

From Ms Duffy Ayers   *28 February 1975*

Sir,

Early today thousands of people were queueing outside the Turner exhibition at the Royal Academy, now in its last week. At 9.30 a.m. before the doors were opened to us all and the queue was turning back on itself like a great snake, a black car drew up and parked quickly – a keeper approached and out leapt Jeremy Thorpe, glanced embarrassedly at us all, ran up the steps as fast as he could and dived inside. Presumably to see this great show in peace and quiet, undisturbed by the common people (not so common really as most were reading *The Times* or *Guardian*). Surely the VIPs, especially politicians, could slip into these exhibitions at some other time and not be seen to be so privileged. Even our greatest *living* artist, Henry Moore, joined the queue like an ordinary mortal. Is an MP more important than an OM?

Yours sincerely,
DUFFY AYERS

From Mr Kenneth Gregory   *3 March 1975*

Sir,

Moore queues, Thorpe does not: Ms Ayers asks if an MP is more important than an OM. Of course, dear lady, there are twice as many OMs as Liberal MPs.

Yours faithfully,
KENNETH GREGORY

Ladybirds Galore

From Mr Michael Hardy   *20 April 1976*

Sir,

Why are there so many ladybirds in my garden this spring? Is this another manifestation of Women's Lib?

Yours faithfully,
MICHAEL HARDY

From Miss Margaret Macleod *22 April 1976*

Sir,

The delightful abundance of ladybirds in our gardens to which Mr Michael Hardy refers may be due to the fact that the late frosts last year drove the aphides to the ground and spraying was virtually unnecessary for the rest of the season.

Now the aphides as well as the ladybirds have powerfully re-emerged and we are faced with the problem – shall we once again commit wholesale slaughter, or shall we wait awhile and give the ladybirds a chance to show that they can do the job for which nature intended them? I for one will wait, praying in the meantime that someone will invent a selective insecticide, and remember that a peasant in Tirol once told me that a multitude of ladybirds signifies great happenings to come.

Yours faithfully,
MARGARET MACLEOD

From Mrs John Ballender *26 April 1976*

Sir,

Oh, Mr Hardy, Ladybirds indeed! Personbirds, surely?

Yours faithfully,
DAPHNE BALLENDER

Background to Mugging

From Mr J. L. Yeldham *23 April 1976*

Sir,

If Mr Ennals is right in attributing the growth of mugging to social conditions such as bad housing, old schools and lack of employment opportunity, then is it not an irresistible conclusion that 40 or 50 years ago, when mugging was on a very minor scale, social conditions must have been superior to those of today? Either both conclusions are right or both are wrong.

Yours faithfully,
J. L. YELDHAM

Wealth Tax Study: Why the TUC?

From The Master of Jesus College, Cambridge
                                                    9 December 1976
Sir,

The news from Whitehall grows daily more incredible. We have just been told that the Government and the TUC jointly are going to study the possibility of a wealth tax. The TUC? What qualifications, let alone right, do they have for such a task?

Since lunacy has now plainly taken over, perhaps the Government might be interested in starting up some more studies? For example, the Government – and the MCC, on the Northern Ireland problem – and the CBI, on the unseating of moderate Labour members – and the RSPCA, on devolution – and the RAC, on the IMF loan – and the WVS, on fast breeder reactors?

                                            Yours faithfully,
                                            ALAN COTTRELL

Booking a Hotel Room

From Professor John Hutchinson   *2 August 1977*

[writing from the Graduate School of Management, University of California at Los Angeles]

Sir,

I was recently in London to hold discussions *inter alia* on the expansion of North American investment and trade in the United Kingdom, my homeland.

I had a meeting in Newcastle and went to a travel agency in the West End to buy my train ticket. I also asked the lady behind the counter (I think it was a female) if she could reserve me a room at the Royal Station Hotel in Newcastle.

'Well, not really,' she said.

'What do you mean, not really?'

'Well, you'd have to pay us for the room now. Then when you got to Newcastle you'd have to pay the hotel. Then you'd have to come back here and ask us for a refund. But you can't do it anyway, because you haven't got an account with us.'

Where, Sir, do we go from here?

                                            Yours faithfully,
                                            JOHN HUTCHINSON

241

Where in the World?

From Mr Herbert C. Tobin   *25 July 1977*

Sir,

There are doubtless many who, like myself, deplore the habit – which unfortunately is becoming increasingly common – of referring to foreign countries not by the names by which they have been known for generations and indeed for centuries to the English-speaking world, but by the local usage of the countries concerned. I may instance the abandonment of the ancient and famous names of Ceylon, Persia, and Siam in favour of Sri Lanka, Iran, and Thailand, or the increasing use of Romania instead of Rumania (or Roumania).

If it be objected that the countries concerned wish to be known abroad by the names familiar to their nationals, we can with equal logic start speaking and writing of Sverige, Suomi, España, Hellas, Shqiperi, Misr, Bharat, and Nippon instead of Sweden, Finland, Spain, Greece, Albania, Egypt, India, and Japan, among many other examples.

Further progression along this fashionable but undesirable path will no doubt lead us in due course to speak and write of Bruxelles, Den Haag, Köln, Firenze, Venezia, Napoli, Wien, and Praha instead of Brussels, The Hague, Cologne, Florence, Venice, Naples, Vienna, and Prague – also among many other examples. And if we are to be guided by strict logicality we should speak not of Persian and Siamese cats but of Iranian cats and Thai cats, whilst Persian rugs and carpets will have to give place to Iranian ones.

Sir Winston Churchill, when wartime Prime Minister, sent a minute to the Foreign Office in April 1945 (it can be found among the Appendices to the sixth volume of *The Second World War*) worded as follows:

'I do not consider that names that have been familiar for generations in England should be altered . . . Constantinople should never be abandoned, though for stupid people Istanbul may be written in brackets after it. As for Angora, long familiar with us through the Angora cats, I will resist to the utmost of my power its degradation to Ankara. . . . If we do not make a stand, we shall . . . be asked to call Leghorn Livorno, and the BBC will be pronouncing Paris "Paree".'

Four years earlier, amidst many other preoccupations, Sir Winston on two occasions asked the Foreign Office in 1941 to inform him why Siam was 'buried under the name of

Thailand' and what were 'the historic merits of these two names'. I believe also that during his post-war Premiership in the 1950s, Sir Winston gave instructions that (except in intergovernmental communications) the designation Persia was to be used, and not Iran.

With that illustrious example before us, may one make a plea that, where a recognized English form exists for names of foreign countries, cities, or geographical features, it should not be departed from except for very good reasons.

Yours faithfully,
HERBERT C. TOBIN

BR Dialogue

From Mr Winston Fletcher   *4 October 1977*

Sir,

On the fecund subject of overmanning and productivity I thought that you would wish to have recorded for posterity the following conversation which occurred yesterday evening on a train from Paddington.

Guard to barperson: Tony's serving toast, on the other train.

Barperson: Toast? On his own? I'll have the union on him.

Guard (apparently taken aback by the vehemence of the barperson's reply): Well his customers seem to like it.

Barperson: Pleasing customers is all very well, but you can go too far. Making toast's a two-man job.

Only the reprobate toastmaker's name has been changed, in the probably forlorn hope that it may still be possible to protect him.

Yours faithfully,
WINSTON FLETCHER

The Reviewer's Approach

From Mr Christopher Gandy   *5 October 1977*

Sir,

Your newspaper is not yet subsidized by the Socialist Workers' Party, so why not employ reviewers who value books for themselves, and writers *as* writers, not as 'social documents' and 'products of their class'? Your review of Osbert Sitwell's autobiography by Kay Dick is not, I believe, your first to treat literature in this drab, disagreeable and uninformative way. Who would guess from it that the book is in marvellous English, teeming with lyrical description, acute analysis of people and hilarious anecdote, or that its author often satirized his native milieu?

What would a Dick of previous generations, or Proto-Dick, have made of earlier masterpieces? A few conjectures:

'If music be the food of love, play on, give me excess of it.'
Proto-Dick 'The Duke was of course used to excess of food, but too philistine to want excess of music except to serve his sexual appetites. Peacocks and drabs were his for the guzzling and fondling. Meanwhile in the Illyrian slave-galleys' etc., etc.

'I stood tiptoe on a little hill.'
Proto-Dick 'He would have done better to stand flat-footed on a slag-heap. For while this consumptive young Cockney was a-twittering, in the industrial north the satanic mills were belching forth' etc., etc.

Any one can do their own Proto-Dick on Trollope and Thackeray, but what about the radical Dickens? – 'The little room into which they were shown for dinner was delightful. Everything was delightful. The park was delightful, the dishes of fish were delightful, the wine was delightful' (*Our Mutual Friend*, ch. 8).
Proto-Dick 'The successful writer, now basking in fame and fashionable dinner parties and battening on royalties five times the compositors' wages, omits to remind us – did he any longer care? – that the park gardener got two pence an hour, the fisherman six pence a stone, the vineyard workers one sou a day if they were lucky' etc., etc.

Dost think that because thou hast elephantiasis of the 'social conscience' there shall be no more cakes and ale?

I am Sir, etc.,
CHRISTOPHER GANDY

'Wogs'

From Dr G. E. Diggle   *27 October 1977*

Sir,

Your readers may care to know the etymology of 'wogs'. The term was first used to denote those Workers On Government Service engaged in the construction of the Suez Canal. My 700,000 colleagues and I in the Civil Service are, of course, wogs.

Yours faithfully,
GEOFFREY DIGGLE

Economic Evidence

From Mr William Waldegrave   *12 December 1977*

[Conservative Member for Bristol West since 1979]

Sir,

Mr David Lea, of the TUC Economic Department, said in his oral evidence to the Wilson Committee: 'I do not think we can say it is a black or white situation but in the 1980s what we are emphasizing is that we are in a whole new ball game when we hope we will have a growth scenario when we believe that profitability in a secular as well as in a cyclical sense will be important.' (Wilson Committee Evidence, Vol. 2, HMSO, p. 93.)

Mr Lea is, I believe, Mr Len Murray's key adviser on economic and industrial matters at a time when the TUC is expanding its ambitions towards an ever greater role in economic policy. Some even say that there is a chance that he may be Mr Murray's successor.

I have read the sentence quoted above a good many times. I don't get any nearer to understanding it. It is not untypical of Mr Lea's evidence. Perhaps others will be better than I am at extracting meaning from it. But surely it must be a matter of some concern that people as powerful as Mr Murray and his TUC colleagues draw their ideas from thinking which appears as incoherent as this?

Yours faithfully,
WILLIAM WALDEGRAVE

A Tale of Two Pictures

[To mark the occasion of Sir Winston Churchill's eightieth birthday in 1954, Parliament presented him with his portrait by Graham Sutherland. Both Churchill and his wife disliked the painting, and it was on Lady Spencer-Churchill's initiative that the portrait was destroyed before Sir Winston's death]

From Mr. G. S. Whittet   *17 January 1978*

[former Editor, *The Studio* and *Studio International*]

Sir,

Soon after the presentation I was invited to view the portrait by Sutherland at Churchill's home in Hyde Park Gate. There in the garden drawing-room, fortified by a glass of sherry, I examined the picture alone for some time. Now looking up the number of the magazine I find I described it as 'an unconventional work of an unconventional sitter'. Its chief defect was that it looked unfinished in as much as his feet were concealed in a carpet that seemed to have sprouted a dun-coloured grass – the artist had obviously been unhappy about them and they had been painted over since it would have been impossible to 'cut off' his legs below the knees without radically altering the proportions and placing of the picture on the canvas.

One has to remember that the portrait was a gift to Churchill by colleagues past and present in Parliament as a token of their affection for him as a man of long service in that institution. It was not a state or official portrait but a personal symbol of good will and respect of which there was little evidence in the painting; I wrote the 'mood and the manner of the study do not awaken sympathy or warmth' as anyone looking at the colour reproduction accompanying my critical comments may confirm. Also, Churchill had a keen sense of history and his own place in it; lacking a present-day Holbein, he and his wife were not going to risk being preserved for posterity in a painting that they felt did neither him nor the artist full justice.

As footnote to the above, soon after I had viewed the portrait I visited Arthur Jeffress, the art dealer, who told me that a portrait of him by Sutherland had actually been begun and 'laid in' on the canvas the artist then used for Churchill – not that it mattered, for that initial sketch was undetectable.

246

Jeffress asked me not to mention this in print and I didn't until some six years later after he had died. As I said then it would have been another reason for the Old Man to have disliked the portrait though by that time apparently it did not exist.

Yours, etc.,

G. S. WHITTET

[In February 1974 Vermeer's *The Guitar Player* was stolen from Kenwood House.

Later a letter announced that the picture would be destroyed on St Patrick's Day unless the Price sisters, Dolours and Marian, on hunger strike in Brixton prison after being convicted of taking part in London bombings, were returned to Northern Ireland to complete their sentences]

From Mr R. G. T. Lindkvist　　　　　　　*15 March 1974*

Sir,

Mr Murray Mindlin (14 March) gives voice to the anguish one feels over the fate threatening the Vermeer painting, and he quite correctly spots an ideology and a logic at work. But is that logic impregnable? I think it right to argue that the thieves, were they to set fire to the Vermeer, would simultaneously see their own framework of logical thought perish in the flames.

Take the very act of stealing the painting. As it was not an act perpetrated for criminal gain as commonly understood, I assume it to fall within the category of creative protest which, some will argue, is an art form. Well, and I am not joking, this places the thieves and the painter Vermeer in the same group where members have the same rights of expression. Therefore, whatever damage they do to the painting they also do to their own action and to any right they may argue they had or have to take that or any consequential action. I take the thieves seriously. Do they?

This is quite apart from another argument militating against them: by hitching any success of their venture to a star priced at £1,000,000 they have, of course, *de facto* accepted the values of the capitalist society they profess to be fighting.

Yours faithfully,

T. LINDKVIST

247

[On 9 May 1974 the Vermeer was discovered in the grave-
yard of St Bartholomew's Church, Smithfield – damp and
with a slight cut but otherwise undamaged]

Music on Radio 3

From Mr David Shayer   *18 February 1978*

Sir,

Those of us who see Radio 3 as an island of normality in a
media ocean of unreal trivia can only fear the worst after
reading Stephen Hearst's state-of-the-waveband message in
your columns on Saturday 11 February.

It is not the speechday metaphors ('the good ship Radio 3')
which depress so much as the impression Mr Hearst gives of
a desire to convince the world at large (made up of other BBC
policy makers no doubt, together with all regular followers
of Radios 1, 2, 4 and local radio) that Radio 3 and its listeners
are truly grateful, bear the stigma of their 'cultural blessed-
ness' with humility, and will occupy their appointed station
with heartfelt deference. It is all too common nowadays to
have the populist finger wagged while we are reminded that
'it is unfair to expect the majority to tolerate and therefore
subsidize the bizarre, eccentric and undemocratic tastes of the
educated minority', but to hear this sort of thing, with its
tacit assumption that majority taste must be the starting-point
in all discussion, from the Controller of Radio 3 himself is a
sad experience.

Yours faithfully,
DAVID SHAYER

From Mr Toby Jessel   *2 February 1978*

[Conservative MP for Twickenham, writing from King
Edward VII's Hospital for Officers]

Sir,

Recovering here from an operation after a ski accident, and
awoken today (30 January) by hospital crack-of-dawn routine,
Radio 4 greeted me with chilling descriptions of the worst
snowstorms to hit Britain in 30 years.

Never has any skier moved so fast in switching over to
Radio 3, and a finely moving performance of Schumann's

2nd Symphony. It made my morning. To hell with the morons who want to cut it, and long live Mr Stephen Hearst, and his splendid team on Radio 3 who provide us with such a wonderful variety of good music.

Yours faithfully,
TOBY JESSEL

[There are no morons in Twickenham]

From Mr C. J. Harris   *30 January 1978*

Sir,
   Could I suggest that nothing written after 1800 should be played before 0800?

Yours faithfully,
CHRIS HARRIS

Package Holiday

From the Reverend I. J. M. Haire   *3 February 1978*

[Missionary to Halmahera, Indonesia]

Sir,
   Yesterday (Monday, 23 January) I received, in this Northern Moluccan island in Eastern Indonesia, a parcel posted in Belfast on Saturday, 8 June 1974. It took exactly three years, seven months and 15 days on its journey. I wonder if this is a record, at least for the fast-moving seventies?

Yours faithfully,
JAMES HAÍRE

[On 5 February 1970 (*The First Cuckoo*) the Dean of Canterbury reported the arrival of a letter, for forwarding, addressed to T. A. Becket, Esq. – that is a delay of over 800 years. As the Dean did not mention the letter's postmark, Mr Haire may claim his record]

Noise Level in Entertainment

From Professor Ivor H. Mills   *12 June 1978*

[Professor of Medicine, University of Cambridge Clinical School]

Sir,

I have followed with great interest your correspondence on this subject. It is striking that almost everyone deplores the intensity of sound now inflicted upon us in places of entertainment and yet no one asks why and how such a state of affairs came about.

I believe it started in the middle sixties when discotheques with excessive amplification of music became synonymous with the meeting places of teenagers. To enter such a place to collect a teenage child was then an auditory painful experience. Was this a device to keep the grown-ups out? And if it was, how did the teenagers survive in an atmosphere that we found painful?

The answers to these questions may be found in two different studies: one is the work of the Medical Research Council Applied Psychology Unit in Cambridge and the other is the study of the evolution of various techniques which young people have used in the last decade to produce excitement in the brain. The MRC unit has shown in a number of studies that the efficiency of the human brain falls as a result of sleep deprivation and it also falls in such things as tracking or reasoning tests when the person is exposed to very loud 'white noise'. However, when the tired brain is subjected to the intense noise it raises its efficiency and the person becomes more accurate in the tests. Similar types of results came from the study of sleep loss in young doctors. With five hours' loss of sleep over a three-day period they had a distinct fall-off in a verbal reasoning test but no fall-off in a test of medical judgement. When given the verbal reasoning test *after* the medical judgement test their mental efficiency was so raised by the challenge to medical ability that they did well in the verbal reasoning tests.

Among the variety of devices used by young people today to stimulate and excite the brain, one of the commonest is self-starvation. This was shown by Benedict in 1915 to increase mental excitement and by 14 days to produce an increase in efficiency and accuracy in handling mental problems. No doubt this explains why we found that 75 per cent of girls with anorexia nervosa start crash dieting in the year in which they are working for a major examination.

Other devices used by young people for mental excitement are challenging authority, starting rows or fights and even occasionally slashing themselves or stubbing out cigarettes on the back of the hand. Excessively loud noise clearly excites the flagging brain and may make it more efficient. No doubt the proportion of young people in places of entertainment encourages the management to turn up the volume of sound to suit the young who get a kick out of intense noise.

We all like mental excitement and commonly use drugs such as caffeine in coffee and nicotine in tobacco to produce mental stimulation and increased mental efficiency. Though intense noise may be damaging to the hearing mechanism, it may be no worse than escaping from reality with illegal drugs.

Yours faithfully,
IVOR H. MILLS

Vicarial Bounds

From Mr D. I. Carter   *23 January 1978*

Sir,

I see from *The Times* of 14 January that the appointment has been announced of the new Vicar of Upton Snodsbury with Broughton Hackett and Naunton Beauchamp and Grafton Flyford with North Piddle and Flyford Flavell.

Is this, Sir, a record?

Yours faithfully,
D. I. CARTER

From the Reverend Reginald Lee   *25 January 1978*

Sir,

If in using the word 'record', Mr D. I. Carter means the record number of churches in the charge of one incumbent, then the answer to his question is in the negative.

As a contender for such a record, the Tarrant Valley Benefice here in Dorset should merit serious consideration. This benefice contains the churches of Tarrant Grenvile, Tarrant Hinton, Tarrant Monkton, Tarrant Rushton, Tarrant Keynston and Tarrant Crawford and runs throughout the length of this beautiful valley.

Yours faithfully,
REGINALD LEE

Advertising Bad Spelling

From Mr F. T. Meacock   *1 February 1978*

Sir,

Why are the pundits so surprised about the prevalence of bad spelling from our youngsters? For years we have been officially encouraged to drinka pinta milka day. From such an example what can they expect?

Yours faithfully,
F. T. MEACOCK

From Mr Bertrand T. Whitehead   *4 February 1978*

Sir,

Twenty years ago, when I adapted the Middle English injunction, 'Drinke pynte mylke daie', I little thought that I would be held responsible for the poor spelling of a whole subsequent generation.

Those who have benefited from the millions of pounds spent on public education might now expect to be 'officially encouraged' in some such way as 'Consumers are recommended to maintain a diurnal input of 567 ml of lactic beverages'.

But which is the more literate?

Yours faithfully,
BERTRAND T. WHITEHEAD

From Mr Kenneth Pinnock   *13 February 1978*

Sir,

The author of the 'drinka pinta milka' slogan does well to defend himself. The decline of spelling is no fault of his. It is a nation-wide phenomenon, of which *The Times* itself gives almost daily evidence. Today, for instance, one finds 'enourmous' and 'arguement'; 'principle' and 'principal' are commonly confused; and there was one occasion last summer when a front-page headline referred to 'Bismark' while later pages contained such errors as 'dispersed' (for 'disbursed') and – incredibly – 'court-marshalled'.

For those who deal with the printed word this is a worrying trend, and it was not surprising to find recently that a famous publishing house, in advertising for an editorial secretary, insisted that candidates must have 'a high standard of English grammar and a literate education'. The message was clear – or would have been, if only 'grammar' had not appeared in the advertisement as 'grammer'.

Yours faithfully,
KENNETH PINNOCK

[The Old Etonian cricket commentator Brian Johnston often informs the nation he is off for a 'cuppa']

Boys' Papers and Class

From Mr Stephen Corrin   *31 January 1978*

Sir,

As an avid reader of *The Magnet, The Gem* and all the other celebrated boys' papers that featured the three schools, Greyfriars, St Jim's and Rookwood, I must say that Reith Lecturer Professor A. H. Halsey (as reported by you yesterday, 26 January) is talking through his hat when he says that 'for working-class boys *The Magnet* and *The Gem* exalted the manners of public school boys'. Most of my schoolmates in Tredegar, Mon., in those far-off days were sons of miners or other cruelly underpaid workers and we neither knew nor cared what a public school was. We read the adventures of Harry Wharton, Tom Merry and Jimmy Silver simply because they were 'ripping yarns' and allowed us to indulge in a fantasy world remote from the sort of lives we led. Exaltation of manners had nothing at all to do with it. Why can't sociologists refrain from making these glib generalizations?

Yours sincerely,
STEPHEN CORRIN

Anglophones' Accents

From Lord O'Neill of the Maine   *29 June 1978*

Sir,

Thank you for your leader in *The Times* today (28 June) on today's methods of speech in Britain and America. I have always been interested in differences between 'British English' and 'American English'; but the general assumption that America has changed the 'English' accent more than we have since 1776 does not, I believe, bear investigation.

My mother's family, whose grandparents (and even parents) spoke an old-fashioned upper-class English, said things like 'yallah' instead of yellow, 'cawfie' instead of coffee, and 'awfice' instead of office. My mother conducted a long and not always successful battle against the way I was being taught at Eton to pronounce certain words, and although she succeeded with words such as 'lorst' instead of lost, and 'sorlt' instead of salt, to her horror I learnt to say laundry instead of 'larndry' and launch instead of 'larnch'.

I remember some 12 years ago my wife and I paid a visit to Williamsburg, Virginia, and there we were shown a film based on the life of Patrick Henry and his part in the battle for independence. His mother, still loyal to George III, was portrayed speaking in a 1960 'English' accent, while her revolutionary son spoke in a 1960 American accent. I pointed this out to astonished officials, who appeared to believe that the 'Oxford' accent had already been invented in 1776.

Some people think that the English spoken in co. Armagh is today the nearest thing left to the accent used by the Elizabethans. At the time of the Declaration of Independence, about a quarter of the three million, or so, Americans had come on from the 'Plantation' of Ulster, and it is not without interest that many Northern Irish who joined the British forces during the war were constantly mistaken for Canadians.

The 'Establishment' in Britain today does not speak with an 'English' accent, but with an 'Oxford' accent.

Yours, etc.,
O'NEILL OF THE MAINE

The Sound of Jekyll

From Mr Ernest Mehew   *28 November 1980*

Sir,

Mr Roger Lancelyn Green (25 November) asks whether it is known how Robert Louis Stevenson intended the name of Dr Jekyll should be pronounced. Fortunately a reporter from the *San Francisco Examiner*, who interviewed Stevenson in his hotel bedroom in San Francisco on 7 June 1888, asked him that very question:

'There has been considerable discussion, Mr Stevenson, as to the pronunciation of Dr Jekyll's name. Which do you consider to be correct?'

Stevenson (described as propped up in bed 'wearing a white woollen nightdress and a tired look') replied: 'By all means let the name be pronounced as though it spelt "Jee-kill", not "Jek-ill". Jekyll is a very good family name in England, and over there it is pronounced in the manner stated.'

Yours faithfully,
ERNEST MEHEW

Zips?

[The sight of two televised batsmen chatting – presumably about tactics – in the middle of a cricket pitch intrigued correspondents]

From the Captain, Poet's and Peasants'
Cricket Club   *19 August 1980*

Sir,
Not all mid-wicket conferences concern matters of import. Last season, I once came to the wicket when the score was 12 for 5. The other batsman, who had been there from the outset, solemnly beckoned me to mid-wicket to give, I assumed, advice as to what I should do. 'I'm sorry to trouble you', he said, 'but I've just lost a fly-button. Would you mind keeping a look-out for it?' Unfortunately, I did not remain long enough to assist him in the search.

Yours faithfully,
DAVID A. PEARL

[This letter was sent from Lincoln's Inn, where, at the close of the home side's innings, the pitch is tended not with a roller but a vacuum cleaner]

Stale News from British Airways

From Miss Jean Lewis   *28 November 1980*

Sir,
Marie-Antoinette is alive, well and financial adviser to British Airways.
Boarding the morning flight from Düsseldorf to Heathrow the other day I was presented with the previous day's newspaper. It was no mistake. 'Today's papers are for First Class

passengers only' I was told. 'Second Class passengers can read yesterday's.'

Could someone inform the lady that stale news is just as bad as stale cake?

Yours faithfully,
JEAN LEWIS

[Very stale news in *The Times* would captivate: Walkley on a new play by Bernard Shaw, Darwin on Bobby Jones, Levin on the Richmond dustmen]

World Service

From Mr John Le Carré   *1 July 1981*

Sir,

At a moment when, thanks to the failure of diplomacy, we are spending £33·7m a *day* (and rising) on defence, and wondering whether we are getting value, the Foreign Office is aiming to save £3m *a year* by cutting BBC foreign language broadcasts to three of the most important unaligned countries of the world: Burma, Somalia and Brazil. At a saving of £10,000, which is a fraction of the cost of keeping a very average ambassador in the style to which he is not accustomed, they are also disconnecting Malta.

By what conceivable right? Are we to believe it is not worth one tenth of our daily defence expenditure to be revered as the distributors of sober, accurate and impartial news to unaligned countries who are otherwise without it?

Does the Foreign Office itself believe that the pulp distributed by its information services and spokesmen commands a particle of the same respect, let alone the same audience? Have we forgotten that two years ago the Foreign Office ordered cuts in the Turkish broadcasts, only to come running back a year later, asking for them to be expanded?

The BBC's foreign language broadcasts achieve something which goes far beyond the capacity of any foreign office. They enter the homes of thousands of ordinary people. They are taken to their hearts. They inform and educate. They set standards of objectivity. They inspire gratitude and even, now and then, actual love, as any traveller to those regions can establish for himself.

Really, it is obscene to imagine that the Foreign Office,

whose emissaries have scant contact, at best, with the ordinary people of the countries to which they are accredited, should presume to sit in judgement over our most effective, popular and trusted spokesman.

If Mrs Thatcher is looking to bring reason to bureaucracy, let her do it here, and sharply. Better to shed an embassy or two, and slim a few more, than sack our real ambassadors.

Yours faithfully,
JOHN LE CARRÉ

[John Le Carré was a member of HM Foreign Service 1960–64]

West Indians in School

From Mrs S. Best   *27 June 1981*

Sir,

West Indian kids fail to do well in school. First, lack of discipline all over the place; at an early age they are all taught in school that parents are too strict; they had Victorian up-bringing (although Victoria died 22/1/01); parents do not understand them.

The biggest culprits are the welfare officers who leave little white babies to be battered to death but can't wait to take black kids from their home to put them with nice white aunties and uncles, where they are allowed to run wild in most cases. They can't relate to new environment, but worst of all there comes 18th birthday, no more artificial love and affection, so they are thrown in at the deep end. The few misfits glamorize their position.

So parents fail to do their duties for fear of their children being taken away from them. So the young darlings play up and blackmail parents into giving in (if not they'll tell Miss or Sir and they'll call the Welfare) or run away and lie on parents and the court will be told Topsy or Sambo needs love and affection as the blacks are too illiterate to provide same.

Leave blacks alone and children will come OK. Let them realize there is nowhere to run. They must have discipline.

As for Asians, most were not born here. Wait for the next generation before you pass judgement. Our kids have the same 4lbs of grey and white matter in the hollow of the skull so let them use it. The whites are afraid, they also look towards USA too much. A lot of the teachers do not seem to know much themselves.

Respectfully yours,
S. BEST
(West Indian parent)

English Theatre's Blow to the Heart

[On 28 June 1957 the critic Alan Dent bewailed the impending destruction of the St James's Theatre – see *The First Cuckoo*]

From M Jean-Louis Barrault   *15 May 1981*

Sir,

May we express, with appropriate modesty, our emotion at the threatened disappearance of the Old Vic?

The Old Vic is part and parcel of the heart of London's theatrical life, and London is one of the world's true capitals of the art of theatre.

Every evening, at sunset, the spirit of English theatre awakes and, just over the Old Vic, hover the spirits of Shakespeare, the Elizabethans and the Restoration playwrights, whose links with today's dramatic poets have never been severed.

How many happy memories we recall of evenings spent at the Old Vic, especially of the magnificent post-war period when Sir Laurence Olivier, Sir John Gielgud, Sir Ralph Richardson and their colleagues brought it to life! We have great memories, too, of the season when our own company had the honour of playing there.

Today we emphasize our fraternal solidarity with English actors in their pleas that the Old Vic should not be closed. The soul is fragile without the body; and the Old Vic company forms, as it were, part of the body of English theatre.

Such an act would not only be cruel, it would darken the glow of British theatre in the world at large which we love, admire and need.

We would like our English friends to know that we are with them in their request, the aim of which is only to serve the artistic genius of England.

Yours etc.,
JEAN-LOUIS BARRAULT
Renaud-Barrault Compagnie, Théâtre du Rond-Point

[The great *comédian-administrateur* was more fortunate than the critic. On 5 August 1982 Mr Ed Mervish, the owner of Honest Ed's discount store and the Royal Alexandra Theatre, Toronto, bought the Old Vic for £550,000. He plans to fill the theatre with canopy lights to make it sparkle]

Trail Blazers

From Mrs M. Keyes   *17 December 1981*

Sir,

On Friday morning I was amazed to see, along with dozens of other passengers at Northwick Park station, my train approaching the platform preceded by two men walking slowly along the line scraping snow off the rails with spades. Have we reached the ultimate in British technology?

Yours faithfully,
RITA KEYES

Ruritania

⬥

[On 31 July 1976 *The Times* published *Land of Hope and Glory*, a long and brilliant reassessment 'of a neglected corner in the field of Eastern European Studies and its discoverer and historian, Anthony Hope', by the paper's former Foreign Editor E. C. Hodgkin.

'. . . For a long time I used to identify Ruritania with Romania, and I suspect a good many others did too. This was partly due, I suppose, to a similarity of names, and partly because in the days of good King Carol Romania seemed to fit quite neatly the defini- tion of Ruritania given in the *Oxford Dictionary of Etymology*: "A petty state, esp. as a scene of court romance and intrigue". But was I right in placing Ruritania in the Balkans? . . .'

Historians, both professional and amateur, among *Times* readers soon took over]

From Dr Emma Mason   *4 August 1976*

[Birkbeck College, University of London]

Sir,

E. C. Hodgkin's reappraisal of Ruritanian studies is too hasty in rejecting Romania's prior claims to identification with that best-known of all Balkans states. In the 1890s, the Romanian king, like his Ruritanian counterpart, was both Roman Catholic and German-speaking, and the boulevards of Bucharest, like those of Strelsau, were in their prime. Immi- grants from the large Teutonic minority in Transylvania (at that time outside the frontiers of Romania) doubtless account for the bevy of efficient huntsmen and retainers with German names then in the service of the Elphbergs.

Several of Rupert's most splendid dress uniforms hit the eye as one enters the History Museum in Bucharest, and Peles Castle is Zenda to the last detail (except for the moat, but then we've been having long hot summers recently). Moreover, Princess Marie of Edinburgh's marriage to the Romanian crown prince brought the remarkable doings of the Romanian court to the notice of the English public shortly before Anthony Hope began to write *The Prisoner of Zenda.*

Students of Ruritanian political sociology remain unconvinced by the rival claims brought forward on Austria's behalf – and surely no one ever travelled from Paris to Vienna via Dresden.

Yours faithfully,
EMMA MASON

From Mr J. A. Jowett   *9 August 1976*

Sir,
   Your former Foreign Editor does well to remind us that Ruritania was not Balkan but Austrian in character and polity, both civil and religious; the comfort which he derives from this may, however, be misconceived. When this topic was discussed 12 or 13 years ago, one student, as I recall, would have numbered Strelsau among the Siebenburgen but for Rassendyll having boarded the sleeper at Dresden. Yet a map of central Europe can readily indicate where such a train could have desposited him in the early morning: the rump of Silesia, sometimes called the Teschenland, which was not acquired by Frederick the Great. It would not be difficult to picture the dynasty's ancestral keep perched on a crag in the West Beskias and one may fairly suppose the Rudolf who reigned in Strelsau at the time of the Partitions received such accessions of territory as would qualify his nineteenth-century successors to exchange ambassadors with her Britannic Majesty.

   Sadly, all this means that Ruritania would be behind the curtain and one's only hope would repose on the capacity of her subjects to temper communism with Schlamperei.

I am, Sir, your obedient servant,
J. A. JOWETT

From Mr Alan Palmer   *11 August 1976*

Sir,
   Mr E. C. Hodgkin's essay on the fundamentals of Ruritanian Studies made delightful Saturday reading. Two recent events in Austria – both noticed by the London press – probably stimulated Anthony Hope's imagination during that memorable walk on 28 November 1893, when the Zenda tale 'came into his head'. The first of these was the dismissal a fortnight

previously of Count Taaffe, Franz Josef's right-hand man for the past fourteen years. Comment on Taaffe's fall revived interest in the Mayerling tragedy since he was the minister suspected of having attempted to hush up the Crown Prince's suicide.

The second event is more significant. News reached London on 17 November that Prince Alexander of Battenberg had died suddenly from peritonitis in Styria. The Battenbergs, with close family links to Queen Victoria's children, had long aroused interest among the British: Prince Alexander's adventures in Bulgaria in 1885–6 excited London, and the gossips enjoyed tales of his romances. His body was conveyed from Styria for interment in the cathedral at Sofia. Details of this impressive ceremony appeared in the English newspapers on 28 November.

Surely the romantic Elphbergs have more in common with the Battenberg dynasty than with the Habsburgs who, despite Mayerling, remained staidly stiff-lipped? Yet Hope needed a predominantly Habsburg setting for his tale of mistaken identity. He could not expect to hold English readers if he placed it somewhere so wildly unfamiliar as the Balkans. It is interesting that *The Prisoner of Zenda* should have been published in April 1894, within a few days of the opening night of *Arms and the Man* at the Avenue Theatre. Bulgaria and the Balkans might be good enough for chocolate soldiers: the Rassendylls could only flourish in a kingdom where the swordplay was more polished. Ruritania had to be in central Europe, or not at all.

Yours sincerely,
ALAN PALMER

From Doctor W. H. Zawadzki   *11 August 1976*

[Wolfson College, Oxford]

Sir,

Dr E. Mason's learned arguments on behalf of Romania are very shaky. Students of Ruritanian history also find it difficult to believe that a Cardinal Archbishop could be the leading churchman of a country whose established religion was Orthodoxy. And why should one not travel from Paris to Vienna via Dresden and see something of Bohemia, that jewel of the Elphberg Crown, on the way?

Yours faithfully,
W. H. ZAWADZKI

Sir,

Before your splendid Ruritanian correspondence draws to its close – perhaps with the revelation that *The Prisoner of Zenda* was written by Mr Thomas Keating in a brief moment of leisure while engaged on a busy sketching holiday at Shoreham – may I put forward the claims of Bavaria as the source of Anthony Hope's inspiration?

In 1893 Bavaria like Ruritania was a Catholic German-speaking Kingdom of moderate but significant size. Munich like Strelsau was the seat of a Cardinal Archbishop. The nineteenth-century dynastic adventures of the House of Wittelsbach have the true Elphberg flavour. But it is when one comes to study the events of four days in June 1886 that the most striking parallels emerge.

We see a conspiracy organized by Count von Holnstein (Rupert of Hentzau) to install Prince Luitpoid (Black Michael) as Regent by having King Ludwig II (Rudolf) certified as incapable and insane. On 10 June the first attempt to apprehend the King fails. On the eleventh his loyal aide-de-camp Count Dürckheim (Fritz von Tarlenheim) is lured to Munich and arrested. On the twelfth the King is overpowered at Neuschwanstein (the hunting lodge) and taken under escort to Schloss Berg (the castle of Zenda). Finally on the thirteenth the bodies of the King and his medical attendant are found mysteriously drowned in the lake adjoining the castle.

If only it had been in the moat I would consider the Bavarian case as proved, but at least it is *ben trovato*.

Yours faithfully,

Christopher Norman-Butler

Sir,

It just will not do to try and make the realm of the Elphbergs fit into the pattern of any other kingdom. Rassendyll bought a ticket from Paris to Dresden, not just in order to confuse the Paris Correspondent of *The Critic* by taking a roundabout route but simply because Dresden was in fact on the direct route to Strelsau, as Antoinette de Mauban, who was on the same train, proved. By no stretch of the imagination could Dresden be said to be on the direct route either to Munich, Vienna or Bucharest.

No, Sir, I plump for Ruritania in the region of southern Silesia as placed by Mr Jowett. It has the further advantage of being on the Catholic periphery of that magical region of Orthodox kingdoms known then as the Balkans.

Yours faithfully,
AUBREY MOODY

From Mr Kenneth Gregory 18 August 1976

Sir,

It is possible that the arch-Fabian and most quintessentially perfect Wagner-Ibsenite was ignorant of geography and much else. Still, perhaps someone can explain why, when reviewing the stage adaptation of *The Prisoner of Zenda* (St James's Theatre, 7 January 1896), Bernard Shaw should have mentioned how Anthony Hope had 'gone to the shores of the Baltic, and carved an imaginary State of Ruritania out of Mecklenburg'.

Yours faithfully,
KENNETH GREGORY

From Mr Oliver Barnes 20 August 1976

Sir,

Mr Christopher Norman-Butler makes out an excellent though not entirely convincing case for Bavaria's claim to be Hope's Ruritania.

I would have subscribed more wholeheartedly to his view had the Salic Law prevailed in Ruritania as it did in every other Germanic kingdom.

The accession of Queen Flavia makes it clear that whoever the Ruritanians might have been they were certainly not 'Salian Franks'.

Yours faithfully,
OLIVER BARNES

From Captain John Miller and others 27 August 1976

[intervening from the British Army of the Rhine]

Sir,

With regard to the geographical location of Ruritania, we may certainly dismiss any idea that it was the Austro-Hungarian Empire! The Emperor always had naval ADCs in addition to those drawn from the land forces. There is no mention of a navy in either of Hope's novels.

No, we must look for the answer on a smaller scale. Hope may have ignored the unification of the German States in 1866, by using a map drawn prior to that date. Bernard Shaw rightly identifies it as Mecklenburg and may well have had access to the 1863 edition of *Unter Dampf Fahren Im Grossherzogtum* (page 73) by the then famous traveller Charlotte Helsing. This clearly shows the railway connexions as they stretch from Neve Strelitz (Strelsau) through Dresden and Frankfurt-am-Main before dropping down to the French border.

Dornford Yates acknowledged his dept to Hope in providing the inspiration for his Chandos novels based in Reichtenberg. But Yates was less coy about location, and clearly identifies the ground as being Austria.

Yours faithfully,
JOHN MILLER
IAN McPHERSON
CHARLES F. MURISON

From Doctor W. H. Zawadzki   *24 August 1976*

Sir,

With his letter on the Salic Law in Germany Mr Oliver Barnes has made an invaluable contribution to Ruritanian studies. But he should have proceeded one step further and indicated a crucial modification of the Salic Law: Emperor Charles VI's Pragmatic Sanction of 1713 making female descendants of the House of Habsburg eligible as heirs to the Habsburg domains. Hence Maria Theresa's succession in 1740.

The principle of a woman on the throne having been once established, widows on the throne seem the next obvious step – an amendment that Queen Flavia must have introduced for equally pressing reasons of state.

Despite Mr Christopher Norman-Butler's seemingly devastating contribution on Bavaria's behalf, the Austrian claim has not yet been successfully dismissed (and Teschen Silesia, a highly industrialized and predominantly Slavonic rump-province, or Mecklenburg, that gloomy Lutheran grand duchy, just will not do).

Yours faithfully,
W. H. ZAWADZKI

Sir,

Since the contestants in what now must be described as the War of the Ruritanian Succession show no sign of retiring to winter quarters, may I re-enter the field?

The claims of the outsiders, the Balkan States, Mecklenburg and Teschen Silesia, despite the gallant efforts of their adherents, have been found wanting. Bavarian supporters may have been flung into temporary disarray by Mr Oliver Barnes's penetrating letter on the implications of the Salic Law, but anyone conversant, as any advanced Ruritanian scholar must be, with the terms of the Treaty of Aix-la-Chapelle in 1748, will be aware that Bavaria after seven years of warfare was compelled to recognize specifically Charles VI's Pragmatic Sanction. If the Habsburgs for want of a male heir could alter the Salic Law so could and would the Wittelsbachs – a psychological fact which did not escape the attention of Anthony Hope!

The Bavarian case, therefore, though shaken remains essentially intact. The claims of Austria, I regret to say, are seriously if not mortally damaged by the breakfast table conversation at Number 305 Park Lane, W1, recounted in Chapter 1 of *The Prisoner of Zenda*. Mr Rassendyll having read in your newspaper, Sir, of the forthcoming Coronation of King Rudolf the Fifth, decided to break the tradition that no member of his family should visit Ruritania. Let me quote his exact words: 'inasmuch as it had never been my practice to furnish my relatives with an itinerary of my journeys, and in this case I anticipated opposition to my wishes, I gave out that I was going for a ramble in the Tyrol – an old haunt of mine.' This disposes of the Austrian case unless one is prepared to doubt the word of one whom Colonel Sapt regarded as the finest Elphberg of them all.

One question remains: the journey from Paris via Dresden to Ruritania. A careful study of Chapter 2 of Mr Rassendyll's memoirs will reveal that Dresden was not on the direct line to Strelsau or (if I may be so bold) Munich. Both Madame de Morban and he had independent and valid reasons for reaching Ruritania by an indirect route. Both of them broke their journey for a night at Dresden and travelled to Strelsau and Zenda on the following day. Further research in the 1893 continental Bradshaw would no doubt reveal the actual train timetables, but as every Ruritania enthusiast will agree, there comes a moment when investigation must cease. It is better to travel Hope-fully than to arrive!

Yours faithfully,
CHRISTOPHER NORMAN-BUTLER

From Dr I. D. Hill   *2 September 1976*

Sir,

Dr Zawadzki writes (24 August) 'the Austrian claim has not yet been successfully dismissed'. However, with King Rudolf restored to his throne, Rudolf Rassendyll left Ruritania and spent a quiet fortnight, for psychological recovery and to let his beard regrow, in the Tyrol. This is conclusive evidence that, wherever Ruritania may be, it cannot be Austria.

Yours faithfully,
I. D. HILL

From Mr W. E. R. Barnett   *3 September 1976*

Sir,

Ruritanians are a race who generally prefer to keep out of the international news and away from the realities of the twentieth century. They must, however, feel hurt at the suggestions made by your correspondents that they are Austrians, Bavarians, or Mecklenburgers.

The Ruritanians exist where the rules of everyday topography need not apply, lying since 1918 to the south of Poland and to the north of Czechoslovakia, a Slav people widely interbred with the German-speaking ruling class, who have succeeded, despite all probability, in retaining their independence and their Elphberg monarchy through episodes of bolshevism, nationalism, Nazi invasion and Soviet liberation, enjoying friendly but not servile relations with all three worlds.

Yours faithfully,
W. E. R. BARNETT

From Mr Michael G. Heenan   *6 September 1976*

Sir,

May I suggest that the author, having in Chambers' beautifully pedantic word 'discovered' Ruritania, then went to considerable trouble to cover it up again? Rudolf travelled east from Paris to Dresden. There he turned two ways: south for the landscape of his cousin's kingdom, in which he found the Thuringian forests with their little principalities, north to find disguises for the names.

In Brandenburg, the Ukermark and the Mecklenburgs, he found the Slavic *ow* or *au* of Strelsau and Hentzau, and names (or something like their real names) for Marshal Strakenz and the Countess of Strofzin. Compare Strelitz and Stralsund, Schwerin and Stettin and Prentzlau, all between the Elbe and the Oder. It was the Grand Duke of Mecklenburg-Strelitz who in 1894 had a nephew named Michael, not the King of Bavaria or the Emperor of Austria; and it was the Grand Duke of Mecklenburg-Schwerin who had a father-in-law named Michael, not the King of Rumania or the Prince of Bulgaria.

Hope's was the old dilemma of the romantic in love: he wanted the world to know of his discovery, and he wanted to keep it to himself. I seem to remember that this aspect of the book was most elegantly captured in the film* (the 1937 film, I need hardly add) when the unrolling map, clearly showing Rudolf's journey from Paris to Dresden, then quickly faded out . . . overtaken by the dark forests of Thuringia? Or by the gloom of Mecklenburg? We shall never know.

Yours faithfully,
MICHAEL G. HEENAN

[*The 1937 film version saw Ronald Colman as the two Rudolfs, Madeleine Carroll as Flavia, Douglas Fairbanks Jr as Rupert, Raymond Massey as Black Michael, and David Niven as Fritz von Tarlenheim. C. Aubrey Smith, who was Sapt in the 1937 film, had succeeded to the role of Black Michael in George Alexander's production of the stage adaptation at the St James's Theatre in 1896]

From Mr Anthony Wood   *8 September 1976*

Sir,

Anthony Hope provided the answer himself. The true location of Ruritania was in the head of an upper middle-class Englishman in 1893. Her undeniably Germanic character derives from a hazy Victorian image of small princely families, Ludwig-type castles and Mayerling-type hunting lodges, an essentially non-Prussian Germany – foreign, of course, but cosy and with a romantic charm. Within a few years of the publication of *The Prisoner of Zenda* that image was being replaced by another; a Germanic Ruritania would hardly have been conceived by an Englishman, once the building of the German navy had begun, and this is perhaps why for later readers Ruritania mysteriously shifted eastwards to somewhere like Romania. Perhaps, too, it is a sign of the new images at work in Europe today that the Elphbergs can at last move back to their native soil in Munich/Teschen/Vienna.

Yours sincerely,
ANTHONY WOOD

From Mr Roger Lancelyn Green   *9 September 1976*

Sir,

Surely the great charm of Ruritania, that Land of Hope and Glory, is that it cannot be found in any atlas, though it figures large in many a map of the imagination – where I, for one, have little difficulty in finding it on frequent visits:

> 'Though its latitude's rather uncertain,
> And the longitude also is vague,
> The persons I pity who know not the City' –

of Strelsau and the Castle of Zenda.

Ruritania lies somewhere near Andrew Lang's Pantouflia, discovered a few years earlier – and its nearest port is on the 'Sea-coast of Bohemia'.

Yours truly,
ROGER LANCELYN GREEN

From Squadron Leader I. A. McCoubrey   *9 September 1976*

Sir,

I note from your columns today that the debate on Ruritania continues. While its exact geographical location may remain a mystery, I feel sure that its spiritual home at least is at the bottom right-hand corner of your leader page.

Yours faithfully,
IAN A. MCCOUBREY

A Veteran Remembers

['Your grandfather may have told you about the Boer War, which ended all of 80 years ago, in 1901. I am surprised to discover that there are 14 known veterans of that distant campaign still alive; these oldest of old soldiers are to hold their last reunion later this month, before they finally fade away.

Seven of the fourteen are expected to turn up at a lunch at Chelsea Barracks provided by the Army Benevolent Fund; it will be the last gathering ever held of men who went to war while Victoria was still on the throne. . . .

Among the guests will be Georgina White, now in her nineties, daughter of the general who defended Ladysmith; she herself was in the town throughout the siege.'
– from *The Times* Diary, 13 May 1981]

From Mr A. D. Bowers   *20 May 1981*

Sir,

I still manage to look through *The Times* daily (born 25.2.1882). Thank you so much for your note on p. 14 [13 May, London Diary]. I have been to *most of* the reunions since 1901. I am *the only* veteran who fought in the last *big* fight of the Boer War, Battle of Tweefontein (at 4 a.m., 25.12.1901) – practically naked, butt end and bayonet. The Boer C-in-C *himself*, pistol at my head, said he would shoot me if I attempted to escape – I and three others did 'hop off' when our exhausted cavalry arrived after a 14-mile gallop from Elands River Bridge.

What a ghastly bloody sight the camp was after the fight: my fine *new* horse standing on 3½ legs, Captain M. with lower jaw blown away (expanding bullets). I was in the W. Kent Yeomanry (volunteer) then. I rejoined in 1914 in World War 1 and was at once sent away to a special Artillery School and *ultimately* demobilized with rank of Captain RFA.

I fought in *countless* engagements in S. Africa (sometimes two or three or four near or far actions day by day for 18 months) and World War 1 in *very many* of the big battles in Belgium, Ypres and the Somme – for a special job on very bloody *Passchendaele* I was mentioned in despatches – the award is beside me – (the most terrifying battle fought since man came on earth. Men shot themselves to get out of it).

271

Packed like sardines on the crest, a German shell killed many, and at last detonated in the crowded cellar and wounded one of my two signallers in the thigh (*touching me*).

I have a number of relics still of both wars. I write occasionally to Veteran Wood [mentioned in the Diary item]. I regret I can only hobble now and I am 50 per cent blind.

In World War 1 my Col. (Long) appointed me his 'Orderly Officer' (Assistant Adjt. of 14th Army Bde RFA) and I accompanied him on much of his work and inspections and was given many *special* jobs of all sorts. I wrote up two war albums, full of photos.

I am now a widower (since 1975) and live with my widowed daughter in my boyhood home here (after many years in Richmond). Your note on p. 14 stirs up so many fine memories of countless battles (*big* and small). I took a very active interest in the Boer War Veterans for many years.

A. D. BOWERS

[In his 101st year Mr Bowers wrote copiously to *The Second Cuckoo*.]

Implications of Inter-city Rioting

From Mrs Vivien Noakes   *8 July 1981*

Sir,

Before Freud responsibility for all shortcomings fell, often unjustly, upon the miscreant. We now know that such shortcomings often grow from maltreatment of the individual, either directly by another person or through society overall. However, this once necessary shift has now reached absurd lengths, so that no one dare say that a person is responsible for his own deeds without seeming to be unfeeling and reactionary.

In the case of the recent street riots we have heard that unemployment, racial prejudice, the police, outside provocation and that omnipresent factor of post-Freudian society, frustration, are all to blame. Such forces undoubtedly have an important part to play and must be carefully examined. In the end, however, it is surely the individual who stones and loots and burns who is responsible for making the decision to stone and loot and burn.

And yet, ironically, perhaps society is to blame, for as long as these people continue to receive our tacit complicity in what they are doing, until they hear unequivocally that what they are doing is wrong, however provoked they may feel themselves to be, there will be no end to incidents such as those we have been witnessing.

Yours faithfully,
VIVIEN NOAKES

From Dr Alexander Cooke   *8 July 1981*

Sir,

When 250 policemen are injured in a riot, why are there no protests from the Council for Civil Liberties?

Yours faithfully,
ALEXANDER COOKE

Ill-equipped for Life

From Mr U. C. A. Breese   *6 May 1981*

Sir,

I am a 19-year-old school-leaver. I have been working in a hotel as a barman with four A levels and 10 O levels, none of which I have had a chance to use.

Consequently, although I could give my employer a detailed description of various processes of polymerization or tell him how hard he would hit the ground if dropped from a height of 30ft, I would have to ask *him* how to open a current bank account or fill in a cheque. As far as I'm concerned, a mortgage is something that happens to an item of property in a game of Monopoly.

Yes, I know millions have been spent on education over the past 10 years, but still my friends leave school not knowing how to insure their first car and have the registration card transferred in their name. What is a log book? A set of figures which help you multiply and divide more complicated figures?

Perhaps the education authorities could reduce the luxurious standards of school life and have us learn more appropriate subjects, with a view to 'living' after our schooldays. I would like to hear whether other school-leavers have been walking round in complete ignorance due to *their* education!

Yours sincerely,
U. C. A. BREESE

Bats to Beware of

From Colonel Etherwald E. Vella   *29 April 1981*

[consultant pathologist and microbiologist, Royal Army Medical College]

Sir,

Interested as I am ex-officio on the subject of communicable diseases, my attention could not but be riveted on two reports (Science Report on rabies and 'Bats in the attic') which, as it happened, were printed immediately adjacent to each other in your issue of Wednesday, 22 April, p. 14.

Vampire bats (blood-lapping) as vectors of rabies have been known for many years, even to the Spanish Conquistadores in South America; however it was as recently as 1953 that doctors in the United States recognized that non-haematophagous bats could cause rabies in their country.

We in Great Britain are watching with attention and some disquiet the onward march of the present rabies epizootic in Europe – it has now approached to within 50 miles of the French north coast. This epizootic, which began in 1939, is fanned by the red fox, but it may be prudent to remember that reports of the rabies virus being found in insectivorous bats have been recorded from European countries, namely Germany, Yugoslavia, Turkey and possibly Hungary.

I am, Sir, your obedient servant,

WALLY VELLA

Brideshead's Men at Arms

From Mr Andrew d'Antal   *15 October 1981*

Sir,

Having read Michael Ratcliffe's panegyric on *Brideshead Revisited* (13 October), I am not really surprised that he was not inclined to make any critical reference to the military clangers in the opening section of the first instalment. Though I share his enthusiasm for the production as a whole, I cannot let these shocking errors pass without protest.

Having been a sergeant in 1940 and a sergeant-major in 1941, I can confidently assure the producers of *Brideshead Revisited* that a sergeant-major does not wear three stripes, as did the man addressed as sergeant-major by Charles Ryder.

The costume department should surely have known better and provided him with a uniform appropriate to his rank, i.e. with crowns at the lower ends of the sleeves, and of course no stripes at all.

Worse was to follow: Captain Ryder responded to a soldier's salute (indoors) with a salute of his own although his head was bare. Sir, as you well know, as indeed any British schoolboy surely knows, it is only in the armed forces of the United States that such a thing is done.

No British soldier of any rank is allowed to salute if he is not wearing a cap. If the purpose of the captain's gesture is possibly to make *Brideshead Revisited* more easily marketable in the United States, then I would beg to suggest that the price is too high.

Yours truly,
ANDREW D'ANTAL

Bear Facts

From the Reverend Aubrey Moody   *10 February 1981*

Sir,

Surely Mr John Rae is mistaken, in his article on 31 January, in saying that 'Winnie was Christopher Robin's favourite *polar* bear at the London Zoo'. When I was a small boy, before *Winnie-the-Pooh* was written, I was taken as a treat behind the Mappin Terrace where a kindly keeper let a *brown* bear out into the long passage, and then pretended not to see as she made her way to a corn bin, opened the lid and stuck her head inside.

Pretending surprise, the keeper called her and she ambled back to us and gently opened my hand with her paw to get the lump of sugar that she knew would be there. Her name was Winnie and she had been the mascot of a Canadian regiment in the first war.

Yours faithfully,
AUBREY MOODY

Do Scholars Count?

From Professor R. J. C. Atkinson   29 May 1981

[Department of Archeology, University College, Cardiff]

Sir,

If pedantry about the bi-millenary of Virgil's death requires account to be taken of the differing lengths of the Julian and tropical years (16 May), then the right date cannot be either 21 or 22 September 1982.

Two thousand Julian years amount to 730,500 days, from which must be subtracted (for British calendars) the 11 days lost by Act of Parliament in September 1752, and one day each in 1800 and 1900 which in the Gregorian calendar were not lean years.

However, in 2,000 tropical years starting in 19 BC there were only 730,484·51 days. The discrepancy of 2½ days arises because the Gregorian calendar restored the date of the vernal equinox to 21 March (its date at the time of the Council of Nicaea in AD 325), by which time the Julian calendar was out of phase by this amount.

I suggest, therefore, that the right date for a commemoration is 18 September 1982, ignorance of the precise hour of Virgil's death notwithstanding.

Yours more pedantically still,

R. J. C. ATKINSON

Crying Shame

From Mr Steven Joseph   2 November 1981

Sir,

Travelling on the London to Dover service yesterday I heard the guard make the following announcement over the loud-speaker: 'We apologize for the delay to this train. This is entirely due to an incompetent signalman.'

Are we to understand that British Rail are practising a man-management technique long-favoured by the Chinese – achieving greater efficiency from employees through public shaming?

I remain, yours faithfully,

STEVEN JOSEPH

Babes and Sucklings

From Mrs T. D. Shephard   *11 August 1981*

Sir,

Reading today's article (4 August) on breast feeding in
Oxford reminds me, not of my Oxford days, when such problems did not arise, but of finding myself on Singapore docks
queueing for one of the last boats out before the Japanese
arrived.

The scorching tropical sun was beating down, and occasional bombs, and with my baby desperately needing a feed,
I poked my head into a tent full of British 'other ranks' and
explained my need.

'Come in, love,' they all chorused, 'we're all married men
in here.' (They all looked about 18 to me then!)

I was offered an upturned packing case to sit on and thereafter completely ignored.

How has everyone become so much more 'sensitive' in the
last 40 years?

Yours faithfully,
SYLVIA SHEPHARD

BBC Refinement

From Mr C. A. C. Hendriks   *24 September 1937*

Sir,

As an example of the 'naiceness' of the BBC's mind may I
quote from a recent *cri de coeur* – an SOS on Saturday night
last – when instead of a 'wet nurse', or 'foster mother', 'a
source of supply of human milk for new-born twins' was
called for.

Could 'refainement' move further along the path to the
lunatic asylum without actually enforcing an entrance?

Yours etc.,
CECIL A. C. HENDRIKS

Glazed Look

From Mr David Climie   *15 October 1981*

Sir,

In this centenary year of the great and good Sir Pelham Wodehouse I hope I may be permitted to plead, through your columns, for a mark of respect in the shape of a moratorium on the Wooster Monocle Fallacy.

Throughout the whole of the canon I have been unable to find a single reference to Bertie Wooster wearing a monocle. As far as I can see, he does not wear a monocle, he never has worn a monocle, and now it seems highly unlikely that he ever will wear a monocle. Psmith wears a monocle, the Hon. Galahad Threepwood wears a monocle, and a recent poll at the Drones Club reveals that 63·5 of the membership (Catsmeat Pirbright occasionally for theatrical purposes) wear monocles. But the name of B. Wooster, far from leading all the rest, does not even appear down among the wines and spirits.

Clearly, the man is unmonocled. Yet in the two hemispheres available to us I seem to be the only person aware of it. Even the learned Mr Richard Usborne makes no mention of this (admittedly negative) fact. Everybody else is clearly under the impression that the Wooster eye has been behind glass day and night since birth. An actor's first impulse on being asked to portray Bertie is to seize the nearest sheet of window-pane and start cutting discs out of it. Why? The finger points inexorably to the illustrators.

With a few honourable exceptions, Sir Pelham was not lucky with his illustrators. But in all their illustrations, good, bad, indifferent (and including that extraordinary collection of what appear to be waxworks on the Penguin covers), whenever the presence of the *preux chevalier de nos jours* is called for, there he invariably is, eyebrow clenched and ribbon a-dangle. Sir Pelham, ever kindly, seems never to have objected, but to my mind it is equivalent to presenting a Jeeves with a walrus moustache or a Lord Emsworth in a well-pressed natty gents suiting.

Yours faithfully,
DAVID CLIMIE

An Humble Petition

[A *Times* book review brought forth unusual but familiar cadences]

From the Reverend P. J. Ridley   *13 January 1982*

Dearly beloved Sir, the Source of all might, majesty and dominion in these our Times, I, thine unworthy servant, do humbly beseech thee, of thy merciful goodness so to admonish and enlighten thy servant Christopher Staughton that whereas (as it seemeth) he doth verily believe the *Alternative Service Book*, 1980, to have in it the words, 'Do not bring us to the time of trial', he may by thy ghostly counsel be brought to repent of that his most miserable conceit.

And forasmuch as perchance he hath never yet looked with his own eyes into the said Book but goeth (as the saying is) by hearsay, being but a poor scholar yet notwithstanding misliking the said Book from the inclination of his heart, I humbly beseech thee of thy gracious and most bounteous favour so to bestow upon him sufficient alms that he may purchase to himself a fair copy of the same Book, that so he may have the fruition of its most excellent virtue and evermore live to ascribe praise and honour where it is most just and due.

And these things I ask for the sake of sound learning, indifferent judgement and integrity of manners; ever remaining thine obedient servant,

PETER RIDLEY

Evolutionary Dead-end?

From Sir Roland Penrose   *18 February 1982*

[President, Institute of Contemporary Arts]

Sir,

May I be allowed to comment briefly on the dismay I felt, as presumably did many others, when confronted with the new stamp issued for our first-class inland mail. It is good that we should be reminded of great men, giant reptiles and the overriding presence of her Majesty, but the ineptitude of the monochrome design is lamentable.

In the centre we find the hoary appearance of an aged Charles Darwin with the top of the impressive dome of his forehead sliced off and what remains covered with his signature, which is placed so as to invite its obliteration by postmarks. On either side of him creep in caricatures of the heads of two noble chelonians. One of them is apparently attempting to kiss Darwin on the mouth while the other, rearing up towards his left eye, has a diminutive profile of her Majesty, also in sepia, slipping backwards off its nose.

This almost unrecognisable profile of our Sovereign is effectively dwarfed by the price of this small piece of sticky paper placed on high in the opposite corner.

May we know, Sir, who is responsible for this pathetic jumble of disproportionate symbols which in themselves should arouse respect, and add to our national prestige, and can a way be found to stop the appalling deterioration in the design of our stamps and currency?

Yours faithfully,
ROLAND PENROSE

Measure for Measure

*From the Principal and the Vice-Principal
(Administration) and Registrar, University
College, Cardiff* *25 March 1982*

Sir,

On page 12 of your issue of 19 March,

6 Downe House School scholars = 6·5 column centimetres
and

40 Fellows of the Royal Society = 5·5 column centimetres.
Hence,

$$\frac{DHSS}{FRS} = \frac{40 \times 6·5}{6 \times 5·5} = \frac{260}{33} \text{, and}$$

$$1 \text{ DHSS} = 8 \text{ FRS.}$$

Is this the new mathematics or the new technology?

Yours etc.,
C. W. L. BEVAN
L. A. MORITZ

280

Plastic Surgeon's Hungry Allies

[Sir Arthur Everett Shipley, the Master of Christ's College, Cambridge, on 28 January 1915 (see *The First Cuckoo*) reproached Generals Joffre, von Kluck, von Hindenberg, and Grand Duke Nicholas for fighting over some of the best leech areas in Europe]

From Mr D. Dencer   *23 March 1982*

Sir,

Your recent news item on leeches (17 March) interests me because I have been using these little creatures in my practice of plastic surgery for 30 years.

The bugbear of skin flaps is that blood stagnates in them and destroys them. The leech, with his two-fold skills, combats this, first of all by sucking out the sluggish blood, and secondarily by injecting an anti-clotting agent called hyalurodinase into the wound. This means that the wound made by his bite will still drip blood perhaps two days later. All of this helps the plastic surgeon very considerably.

Reasonably, therefore, one must be kind to leeches. They don't come from Hungary, as your informant suggests; they come from Africa. Don't you remember Humphrey Bogart climbing back into the African Queen with his back covered with leeches? Therefore they must be kept warm. We keep our leeches in a warm cupboard and periodically they are taken into the sunshine.

Long ago I knew a pharmacist who felt very keenly about his leeches. He would roll up his sleeve and feed them off his arm as a special treat. I remember, still, watching the sensual peristaltic movements of these gleaming dark-green bodies as they engorged themselves, it would seem in a sort of haemorrhagic orgasm.

You have to be very careful with leeches, because each end is very alike. When you want a leech to bite you must present the right end. They like to sit on their bottoms and bite with their mouths. If, through anatomical ignorance, you try to reverse the process you will end up with a resentful, sullen and dispirited leech.

My ward sister starts them off with milk or jam. She tells me that a little jam on the skin will start them off with enthusiasm, and many a skin flap in peril has been saved by these small, little-known simple creatures.

Yours faithfully,
D. DENCER

Name Dropping

From Mr John Cope   *28 April 1982*

Sir,

In one single week's news items I have heard the following names preceded by the title 'Mister', and in one case 'Sir': Andy, Ben, Bert, Bill, Bob, Dick, Ed, Fred, Freddie, Geoff, Jack, Jim, Ken, Max, Mike, Pat, Ray, Reg, Rob, Ron, Sam, Sid, Stan, Steve, Terry, Tiny, Tom, Tony, Vic, Viv and Will.

Are we to understand that at their baptisms not one of these people was given a real Christian name?

Yours etc.,
JOHN COPE

[On 12 October 1963 *The Times* published a letter from 'Anthony Wedgwood Benn'; a decade later, the same MP was 'Tony Benn']

Organ Symphony

From the Reverend D. G. Richards   *1 May 1982*

Sir,

In 1973 there was a concert and organ recital in the church of SS Peter and Paul, Neath. Next the church was the fire station. During the playing of a piece by Bach the fire siren sounded; with great presence of mind and skill the organist changed key with the siren and earned spontaneous applause. Not true Bach but great fun.

Yours faithfully,
DEREK RICHARDS

From Mr P. A. Gascoin   *5 May 1982*

Sir,

Against the possibility that concerts or organ recitals at SS Peter and Paul, Neath, may again coincide with alarms at the adjacent fire station, would not Mr Richards's organist friend be well advised to practise a rapid substitution of Parry's 'Blest Pair of Sirens' for whatever is on the programme (again with appropriate transposition of key)?

Yours faithfully,
P. A. GASCOIN

From Mr George E. Hill   *8 May 1982*

Sir,

I am the organist at a local crematorium, and at a recent ceremony I was asked to play Bach's 'Sheep may safely graze'. I dutifully did so.

I discovered, later, that the lamented deceased had been a New Zealand lamb importer!

Yours faithfully,
GEORGE E. HILL

Right Hand – Left Hand

From Mr Tim Hembry   *11 June 1982*

Sir,

I would be interested to hear from anyone who could explain to me a query I have had for some time now. It is to do with the terms 'right-handed' and 'left-handed' in referring to batsmen in cricket. I myself being a 'left-handed' batsman.

One is called 'left-handed' if one has his front foot (right), shoulder (right), and the top hand, which is supposed to be the one which does the work, is also the right hand.

It only seems sensible to me for a 'left-handed' batsman in fact to be called 'right-handed' and vice versa. It also seems sensible that if one is right-handed normally for writing, etc., one should be taught to bat 'left-handed' as one's right arm is stronger and would be the 'top hand'.

Therefore if one is 'left-handed' normally one should bat 'right-handed', again for the same reason and surely this would help one to play over the ball and keep it down. As yet no one has been able to explain to me the reason for this phraseology. Is this because there is no logical answer?

Yours sincerely,
TIM HEMBRY

From Professor P. H. Spencer-Silver   *19 June 1982*

[Department of Anatomy, The Middlesex Hospital Medical School]

Sir,

Mr Tim Hembry will be pleased to know that there is a certain logic in answer to his concatenation of questions concerning the stance at the wicket of right-handed batpersons. The key to understanding is to be found in the posture of the spinal column.

The position is that in most right-handed people there is a slight asymmetry of the spine as a result of which the left shoulder is held a little higher than the right. When grasping a bat handle the left hand therefore only fits comfortably above the right. At the wicket the raising of the left shoulder is merely brought about by an enhancement of the asymmetry of the spine with which the body is already at ease. Such a starting position feels right, and the movements which flow from it are slick and dextrous.

To grasp the handle with hands reversed (which is required when facing the bowling from the 'wrong' side) requires an elevation of the right shoulder brought about by a twist of the spinal column in an unwonted direction. Such a starting position feels all wrong, and movements based on it cannot flow but instead are clumsy and maladroit.

Let me say about phraseology that by definition right-handed batpersons are those who bat the same way round as most other right-handers (even if they write left-handed). Also the posture of the back and the asymmetry of the shoulders can best be pondered not on the cricket field but on the golf course. French cricket is also worth thinking about.

Yours faithfully,
P. H. SPENCER-SILVER

['Batpersons' suggests that the Middlesex Hospital Medical School XI is a mixed one. Traditionalists may prefer the word 'bat'; Wilfred Rhodes said of Ranjitsinhji – and of Trumper, Hobbs and Bradman, "e were good bat'.]

Sir,

Left-handers are always a nuisance at a Chinese banquet. The most serious problem arises when precious superior sharks-fin is served since this must be most delicately brought up to the mouth with one's chopsticks and when they are left-handers their left-hand neighbours are invariably impeded in their intake.

This was the sole reason why my great-grandmother and grandmother never sat anyone important to the left of my brother, who is left-handed. Indeed, Chinese of their generation thought left-handers were improperly brought up and should be frowned upon.

My brother was perpetually instructed to change over to his right hand. He now unhelpably does everything with his left hand but writes with his right hand – in, I think, a most dreadful handwriting. He admits it, too, but consoles himself with the fact that when writing Chinese he doesn't get ink on his hand, since we write from right to left.

Yours faithfully,
DAVID TANG

The Falklands

————◆————

[On 2 April 1982 the British Government announced that it was assembling a large naval task force in response to Argentina's seizure of the Falkland Islands in the South Atlantic]

From Dr Anthony Storr   *18 May 1982*

Sir,
British forces are poised to invade islands which we have neglected, do not seem to want, and, in the long run, are incapable of defending against further attack. Even if we repossess the islands, is it likely that any Falklanders will wish to continue to live under perpetual threat?

As a pragmatic solution, the Government should offer the remaining islanders sufficient funds to resettle them in other parts of the world where they could pursue their accustomed way of life. The cost would be less than that of replacing the *Sheffield*, and the saving in life considerable.

In the heat of resentment, we have lost our sense of proportion. We can afford to let General Galtieri strut and swagger. We cannot and should not squander our resources and sacrifice so many young lives for objectives which cannot be sustained.

Yours faithfully,
ANTHONY STORR

Learning from the Falklands conflict

From Mr Ronald Higgins   *14 June 1982*

Sir,
Let us at once resolve that as soon as the reciprocal killing in the South Atlantic is over we shall not inquire solely into the origins of the conflict and the appropriateness or otherwise of the British response, but into larger questions of profound consequence for the general human future.

Why precisely was our faith in the effectiveness of nonviolent collective action against the Argentine aggression so small? What measures should now be devised and pursued, not least by the UK, to correct the shortcomings? What should be learnt from the extraordinary eruption of public anger and will for battle in this the most mature of all the democracies? How far has rhetoric about principle obscured affront to tribal pride and disrupted the workings of far-sighted prudence?

We are not least prone to do wrong when we are in the right. Neither the undoubted agonies of the decision takers nor the spilled blood of our servicemen should qualify the need to examine afresh the rationale, ethics and psychology of war in what is now a permanently nuclear, global and volatile context. Our generation is challenged as none before it to redefine security and to create robustly effective alternatives to the use of main force.

Yours sincerely,
RONALD HIGGINS

Far South below the Line

From Rear-Admiral John Hervey　　　　　*21 June 1982*

Sir,

With apologies to Rudyard Kipling's 'The Dutch in the Medway':

> If wars were won by boasting,
> Or victory by a speech,
> Or safety found in voting sound,
> How long would be our reach!
> But honour and dominion
> Are not maintained so,
> They're only got by sword and shot,
> *And this the Argies know!*
>
> The moneys that should arm us
> You spent on other things,
> How can you then have sailor-men
> And ships with mighty wings?
> The treasure's all in Europe
> And fat the Germans grow –
> We cannot serve you if we lack,
> *And this the Argies know!*

There are ships in every harbour
That are simply 'standing by',
And, when we want to update 'em,
We're not allowed to try.
And if we were, the welders,
The carpenters also,
For lack of pay were sent away,
And this the Argies know!

Mere missiles, guns and bullets,
We scarce can get at all,
Their price was spent, to our detriment,
In re-ordering Whitehall,
While we in the Americas
From door to door must go,
Beseeching friends for odds and ends –
And this the Argies know!

Nott wants to flog our carriers
And plans to axe our men –
As for the loyal Opposition
It's in the hands of Wedgwood Benn.
But now the Argy aircraft
Have given our fleet a blow,
There's going to be a reckoning –
And this the Commons know!

Yours etc.,
JOHN HERVEY

Falklands Thanksgiving – But for What?

From the Bishop of Lincoln   8 July 1982

Sir,

While recognizing the good intentions of those planning a
national service at St Paul's Cathedral to mark the end of the
Falklands war, I have anxieties about what may be planned.
It is to be a service of Thanksgiving, Remembrance and
Reconciliation. 'Thanksgiving for what?' is the question of
my anxiety. For restored peace, yes: for exceptional efficiency,
endurance and heroism of the Armed Forces, yes indeed: for
the general steadfastness and courage of those in authority,

once committed, yes. But, pray God, not in any nationalistic spirit, for winning a war.

Wars can sometimes win certain things, but they always lose far more – lives, national substance, and the general integrity of the human race. I therefore plead with the planners to include in the service a serious note of reflection on how this and any war pinpoints the tragic frailty of the human race, that continues to find no better ultimate solution to its tensions than mutual destruction. And let there be in the service no spurious connection between the resolution of the Falklands tension and other tensions besetting us at home.

In citing 'the human race' we must not oversimplify a profoundly complex tangle of personal and social forces. But our own hearts are part of that complexity, however swayed by forces which often seem beyond their control. A service in church is surely an occasion for expressing this realism about ourselves which Christians call penitence. It is a realism which makes us one, in our need, with the rest of mankind, including those in Argentina. For some this may point to that other realism, about God, which Christians call Faith and Hope.

Yours sincerely,

✠SIMON LINCOLN

Thanksgiving Choice

From Canon H. L. H. Townshend   *14 July 1982*

Sir,

As it is clearly going to be impossible to reconcile the conflicting points of view about the composition of the Service of Thanksgiving for 26 July, might it not be an idea to have two simultaneous services, the first in St Paul's, containing the elements of penitence and reconciliation as well as thanksgiving, and the second at Stonehenge, at which 'Rule Britannia' and 'Land of Hope and Glory' could be sung with great gusto by the assembled company?

Everyone should then be happy, as they would have a choice.

I am, Sir, yours faithfully,

H. L. H. TOWNSHEND

[see letter for 28 September 1918]

Questions on Falklands Thanksgiving

From Mr Alan Clark, MP   *26 July 1982*
[Conservative Member for Plymouth, Sutton]

Sir,

Most of your readers will understand how eager David Watt must have been to assert that 'the Falkland spirit is on the wane' (23 July). For in common with the majority of intellectuals and established figures of his generation – with the honourable, and significant exception of yourself, Sir – he has been implacably opposed to the whole 'adventure' since its inception. First openly '. . . these paltry Islands' then, as the operation proceeded successfully, by slight and innuendo.

Let us assume that this attitude originates in conviction rather than malice; in the fact that during the last 40 years no British government has ever felt able to take major foreign policy initiatives, still less military action, without consultation and deferral to other nations, and this has become the accepted norm. And that any assertion of the national will has certain non-specific, but undesirable moral overtones.

I suggest that this argument is completely inverted. Far from being on the wane, the Falkland spirit – by which I understand a quiet pride, disseminated at all levels in society (outside the Athaeneum) in our country's proven ability to assert its independence, to rescue its own nationals, and to shed blood through the skills and valour of its servicemen in defence of the principles to which the West is committed – not only flourishes but is wholly beneficial.

It is this background which allows an amused toleration of the various silly-season diversions which Mr Watt identifies, and restrains too hysterical a reaction to the outrages.

But had our nerve failed over the Falklands, the Task Force been recalled and the Islanders delivered, under various pretences, to Argentine rule, then everything that has happened since would be portrayed as still further indicators of decadence. A corrupt and incompetent police force; the Queen herself at risk; the intelligence services still further disconcerted; flagrant and devastating acts of terrorism in the centre of London.

It is not difficult to draft the alternative text of an article by Mr Watt. Instead of gloating over the 'waning' of the Falkland spirit, he would be cautioning us against 'extremist solutions' to deal with these various maladies.

As it is, the dignity and self-confidence which that great victory generated should and do restrain us from excesses in dealing with our own domestic irritants.

I am, Sir, your obedient servant,
ALAN CLARK

Falklands Service – a Question of Emphasis

From Commander R. N. E. Payne, RN   *29 July 1982*

Sir,

The Christian ethic recognizes the concept of a 'just war'. Leaders of the established Church recognized that the Falklands war fell into this category. It follows that they should recognize the success of the Task Force as being God's will.

A thanksgiving service need not preclude prayers for the sufferings of mankind, both Christian and non-Christian, of both sides; but thanksgiving for the deliverance of the temporarily oppressed people of the Falkland Islands by the victorious British force should surely predominate. After all there is still an annual service of thanksgiving for victory granted in the Battle of Britain 1940, this year to be held in Westminster Abbey.

Yours sincerely,
ROBERT PAYNE

Falklands Service Depth of Feeling

From Mrs Sheila D. Abbott   *30 July 1982*

Sir,

As the wife of a soldier turned politician, the daughter and granddaughter of sailors, and an ex-honorary secretary of SSAFA (Soldiers', Sailors' and Airmen's Families Association), I believe I can claim to be a patriot. I found Monday's service to be moving and beautiful, leaving me proud of our nation which in glorious victory could be humble.

Surely one-third of those in St Paul's Cathedral, the relatives of the 254 men who lost their lives in the South Atlantic, along with those servicemen who had survived the conflict, were the most important members of that vast congregation.

Perhaps we should ask *them* if they were dissatisfied. I believe their answer would be the same as that of Captain 'Sam' Salt – 'moving and beautiful'. I don't believe *they* wanted a 'Celebration of Deliverance'. But then, they are not politicians seeking acclaim for battles fought, and votes at the next election.

If the politicians want celebration, then have a victory parade in the street, but in church let us remember in the way in which we did on Monday.

Yours sincerely,
SHEILA D. ABBOTT

The Enemy in Defeat

From Mr John Peter　　　　　　　　　　　*31 July 1982*

Sir,

When Athens crushed the invading Persian armies in the fifth century BC, Aeschylus marked the event by writing *The Persians*. This sombre and lyrical tragedy is set in the Persian court, and celebrates the Athenian victory by showing the enemy demoralized and grief-stricken in tragic defeat after a bloody and misguided campaign.

There is no attempt on the part of the Greek dramatist to exult openly in the victory of his country, even though the Persians had brutally violated the territorial integrity of Athens. The play's mood is one of proud and quiet dignity; its condemnation of the enemy is contained in its grim contemplation of their defeat. I know of no finer example in patriotic literature.

The awful thought now occurs to me that perhaps Aeschylus was a 'wet'. But no, it turns out that he saw active service against the Persians at Marathon when he was 35; and that he fought the Persians again 10 years later, when he was 45, at Artemisium and Salamis.

When the play was performed it gained first prize. This was not the Greek equivalent of the Standard Drama Award: it combined the highest civic, artistic and religious praise the Athenian community could bestow. And it is not too fanciful to assume that leading citizens as well as relations of those who had fallen were among the audience.

I am, Sir, yours faithfully,
JOHN PETER

[Without seeking to define 'wet', it is worth noting that the Archbishop of Canterbury (Dr Runcie), the Home Secretary (Mr Whitelaw), and the two Foreign Secretaries who spanned the Falklands conflict (Lord Carrington and Mr Pym), have one thing in common: as army officers during the Second World War they were all awarded the Military Cross for gallantry]

Truly Thule

From Mr G. M. A. Harrison   *29 June 1982*

[Chief Education Officer, City of Sheffield]

Sir,
   Driven to distraction by hearing BBC voices pronouncing Thule, the South Sandwich Island, to rhyme either with fool or mule, I rang the corporation's pronunciation unit to protest at a rendering that was as ugly as it was unlettered. What causes me to write to you is the awful news that it was the Foreign Office that advised the BBC on this; Thool or Thewl is the convention these days, they are alleged to say. *O tempora, o mores!* It's enough to raise Pytheas, the one to discover the Northern ultimate equivalent, from the dead.

Yours faithfully,
MICHAEL HARRISON

From Mr T. G. Wilde   *29 June 1982*

Sir,
   During recent broadcasts, the BBC has frequently referred to an island in the far South, called THEWL.
   Can this have any connection with the place mentioned by Edgar Allan Poe, in his immortal lines

> 'I have reached these lands but newly
> From that ultimate dim Thule – ...'?

Yours,
T. G. WILDE

From Mr James Young   *7 July 1982*

Sir,

   ... or, rather earlier than Poe, by Virgil (*Georgics I*) where the phrase 'Ultima Thule' occurs as a hexameter ending, thus putting the correct pronunciation beyond all doubt.

Yours faithfully,
JAMES YOUNG

From Mr Jonathan Varcoe   *7 July 1982*

[Director of Music, St Paul's School]

Sir,

   They had no difficulty in knowing the correct pronunciation of Thule in 1600 when Thomas Weelkes published his stunning madrigal the words of which begin: 'Thule, the period of cosmographie'.

The two syllables of Thule are set to two semibreves.

Yours sincerely,
JONATHAN VARCOE

Truly More Than One

From Mr E. Murray   *2 July 1982*

Sir,

   Thule, pronounced to rhyme with cool, is in Greenland, in the Arctic. Thule, to rhyme with newly, is in the Antarctic. This could matter quite a lot to anyone desirous of going to either place.

Yours,
E. MURRAY

National Anthem (moderato)

[*Delete:*   'Confound their politics,
                   Frustrate their knavish tricks'
 Substitute: 'Give up Your faithfulness,
                      Keep us from selfishness']

From Miss Patience Strong   *13 August 1982*

Sir,

As a regular contributor of poetry to several national publications, religious and secular, with over fifty years of professional experience, I consider myself qualified to express an opinion on the new national anthem which is now being offered as an alternative to the one known and loved by millions throughout the Anglo-Saxon world. The main point is that the traditional one is not in fact a national anthem but a prayer and should be sung as such. Anyone who suggests that there is anything wrong in praying for the safety of the Queen and victory over her enemies does not know the Bible in any depth. Treated as a national prayer, I personally resent the intrusion of this new enfeebled version into any service of public worship because it uses the wrong pronoun in addressing Almighty God. This renders it irreverent, therefore unacceptable.

It is bad enough that an alternative Prayer Book has been foisted upon us in place of Cranmer's inspired masterpiece; may God save us from this further spiritual and aesthetic outrage.

As for the point that I heard raised on this morning's radio *Today* programme that 'victorious', 'glorious' and 'over us' were not true rhymes, I would not agree. The three terminal syllables are identical; it is therefore technically and phonetically correct.

Yours faithfully,
PATIENCE STRONG

[On 12 February 1931 the Dean of Worcester informed *The Times* he had received a letter relating to the year's Three Choirs Festival. He would not, of course, permit the second verse of the National Anthem to be sung: 'un-Christian, indecent, disgraceful anywhere, in a church blasphemous, and in a cathedral a brawling obscenity']

Once For All

From Mr John Ticehurst   *1 September 1982*

Sir,

I was fascinated to read on your front page (28 August), 'Pressure builds for national strike day'.

I have long felt that such a day each year would be an admirable way of getting all the strikes out of the way to everyone's advantage. Might I suggest that the most suitable day would be the May Day Bank holiday, already the most gloomy spot on the vacation calendar.

Such a day would have the added advantage of our not having to hear from endless lines of union leaders how much they hated hurting anyone but themselves, but that they were forced etc., etc. With no radio or television we should be spared the hypocrisy, too. What a good idea.

Yours faithfully,
JOHN TICEHURST

Lost without Trace by Sealink

From Mr Julian Berry   *3 August 1982*

Sir,

My eight months pregnant wife, child, nanny and dog, at the time of writing (1.40 a.m.), are 'lost' on a boat that left Guernsey yesterday morning at 10.30 a.m. and was due to land at Weymouth some five hours later.

Because my wife managed to leave the boat to telephone me, the last I heard was that the boat had arrived at Weymouth; although the foot passengers had got off, the boat had not been allowed to use a dock suitable for the unloading of cars. The reason for the delay is a strike called by some Sealink employees. I have in the last two hours telephoned some 12 different numbers provided by British Rail, Sealink, Weymouth station and Weymouth harbour without being able to obtain a definite statement from anyone of what has happened to those passengers encumbered with cars and trapped on the boat. Whilst respecting the necessity for strikes I have no respect whatsoever for BR's failure to set up an information centre to deal with inquiries about the fate of their passengers.

Is there not a responsibility for those offering shipping
services to provide information, at any time of day or night,
to those who are concerned about the casual victims of industrial disputes? My wife is very heavy with child and therefore
more than normally affected by the delay.

Yours faithfully,
JULIAN BERRY

[From *The Times*, 7 September 1982

BIRTHS

BERRY on 4th September to Diana, wife of Julian Berry
– a daughter Georgia Jane]

Fons et origo

From Sir John Betjeman   *3 August 1982*

[Poet Laureate since 1972]

Sir,
    I am appalled by the news that St Barnabas, Pimlico, is to
become redundant.
    Architecturally it is a jewel of a church, not least the
Comper Lady Chapel. And historically it is central to the
history of the Church of England in the nineteenth century:
riots, Bennet, the Vicar in a *Punch* cartoon, Lord Shaftes-
bury attacking it in pious evangelical horror and, during the
Second World War, Winston Churchill attending the church
for the baptism of his Sandys grandchild. It was from its
vicarage that the *English Hymnal* was produced and it was
always a place of devout prayer.
    The church needs to continue as a living focus of love –
God's love and ours for him. And it is in the centre of literally
hundreds of working-class flats whose inhabitants are the
congregation.

Yours faithfully,
JOHN BETJEMAN

'Nothing wrong with Wimbledon'

From Mr Budge Patty   *24 June 1982*

[winner of the Gentlemen's Singles championship at Wimbledon 1950]

Sir,

Having played and been a spectator at the Championships at Wimbledon for more than three decades I am bewildered by the attacks a few players have levied against the All England Lawn Tennis Club. I am at a loss as to what motivated this attitude.

With a feeling of responsibility (perhaps misguided) engendered by what lawn tennis has meant to me, I have made some inquiries. It is axiomatic in the tennis and athletic world that few tournaments match the high standards of the All England Club.

It is splendid that players are finally more than adequately compensated and that there is virtually no difference between being an amateur and a professional player. But the new generation of players do not realize that it was the All England Club that truly opened the big tournaments to professionals.

Previously, professionals (other than instructors) made a living through lawn tennis – Tilden, Perry, Vines, Gonzales, Kramer, Hoad, Rosewall, Laver, to name a few – by barnstorming.

They played in arenas, gymnasiums, theatre stages, on canvas surfaces (if they were lucky), with inadequate light, and often inadequate money.

Fortunately those days are over. Then why is Wimbledon being denigrated? A few players beef that it takes weeks to get used to grass courts, and then they quickly have to play on a different surface. Also, that there are not adequate practice facilities.

Until the past year this does not seem to have bothered anyone. Before the Championships there is a fine grass tournament at Queen's Club (and other tournaments) or the players can just practise there and at other clubs. There are scores of grass courts for practice within a half-hour drive.

How much practice is required when changing surfaces? Of course each player has his favourite surface. Some consider grass the most difficult but if you are any kind of champion a week would do it. It never seemed to bother Perry, Budge, Laver, Drobny, Borg, etc.

It is odd that the women players have not complained about grass courts, or the manner in which they are treated by the All England Club. I am disappointed that Lendl is not playing. I did not see him last year: he lost in the first round. Many top players have lost in the early rounds and not blamed the grass courts. A truly great player should know how to adapt his game. If he can't then he's not.

Reporters have to write interesting articles. From experience I learned they sometimes do this by asking leading questions, such as: 'What's wrong with Wimbledon?' My answer to that question is that there is nothing wrong.

For scores of years competing on the lawns of the All England Club has been for a player what it must be like for a Mohamedan to go to Mecca. There is no greater honour for a tennis player than to win the Wimbledon Championship.

Yours etc.,
BUDGE PATTY

From Mr H. W. Austin   *26 June 1982*

[finalist in the Gentlemen's Singles 1932 and 1938]

Sir,
A story is told of an incident in a match when Don Budge was playing Gottfried von Cramm.

Budge questioned a line decision which he felt had been wrongly given in his favour.

After the match Gottfried took him to task. 'That was very unsporting of you,' he told Don.

'But Gottfried,' replied Don, 'I was questioning a decision given in my favour!'

'I know,' replied Gottfried. 'But think how you embarrassed the linesman.'

Yours faithfully,
BUNNY AUSTIN

Tags on 'Lags'

From Mr Tom Stacey   *16 October 1982*

Sir,
Last week's article on prisons by George Brock (6 October) was headed 'Ideas but little more'. Ideas are what we are

dreadfully short of. We know that the prison population is rising, that the cost of keeping a man in jail is robbing the taxpayer, and – worst of all – that prison elevates the criminal option: it deters few and outcasts many. We are flummoxed.

An old lag of a prison visitor like me has come to believe he can soon distinguish between the wicked or dangerous on the one hand, and the relatively harmless, congenitally or temporarily disordered or disorderly on the other. Such *misérables* of the latter category clutter our jails by the thousands. I wish to advocate tagging such an offender.

Instead of going to prison he would wear something. The offender's tag would be a metal band, like half a pair of handcuffs, that would encompass the wrist or ankle or even the neck. It might or might not be necessarily visible. It would be the offender's option in place of a prison sentence. It would be removed by the court, police station or probation office at the end of the sentence.

It would not be purposely uncomfortable. It would be made of hard metal, or – in the case discussed below – it could be of plastic. To tear it off would be treated as gravely as escaping from prison.

As with that (relatively tiny) proportion of offenders now serving part of their sentence on parole, the tag wearer would agree to reside in a certain place, report at regular intervals, and inform authority if he changed his domicile.

The offender's tag could contain an electronic receiver which (I assure the reader) need be no larger than the last joint of the forefinger. The offender could thus be reminded of his commitment to report. This system could be relatively cheaply developed pick-a-back on the existing British Telecom paging system, by which signals are passed through the network of telephone exchanges.

Theoretically (but not yet practically) it could transmit a signal at certain intervals which would enable computerized monitors to fix the whereabouts precisely of the wearer, alert authority in the case of interference with the tag, or in the case of the wearer leaving the agreed radius or being in close proximity with other tag wearers.

Let me not, however, exceed my own radius. I can already hear the baying and yelping of the civil liberties lobby. To those compassionate fellow citizens I venture to say: I do not believe most of you are familiar with the inevitable brutality of the alternative – namely, prison life. Allow me, for the present, to do no more than offer my offender's tag as a

301

voluntary method of doubling that third of the sentence that an appropriate convict may now serve on parole.

When such a moderate unbolting of doors is seen to work, then perhaps the offender's tag may allow certain offenders, nowadays jailed – my wasting recidivist – to be spared incarceration altogether. If such a man had a job, he would have a chance of holding on to it. If there were those who might love him, he would not be torn from them. He might be disgraced for a spell in his own eyes and others', but he would no longer be obliterated.

After 10,000 years of the dungeon mentality let us try something new, a manifestation of man's advance. Let us try it with the utmost caution, praying the while to St Leonard.

I have established at this address the Offender's Tag Trust which I propose to make a vehicle for stimulating research into this alternative to prison, and promoting its use world-wide.

Yours faithfully,
TOM STACEY

Burlington Toppers

From Mr Jim Agnew   *4 September 1982*

Sir,

As Chief Beadle of the Burlington Arcade, Piccadilly, may I enlist the support of your readers for the defence of our top hats, which are in peril.

The Beadles, which I have the honour to command, are the smallest police force in the world, with only three constables. We have policed the good manners of the public since 1819. Here no one whistles, hums or makes merry loudly. Even those who break our laws are told off courteously. Some Americans call us 'courtesy cops', vulgarly perhaps, but with no ill will and we are not offended.

But it is a sad fact that the London of the past and its characters are fast disappearing; which is why we Beadles refuse to move with the times – for the sake of tourists who come to see us.

Our uniforms are still tailored to an Edwardian cut by our arcade tailors, the fastidious Victor and Keith Brand, who are not related.

Each uniform costs £800 compared with the paltry £78 per uniform of the Metropolitan Police. Our top hats cost £380 each, but now, alas, we learn of a move afoot to replace them with economy toppers at £170.

As an ex-sergeant major I believe that to cheapen the headgear of London's only surviving top-hatted police constables is as sacrilegious as taking away a guardsman's bearskin at the changing of the guard and giving him a stetson to wear, because it's cheaper.

Yours faithfully,
JIM AGNEW

[Three days later *The Times* reported: 'There being no hatters among the arcade's list of shopkeepers, Messrs James Lock in St James's Street nearby immediately offered to provide a top hat from their own workshops for the cost of a bowler. The offer was graciously accepted, and Mr Ray Soley, the junior beadle, will have it in a month.']

'Yours Till the Cows Come Home'

From Mrs Jan Pahl   5 August 1982

Sir,

The English language is a subtle and flexible instrument, but it does have various lacunae; I am writing to invite your readers to repair one such gap. I am concerned that there seems to be no way of ending a letter with a phrase which conveys the idea of 'in friendship' or 'with warm and friendly feelings'.

There is 'love from', but that is perhaps a little naive; there is 'with kind regards' but that seems rather formal; 'best wishes' is too like a Christmas card, and 'yours ever' implies all sorts of long-term commitments; *amicalement* comes closest to the phrase I mean – but I want something in English.

Yours sincerely,
JAN PAHL

From Mr Vivian Vale   9 August 1982

Sir,

A well-tried French acquaintance of ours invariably ends her English letters to us with 'Yours friendly', which we love. But perhaps Mrs Pahl might prefer to employ the simple American coda of 'Cordially'?

Yours faithfully,
VIVIAN VALE

From Dr J. R. Butler   9 August 1982

Sir,

I once taught an attentive student who ended her little notes to me with the valediction 'Yours eventually'. I assumed that this was intended to convey warm and friendly feelings.

Yours sincerely,
J. R. BUTLER

Sir,

Jan Pahl wants a letter-ending to convey friendship, not love or formality. How about 'yours cordially', with which I have been ending letters for years (including one to her)?

The 'yours' form is capable of all sorts of individual variations: 'yours apologetically', 'yours disgustedly', 'yours in sackcloth and ashes', 'yours delightedly' and I have used them all. But perhaps 'yours' itself is absurd; so what about just 'Cordially'?

Until this is an accepted form, however, I remain,

Yours cheerfully,
KATHARINE WHITEHORN

Sir,

Mrs Pahl finds a gap in English in ways of signing off her letters. There is no gap in the language; it is a question of looking a little further to find an expression unhappily fallen into desuetude. When I wish to convey 'warm and friendly feelings' to my correspondent, I sign myself

Yours affectionately,
PAMELA JERRAM

Sir,

Is 'Yours affectionately' *too* affectionate for Mrs Pahl? It offers warmth of feeling without pushiness.

Incidentally, why never '*Dear* Sir' nowadays – even when one is feeling particularly friendly towards *The Times*?

Yours sincerely,
BRIGID GRAFTON GREEN

[Writing to *The Times*, 17 January 1930, Mr E. S. Campbell began 'Dear Sir' and ended 'Yours affectionately' – see *The First Cuckoo*]

Sir,

I have always thought of Evelyn Waugh's immortal phrase 'with love or what you will' as the ultimate end to my correspondence.

It has disarmed my sternest critic and redeemed my dullest prose.

> Yours faithfully,
> PHILIP A. DAVIES

Sir,

> Amiably yours,
> GEORGE GALE

[The Cuckoo-in-Chief is grateful to the *Daily Express* for the only non-letter to appear in the correspondence columns of *The Times*]

Sir,

Mrs Jan Pahl, who seeks an English equivalent for *amicalement* with which to end her letters, may be interested to know that when I was a District Officer in Barotseland in the nineteen-fifties all official letters in English to the local African chief commenced with the salutation 'My Friend' and ended 'I am Your Friend'.

I never discovered the origin of this strange mode of address, which was in frequent use at the time but may be a little too regal for Mrs Pahl's purposes.

> Yours sincerely,
> JOHN HOUSDEN

Sir,

My son, who is 22, began writing to me a year or so ago with the ending: 'Your friend, William'. This seems to be a simple and unaffected ending that conveys the desired feeling.

> Your friend,
> IAN MILLS

From Mr Bernard Kaukas   *17 August 1982*

Sir (and Mrs Jan Pahl):
  Yours till the cows come home.

Yours sincerely,
BERNARD KAUKAS

From Mr David Peace   *19 August 1982*

Sir,
  I hope it may help Mrs Pahl to hear of the endings of two
letters I found especially engaging. A servant ended a letter
to George IV, 'Invariably Yours'. (Incidentally it began, 'My
dearest Sir...') And I will end this letter as did my 10-year-
old granddaughter,

Ever wishing good,
DAVID PEACE

From Mr Gervase Craven   *19 August 1982*

Sir,
  Some years ago a young distant relative wrote to thank me
for a Christmas present. With an obvious wish to express
some sentiment of friendliness, without appearing too effusive,
she brought her letter to a close with the words 'most of my
love'.

Yours faithfully,
GERVASE CRAVEN

From Mrs Phyllis Gascoin   *21 August 1982*

Sir,
  Mrs Pahl is perfectly correct. There *is* a gap in the language.
The problem is one of long standing.
  Did not Miss Austen, in the person of Miss Mary Crawford,
say to Fanny Price: 'You must give my compliments to him.
Yes, I think it must be compliments. Is there not a something
wanted, Miss Price, in our language – a something between
compliments and love, to suit the sort of friendly acquaintance
we have had together? ... But compliments may be sufficient
here.'
  I present my compliments to your correspondents and to
yourself, and sign myself *simpliciter*.

PHYLLIS GASCOIN

From the Under-Sheriff of Greater London   24 August 1982

Sir,

I remember a lady anxious for a reply from my office to her letter seeking to be excused from jury service as she was eight months pregnant, ending appropriately,

'Yours expectantly',
ALASTAIR BLACK

From Vice-Admiral Sir Louis Le Bailly   25 August 1982

Sir,

During the period he was spring cleaning the Royal Navy, Admiral Jackie Fisher didn't do too badly.

To Viscount Esher: 'Yours till a cinder'.

To J. A. Spender: 'Yours till the Angels smile on us'.

To F. E. G. Ponsonby: 'Yours till death'.

To George Lambert: 'Yours till Hell freezes'.

From 1908 onwards the last appeared most frequently.

Yours faithfully,
LOUIS LE BAILLY

From Dr R. W. K. Paterson   31 August 1982

Sir,

When the contents are appropriate, we can end our letters, as our Victorian forefathers often did, by giving a final encore to the dominant theme or delicately reiterating the emotional gist: by, for example, 'Yours in great distress of mind' or 'Yours in heartfelt gratitude and relief'. In this way we can, so to speak, round off our letters pointedly.

Yours in earnest hope of publication,
R. W. K. PATERSON

From Mr Stelio Hourmouzios   14 August 1982

Sir,

Mrs Pahl is treading on delicate ground. The moment you depart from the accepted forms of salutation you inevitably endow any new formulas with some specific value, whereas the present time-honoured conventional forms, inane as they are, no longer have any significance in themselves.

We could, of course, revert to the extravagant protestations that our great-grandfathers liked to use when rounding off a letter, but life is too short for that; and quite honestly I do not see members of our contemporary society tamely subscribing themselves as most obedient, humble servants.

Believe me to be, Sir,
Not your anything but simply
STELIO HOURMOUZIOS

INDEX OF SUBJECTS

wages of bedmakers (at Cambridge c. 1919) 74–5; differentials in 207–9, 219–20, 235–6; of labourers (1919) 73

war profits, abolition of 57–8

war: reflections on 288, 290; types of 171–2

wealth tax, Government-TUC combined study of 241

wedding fees 96

West Indian children, upbringing of 257–8

wife-sale, an instance of 97

wigs, and women barristers 81–2

Wimbledon lawn tennis championships, denigration of 299–300

Winnie-the-Pooh, original model for 275

wireless: *see* radio

'wogs', etymology of 245

women: baristers, and wigs 81–2; and co-educational medical training 79; and recruitment for WWI, their role in 54; and riding, cross-saddle versus side-saddle 51–2

women's colleges, characteristics of, stories to illustrate 227–30

women's suffrage 26–7

Wooster, Bertie (fictional character), unmonocled 278

workmen, and transistor radios 199

World Service (BBC), cuts in 256–7

World War I (1914–18): censorship of letters during 56; and commissions to schoolboys 58–9; German feeling re 54; profiteers from, action against 57–8; soldiers: execution of 61–2; support for foxhunting by 55–6; swords of dead, non-receipt of 59; travelling conditions 64–5; a veteran remembers 271–2; Stonehenge as a memorial to 64; volunteers for, the English girl's role 54–5

World War II (1939–45): bureaucratic blunders during 128–30; censorship of books/letters/newspapers during 56, 127; monotonous diet during 140; servicemen: humiliating position of 135–6; respect for dead, by enemy 138–9; waste paper campaign 133–4

'Wykehamist and the Chair' (story), idle banter concerning 225–30

Wykehamists, character of, stories to illustrate 225–7

Yales, horns of 88–9

'Year in Retrospect' (1961), omission from 182–3

INDEX OF CORRESPONDENTS

Also in Unwin Paperbacks

THE FIRST CUCKOO
Letters to The Times since 1900

Revised Edition

Chosen and introduced by Kenneth Gregory
Foreword by Bernard Levin

The first edition of witty, entertaining and memorable correspondence to *The Times* was greeted with great critical enthusiasm and went on to become a best-seller. Now Kenneth Gregory
has brought up-to-date his selection of the most witty, amusing
and memorable letters to *The Times* since 1900. Among the 'top
people' whose eloquence fills these pages figure a host of writers,
artists, sportsmen, statesmen and public personalities. There is
Conan Doyle on a military invention, Neville Chamberlain on
the grey wagtail, Winston Churchill on corporal punishment,
Bernard Berenson on art forgeries, H. G. Wells on strike-
breaking, T. S. Eliot and Malcolm Muggeridge on television,
Vita Sackville-West on stamps as wallpaper, Field-Marshal
Montgomery on skiing.
    Among the letters he has chosen from the past five years are
ones on toads, tea-boys, triremes, gnomes, postage stamps,
British Rail, chamber-pots, knitting, foreigners and trade unions
— from correspondents as diverse as Kenneth Clark, Beverley
Nichols, Professor Hayek and Graham Greene — and of course
more about the sighting of the first cuckoo in Spring.

'Wholly fascinating...there is no end to the astonishments.'
                                    Arthur Marshall—New Statesman

'The most enjoyable anthology for many a day.'
                                    E. S. Turner—The Listener

'Hilarious.'
                                    Alistair Cooke